The New Extremism in Cinema
From France to Europe

Edited by Tanya Horeck and Tina Kendall

Edinburgh University Press

© editorial matter and organisation Tanya Horeck and Tina Kendall 2011
© the chapters their several authors 2011
© 'Flesh and Blood' *Artforum* 2004

Edinburgh University Press Ltd
22 George Square, Edinburgh

www.euppublishing.com

Typeset in 11/13 Monotype Ehrhardt
by Servis Filmsetting Ltd, Stockport, Cheshire

A CIP record for this book is available from the British Library

ISBN 978 0 7486 4160 4 (hardback)

The right of the contributors
to be identified as author of this work
has been asserted in accordance with
the Copyright, Designs and Patents Act 1988.

Contents

Acknowledgements   v

1 Introduction   1
  Tanya Horeck and Tina Kendall
2 Flesh and Blood: Sex and Violence in Recent French Cinema   18
  James Quandt

Part I   French Cinema and the New Extremism

3 The Wounded Screen   29
  Martine Beugnet
4 Reframing Bataille: On Tacky Spectatorship in the New European
  Extremism   43
  Tina Kendall
5 Beyond Anti-Americanism, Beyond Euro-Centrism: Locating
  Bruno Dumont's *Twentynine Palms* in the Context of European
  Cinematic Extremism   55
  Neil Archer

**Part II   Becoming Animal: Posthumanism and the New
  Extremism**

6 Shadows of Being in *Sombre*: Archetypes, Wolf-Men and Bare Life   69
  Jenny Chamarette
7 Eastern Extreme: The Presentation of Eastern Europe as a Site of
  Monstrosity in *La Vie nouvelle* and *Import/Export*   82
  Michael Goddard
8 Naked Women, Slaughtered Animals: Ulrich Seidl and the Limits
  of the Real   93
  Catherine Wheatley

Part III Watching the Extreme: Cultural Reception

9 Watching Rape, Enjoying Watching Rape . . .: How Does a Study of Audience Cha(lle)nge Film Studies Approaches?   105
Martin Barker

10 Censorship, Reception and the Films of Gaspar Noé: The Emergence of the New Extremism in Britain   117
Daniel Hickin

11 'Sex and Violence from a Pair of Furies': The Scandal of *Baise-moi*   130
Leila Wimmer

12 'Close Your Eyes and Tell Me What You See': Sex and Politics in Lukas Moodysson's Films   142
Mariah Larsson

Part IV Ethics and Spectatorship in the New Extremism

13 Lars von Trier's *Dogville*: A Feel-Bad Film   157
Nikolaj Lübecker

14 A 'Passion for the Real': Sex, Affect and Performance in the Films of Andrea Arnold   169
Tanya Horeck

15 Interrogating the Obscene: Extremism and Michael Haneke   180
Lisa Coulthard

16 On the Unwatchable   192
Asbjørn Grønstad

Afterword

17 More Moralism from that 'Wordy Fuck'   209
James Quandt

Notes on Contributors   214
Works Cited   218
Index   231

Acknowledgements

This book emerges out of our mutual interest in filmic representations of sex and violence, and the growing prevalence of a 'new extremism' in contemporary cinema. One of the questions most frequently posed to us during the writing of this book concerned the long-term effects that watching such extreme films might have on us as individuals. Our typical response would be to respond quite cheerfully (often to the bewilderment of our interlocutors) that, for us, it is precisely the intensely visceral, affective and emotional appeal of these 'feel-bad' films that we find most fascinating, and that formed the basis of our intellectual response in this volume. For as challenging – and at times emotionally exhausting – as it can be to watch these sorts of films, this sustained engagement has also been incredibly rewarding. We think this book is testimony to the kinds of intellectual and critical insights that can emerge from bringing the more difficult aspects of personal response to the fore.

Our critical reflections on the films of the new extremism led, in the first instance, to the creation of an MA course, 'The New Extremism: Contemporary European Cinema', and then to an international Film Studies conference, hosted at Anglia Ruskin University in Cambridge, England, in April 2009. We are immensely grateful to all the scholars who attended this conference, some of whom travelled vast distances, from North America, Europe and Australia, to share their research on extreme cinema. Their rich and intellectually stimulating papers formed the inspiration for this book. As we remarked many times throughout the conference, for academics who spend their time steeped in cinematic depictions of extreme sex, violence and general degradation, you are a remarkably lovely, good-humoured and collegial bunch.

Special thanks to our fantastically dynamic friend and colleague Sarah Barrow, who was a co-organiser of the conference and who helped to make it such a successful event. Thanks also to those colleagues at Anglia Ruskin who offered a helping hand and showed their support on the day, especially Kerstin

Bueschges, Annie Morgan-James, Jussi Parikka, Milla Tiainen and Rowland Wymer. A special thanks also to Lee Keable and Fionn Pooler for their invaluable assistance. For watching a host of graphic, gruelling films with us and providing us with such intellectually engaging conversation week in and week out we would like to thank all the students on 'The New Extremism' MA course, in particular Gözde Naiboglu, Will Smith, Toby Venables, Zeljko Vukicevic, Janice Webster, Adrian Horrocks and Claire Henry. The Representation, Identity, Body (RIB) reading group, which met regularly throughout 2009 to talk about affect, was also hugely important for helping us to think through some of the key issues we explore in this book and we would like to say a big thanks to all the RIBers, whose intellectual energy and contributions can be evinced in our thinking about affect and cinema spectatorship.

While this book was initially inspired by our MA course and the subsequent conference at Anglia Ruskin University, many of the chapters included in this collection were commissioned at a later phase, and we are grateful to all those who generously responded to our requests for collaboration, and who brought their research into dialogue with the aims of the collection so seamlessly. Your contributions have enriched this project. We would especially like to express our appreciation to James Quandt for granting us permission to reprint his original 2004 *Artforum* essay, 'Flesh and Blood: Sex and Violence in Recent French Cinema'.

Thanks to Edinburgh University Press, in particular Vicki Donald, who made it all such a painless experience. We owe a debt of gratitude to the anonymous readers of our original book proposal, who provided critically astute comments and who saw the promise of our project. We would also like to extend our thanks to Martine Beugnet for her wonderful enthusiasm and for offering vital advice at some crucial moments. For their reading of our introduction at a late stage, and for offering such perceptive and incisive feedback, we would like to thank Joss Hands and Lisa Coulthard.

Finally, for their unflagging support and their companionship sitting through more extreme films than any partner should probably have to bear, our heartfelt gratitude goes to Hugh Perry and Jamie Andrews.

CHAPTER I

Introduction

Tanya Horeck and Tina Kendall

WHAT IS THE NEW EXTREMISM?

This book explores a diverse body of films that have attracted attention for their graphic and confrontational images of sex and violence, and which can be described as part of a trend towards a 'new extremism' in contemporary European filmmaking. As with the films it is used to describe, the term the new extremism is a highly suggestive and contentious one, which comes loaded with a range of connotations in this post-9/11 age of religious terrorism. Hence, it is important for us to clarify from the start what it means in a specifically cinematic context. In this collection, we are adopting the term 'the new extremism' in the context of contemporary film culture, both as it has been used to describe and often decry the work of a range of French directors – including, for example, Catherine Breillat, Gaspar Noé, Bruno Dumont and Philippe Grandrieux – and to interrogate affinities with the work of European filmmakers such as Michael Haneke, Lukas Moodysson, Lars von Trier and Ulrich Seidl.

Reports of fainting, vomiting and mass walkouts have consistently characterised the reception of this group of art-house films, whose brutal and visceral images appear designed deliberately to shock or provoke the spectator. Although such films have frequently been dismissed as aggressive and reactionary, this book argues that the films of the new extremism and the controversies they engender are indispensable to the critical task of rethinking the terms of contemporary spectatorship. Beyond the collective emphasis in these films on explicit and brutal sex, and on graphic or sadistic violence – features shared by a range of other global film trends such as 'torture porn' (Lockwood 2009), 'the new brutality film' (Gormley 2005) or 'Asia Extreme' cinema (Chi-Yun Shin 2008) – it is first and foremost the uncompromising and highly self-reflexive appeal to the spectator that marks out the specificity of these films for us. We locate the new extremism in cinema, then, not simply with respect to what is shown, but in light of the complex and often contradictory ways in which these films situate sex and violence as a means of interrogating the relationship between films and their spectators in the late twentieth and early twenty-first centuries. In their concerted practice of provocation as a mode of address, the films of the new extremism bring the notion of response to the fore, interrogating, challenging and often destroying the notion of a passive or disinterested spectator in ways that are productive for film theorising today.

FROM (FRENCH) EXTREMITY TO (EUROPEAN) EXTREMISM

Writing in 2004, film programmer and critic James Quandt first coined the term 'the new French extremity' to describe what he saw as a 'growing vogue for shock tactics' in French cinema since the 1990s. Quandt's widely read polemic has been hugely influential in ways not always expected (and at times lamented) by the author. As he wryly observes in this volume in an important new afterword on the subject, his essay 'took on a life never intended'. It prompted a range of responses from popular and scholarly contexts, and the new extremism has since gained widespread notoriety as one of the most important recent trends in French cinema. In his original 2004 essay, reprinted in this book for the first time, Quandt defined this disparate body of filmmaking in the following disparaging terms:

> The critic truffle-snuffing for trends might call it the New French Extremity, this recent tendency to the willfully transgressive by directors like François Ozon, Gaspar Noé, Catherine Breillat, Philippe Grandrieux – and now, alas, Dumont. Bava as much as Bataille, Salo no less than Sade seem the determinants of a cinema suddenly determined to break every taboo, to wade in rivers of viscera and spumes of sperm, to fill each frame with flesh, nubile or gnarled, and subject it to all manner of penetration, mutilation and defilement. (Quandt 2004)

For Quandt, such determined transgression smacked of desperate measures. As he further explained:

> Images and subjects once the provenance of splatter films, exploitation flicks, and porn – gang rapes, bashings and slashings and blindings, hard-ons and vulvas, cannibalism, sadomasochism and incest, fucking and fisting, sluices of cum and gore – proliferate in the high-art environs of a national cinema whose provocations have historically been formal,

political or philosophical . . . Does a kind of irredentist spirit of incitement and confrontation, reviving the hallowed Gallic traditions of the *film maudit*, of *épater les bourgeois* and *amour fou*, account for the shock tactics employed in recent French cinema? Or do they bespeak a cultural crisis, forcing French filmmakers to respond to the death of the ineluctable (French identity, language, ideology, aesthetic forms) with desperate measures? (Quandt 2004)

With this set of challenging questions, Quandt laid down the gauntlet for the discussions that followed, including a response from British film critic Jonathan Romney, who placed such filmmaking in the context of wider aesthetic and philosophical traditions of extremism and transgression in France. Defending many of the same films derided by Quandt, Romney noted that:

it shouldn't be forgotten that many of the films . . . [of the new extremism] are also stylistically extreme and innovative, whether it's in the shades of austere detachment (Breillat, De Van, Honoré), in Noé's lapel-grabbing kineticism, or in the inscrutable experimentalism of Philippe Grandrieux's *La Vie nouvelle*, which resorts to such disorienting tactics as heat photography and long silences. (2004)

While it was Quandt's notion of a new 'extremity' that initiated the debates that were to follow, it is the idea of a 'new extremism' in contemporary filmmaking that has gained more widespread usage, appearing in a number of contexts, including Ginette Vincendeau's 2007 entry on the New French Extremism in *The Cinema Book*. Other scholarly work on this body of films has preferred cognate terms, such as a 'cinema of sensation' (Beugnet 2007a), a '*cinéma du corps*' (Palmer 2006b), '*cinéma brut*' (Russell 2010) or 'extreme realism' (James Williams 2009). Despite the range of terms used to describe the films in question, these scholars seem to agree that the turn towards 'explicit and graphic physicality' constitutes a significant tendency in French cinema since the 1990s (Williams 2009: 188). The hallmarks of this tendency include a 'disregard for genre boundaries', and an inclination to combine an art cinema aesthetic with 'shock tactics traditionally associated with gore, porn, and horror' (Beugnet 2007a: 36). According to Vincendeau, such films also frequently include 'shocking acts', such as rape, necrophilia and self-mutilation (2007: 205). However, many of them tend to represent such subjects through techniques that heighten the sensory and affective involvement of audiences, foregrounding the question of spectatorial response in a way that 'unites the intellectual and the visceral' (James Williams 2009: 188). Scholars such as Scott MacKenzie have explored how the films of the new French extremism 'profoundly question the complicity of the spectator in the acts of voyeurism and desire surrounding the representation of sexuality, violence and, *a fortiori*, rape-on-screen' (2010: 159).

The films associated with the new extremism trend have had an undeniable impact not only on French cinematic production in the twentieth century, but also on the exportability and marketability of French cinema in foreign markets. As Vincendeau writes: 'The label [the new French extremism] helps the export of French cinema, reinforcing cultural stereotypes of Frenchness, while fitting with the global rising tide of sex and violence and appealing to younger audiences' (Vincendeau 2007: 205). If the films of the new extremism in France have been received abroad as a particularly 'French' take on this 'rising tide of sex and violence', a range of European films since the 1990s have employed many of the same confrontational aesthetic strategies, and have also garnered attention for their distinctive takes on cinematic provocation and transgression. Noting affinities between the early work of Gaspar Noé, François Ozon, Thomas Vinterberg and Lars von Trier, for instance, critic Richard Falcon noted in 1999 that 'the new European cinema wants to outrage us' (Falcon 1999: 11). Falcon details what he calls 'an aggressive desire to confront [. . .] audiences, to render the spectator's experience problematic' (ibid.). More recently, European filmmakers such as Michael Haneke, Lukas Moodysson, Thomas Clay, Ulrich Seidl, Yorgos Lanthimos, György Pálfi, Mladen Djordjevic and others have aligned themselves in noteworthy ways with traditions of cinematic provocation, and there is no doubt that the ever more global nature of extreme cinema has inflected the ways that these films have been marketed and received. The recent example of Lars von Trier's *Antichrist* (Denmark, 2009) is a case in point: the film's promotional campaign traded on that film's reputation as 'the most shocking film in the history of the Cannes film festival' (Singh 2009), and the ensuing polemic also demonstrated just how effective such marketing strategies can be, with the film receiving exceptionally high levels of mainstream media coverage.[1] However, the debates around such controversial, gruelling films in this broader context of European cinema have also led to substantial critical reflection and analysis, and recent scholarly work on European filmmakers engages with many of the same questions that have preoccupied scholars of the new extremism in French cinema – questions about spectatorial agency and 'ethical reflexivity' (Wheatley 2009: 2), about the critical 'appeal of moments of unpleasure in cinema' (Bainbridge 2004: 400), or about the ways in which the 'abject heroes or heroines in European cinema' might offer 'a counter-image of what it means to be human' (Elsaesser 2005: 125).

In light of this, one of the central aims of this collection is to open up the concept of a 'new extremism' from French to European cinema. This is the first book-length study of the new extremism, and the volume brings into critical dialogue for the first time a range of European filmmakers who are recognised for their sensational, provocative work, and for pushing at the boundaries of the watchable. In emphasising this move from France to Europe and calling for a consideration of the work of filmmakers from a range of national contexts, we do not mean to push aside questions of specificity – national, aesthetic, socio-economic or political – in favour of an a-historical or decontextualised approach to sex and violence. Rather, we believe that such a move lends critical insight into the different ideological contexts in which such extreme cinematic strategies have been adopted and adapted. Similarly, we want to make clear that we do not see the 'new extremism' as the collective label for a new 'genre' or 'movement'. The work of film directors associated with the new extremism does not amount to a collective 'style', and the films considered in this volume evoke and often deconstruct a range of generic tropes rather than constituting one collectively. Nor do we wish to downplay the differences in style, approach and intent that separate the filmmakers included in this volume. For example, there is a clear need to differentiate the films of Michael Haneke, which, despite their reputation for brutality, are characterised more by visual restraint than by excessive violence or horror, and the 'self-consciously trashy', in-your-face sex and violence of a film like *Baise-moi* (France, 2000), directed by Virginie Despentes and Coralie Trinh Thi, which has been described as 'among the New French Extremity's most graphic and confrontational texts' (Romney 2004). Hence, in this collection, the new extremism is treated as a trend or tendency that brings together a range of aesthetic approaches, themes and concerns, but that does not preclude other ways of categorising or approaching these films.

Finally, we want to specify our particular take on the terms 'new' and 'extremism' that we are adopting. In using this term, we do not wish to suggest that the extremism of these films is unprecedented; nor do we intend to enumerate a comprehensive catalogue of new, or newly extreme, practices or representations. Graphic representation and the tradition of artistic transgression have complex histories, and the definition of what one takes to constitute extreme is notoriously subjective, slippery and bound by historical and social pressures. As many of the contributors to this volume suggest, the extremity evinced by these films is often as much a matter of asserting particular filiations with artistic, cinematic, literary and philosophical forebears as it is of breaking new taboos. However, as Frances Ferguson argues in her study of obscene representation, the idea of newness is something that may also be intrinsic to our understanding of extremity and obscenity, of shock and outrage. By definition, the extreme is dependent on the idea of newness and on the compromising closeness that it is thought to establish between the real and its representation (Ferguson 2004: 152–4). The term the new extremism, then, reflects this bridging position between newness and indebtedness to the past, to a history of transgression and provocation that is renewed and given a visceral immediacy for the present.

AESTHETICS AND POLITICS: THE VALUE OF EXTREMISM

Given the contentious subject matter, and the emphasis on shock effects and unpleasurable sensations, it is not surprising that the response to these films has sometimes had a tendency to polarise debate. A range of pronouncements by the filmmakers in question have also fanned the flames of controversy, as in Bruno Dumont's self-professed goal of mounting a 'terrorist attack' on spectators (Matheou 2005: 17), Michael Haneke's intention to 'rape the spectator into independence' (Frey 2003), or Gaspar Noé's assertion that he is 'happy some people walk out during [his] film' because 'it makes the ones who stay feel strong' (Noé 1999). Such rhetorical pronouncements have often solidified, rather than challenged, the entrenched positions of those who, on the one side, see aesthetic or political merit in this group of challenging films, and those on the other, who consider the films of the new extremism as nothing but ultra-aggressive displays of pomp and circumstance, or the result of cynical marketing ploys designed to 'attract exposure through transgression' (Falcon 1999: 11). For critics such as Falcon and Quandt, these films display nostalgia for the 'authentic' provocations of Buñuel, Fassbinder or Pasolini, but are not able to reconnect with past traditions of cinematic subversion in a meaningful way. Romney, on the other hand, observes that these films:

> can hardly be accused of lacking a political drive – whether it's in the fiercely engaged sexual politics of Breillat's films, the cultural analysis of corporate-image trafficking in Assayas's *Demonlover* or Noé's venomously precise diagnosis of the alienated extreme right in *Seul contre tous*. (Romney 2004)

Though Romney is undoubtedly correct in ascribing a political dimension to many of the films discounted by critics such as Falcon and Quandt, what is curious is the extent to which his description of those films in this quotation seems to drain them of much of their visceral intensity, and to strip them of their essential ambiguity around questions of politics and history. While the films of the new extremism would seem to invite comparisons with earlier filmmakers for whom aesthetic provocation was an explicit form of political activism, they also seem invariably to short-circuit such analogies, such that the line between critique and complicity is increasingly difficult to discern.

As Martine Beugnet points out in her essay for this collection, these films frustrate 'attempts at meaningful contextualisation' in ways that are perhaps problematic and productive in equal measure. In a recent essay entitled 'Traces of the Modern: An Alternative History of French Cinema', Beugnet and Elizabeth Ezra note the extent to which the 'emphasis on the corporeal and the visceral' in the films of the new extremism, and their 'elliptical narratives and absence of psychological motivation' resist 'explicit interpretations and overt political messages' (Beugnet and Ezra 2010: 35). However, this 'resistance to interpretation' does not necessarily imply that these films lack a political context. On the contrary, it is precisely extreme cinema's ability to eschew 'productive recuperation' (Beugnet and Ezra 2010: 35) and to '[engage] us emotionally as well as aesthetically with the irrational and unacceptable' that gives it its critical edge (Beugnet 2007a: 40). For Beugnet, the obscure historical and political dimension of the films of the new extremism needs to be read in a radically new way – as a form of embodied dialogue that takes place between film, spectator and context, and which has to be sensed before it can be understood. In making this argument, Beugnet draws from the work of Adam Lowenstein (2005), whose approach to the modern horror film insists on the powers of visceral shock and sensationalism as means of building up sympathetic identifications with history. By creating oblique and yet powerful correspondences between the body of the film and the body of the spectator, the films of the new extremism might be said to embody both past and contemporary realities in a novel way. In doing so, they call for a sustained consideration of the complex relations between aesthetics and politics as they are constructed through the intimate dialogue between the film and the spectator, and as they are reproduced and reconfigured through the kind of vociferous public debates that these films so often trail in their wake.

AFFECT, ETHICS AND AUDIENCES

Perhaps not surprisingly, given the emphasis on the nature of embodied spectatorial response, the critical concept of affect is central to this collection.[2] As noted in a special issue on 'Affect' in the journal *Body and Society* (2010), recent critical thinking in the social sciences and humanities has been characterised by an 'affective turn'.[3] What such a turn to affect might mean for contemporary film studies is something that is explored in this book: many of the contributors are concerned, in one way or another, with exploring our affective responses to film culture, as well as looking at how such culture works to shape our perceptions. It has not always been thus. As Lisa Cartwright notes in her recent book, *Moral Spectatorship*, 'feeling' has long been 'a suspect area of research for film and media scholars who, since the time of Brechtian distanciation and Althusserian apparatus theory, have worked to institute models that allow us to resist the seductive pull of the medium as it moves us to feel for the other' (2008: 1). Increasingly, however, film scholars coming from a range of approaches, including audience response studies, cognitive science, psychoanalytic film theory, Deleuzian studies and phenomenological philosophy, have become preoccupied with exploring the nature of that seductive pull. As cognitive film theorist Carl Plantinga notes, 'any satisfactory account of film reception and its implications for ideology, rhetoric, ethics, or aesthetics had better be able to take film-elicited affect and emotion into account' (2009: 5). The question of how cinema works on the level of sensation and body attempts to complicate a purely representational understanding of it as a semiotic meaning-making machine. As evidenced by the contributions collected herein, the films of the new extremism help us to rethink cinema as that which is played out on our bodies, and which constructs an appeal to affect, emotion and, indeed, the intellect.

In turn, this appeal to the affective and visceral components of spectatorship has important implications for thinking about the ethical purchase of such extreme films, and the relation that they construct between self and other, spectator and screen. If, as Lisa Downing and Libby Saxton have recently suggested in *Film and Ethics: Foreclosed Encounters*, 'film studies has had surprisingly little to say about ethics' (2010: 11), this collection echoes their suggestion that 'ethics may be integral to film practice, the phenomenology of cinema, and to much film theory' (ibid.). In the films of the new extremism, questions of ethics are brought to the fore: by pushing at the limits of the watchable and the tolerable, these films involve and implicate spectators in particularly intensified ways with what is shown on screen, demanding critical interrogation and ethical and affective response. Although they have often been dismissed as immoral, nasty and irredeemable, much of what is so interesting and disturbing about this group of films is precisely the challenges they pose to commonly held belief systems. In this respect, the films of the new extremism highlight an important distinction, which all too frequently goes unnoticed in public debates about controversial films, between moral and ethical spectatorship. As Michele Aaron notes, moral response is largely involuntary and uncritical, whereas ethics 'is all about thinking through one's relationship to morality rather than just adhering to it' (Aaron 2007: 109). In this respect, the emphasis on violent excess, negativity and heightened moments of unpleasure in the new extremism may in fact be construed as an indispensable facet of its ethical appeal: as Downing and Saxton put it, 'often the most apparently pernicious representations are the ones that can enlist the viewer in particularly nuanced ethical reflection' (2010: 21). Many of the chapters in this book examine these films from this perspective, exploring the complex ways in which the films of the new extremism wreak havoc on moral certainties and established value systems, but without supplying the kind of comforting messages that are to be found in more redemptive or life-affirming films. Instead, such films highlight the 'ethical and creative potential' (Del Rio 2008: 16) of the spectator to think through her own embodied responses to images and to others. The work of ethical reflection, then, is articulated as much through the heated debates surrounding these films as it is through the films themselves. As Downing and Saxton suggest, 'ethical meaning does not reside purely in the flow of images but emerges more urgently in the course of the reception and circulation of these images – in the multifarious encounters between audiences and films' (ibid.: 20).

Following our interest in the notion of affective and ethical response, we believe there is a need to interrogate many of the taken-for-granted claims that have been made about controversial films and their spectators. The task of theoretical investigation into the new extremism needs to be informed and counterbalanced by a rigorous approach to audiences and what they do with or make of the films in question. Martin Barker's work has been at the forefront of this attempt to understand systematically how audiences respond to extreme images, and how those demands for ethical reflection are negotiated in actual contexts and in specific instances of watching. As he argues elsewhere:

> [Audience research] means devoting attention to the accompanying materials to which audiences are exposed even before they reach the theatre. It means addressing the precise ways in which films are brought to audiences. It means focusing on the social and individual conditions under which films are accessed, watched, appreciated, and digested, and how cultural values and worldviews are used as active points of reference in these processes. (Barker and Mathijs 2008: 2)

We view this approach as essential for thinking about the films of the new extremism. Such films, and the controversies they engender, call for a nuanced consideration of the actual contexts of viewing, and of the extra-textual strategies that help either to contain or to amplify their capacity to shock and offend. We maintain that the films associated with the new extremism provide a productive meeting ground for two apparently rival accounts of film audiences: textual-based theories of spectatorship and audience research. In his essay for this volume, Barker, for instance, takes issue with what he describes as a film studies approach to the spectator, which, for him, often makes generalised predictions about viewers and their habits of viewing films. But one of the intriguing things about watching, teaching and writing about this group of films is the way in which they seem to call for a combined approach to the vexed question of spectatorship and audience response. The films of the new extremism enable – and in many cases demand – an approach that attends to concrete facts about audiences, but that also opens these up to theoretical speculation about the wider stakes and implications of those responses.

The essays in this volume reflect this call for a composite approach to thinking about sex and violence in the cinema, approaching the films of the new extremism from a variety of theoretical and methodological perspectives. Our collection begins with the reprint of James Quandt's 2004 essay, 'Flesh and Blood: Sex and Violence in Recent French Cinema'. It is notable that almost all of the essays in this volume refer to Quandt's impassioned essay, even if it is only to set themselves in opposition to its claims, a move that testifies to its enduring significance as a tour de force in polemical writing. Though Quandt's essay refers to the idea of a new 'extremity' in derogatory terms, something that many of the contributors to this volume seek to complicate and nuance further, it is his work that scholars have found so immensely useful to push against when trying to elucidate the central features of an extremist turn in contemporary European filmmaking. Well aware of the 'straw man' status his work has assumed in discussions of the new extremism, Quandt has written an Afterword for this book that addresses the unexpected impact of his essay and considers what kind of cultural meanings the idea of the new extremism has taken on seven years later. As the title of the Afterword, 'More Moralism from that "Wordy Fuck"', may suggest, a recalcitrant Quandt responds to his detractors, and provides us with yet another bold and thought-provoking piece.

The first section of the book, 'French Cinema and the New Extremism', explores the historical, socio-political and cinematic contexts that frame the eruption of a visceral and extreme wave of French filmmaking. In keeping with this book's focus on the move from France to Europe, chapters in this section also consider how the intellectual and cultural influence of France has had an undeniable impact on ways of thinking about and framing European cinematic identities, practices and processes. The opening chapter of this section, 'The Wounded Screen', is by Martine Beugnet, whose critical interventions have played a central role in shaping intellectual thought about French extreme cinema. In this chapter, Beugnet focuses on post-war cinema, considering how an emerging extreme cinema deals with political conflicts and concerns about France's involvement in traumatic historical events in ways very different to the tradition of political, social realist filmmaking. As she writes: 'By contrast, the new extreme's foregrounding of a corporeal, embodied dimension offers a less immediately legible, more visceral connection to the historical context of production.' Beugnet builds on key insights from her book, *Cinema and Sensation: French Film and the Art of Transgression* (2007), regarding the 'sensory overload' of the 'cinema of sensation', by comparing Agnès Varda's classic art film, *Cléo de 5 à 7* (France, 1962) and Claire Denis's 'blood-soaked gore opus', *Trouble Every Day* (France, 2001). She explores how both films, though separated by forty years, work with categories 'emblematic of the postwar cultural shift' identified by Kristin Ross in her important study of postwar French society, *Fast Cars, Clean Bodies* (1999). Through references to disease, both films evoke 'the legacy of French colonial history', and in doing so, each connects 'the individual and the filmic body with the national body and history's festering wounds'.

Tina Kendall's chapter addresses one of the cultural figures who has been central to understandings of sexuality and transgression in France – Georges Bataille. Kendall examines Christophe Honoré's *Ma mère* (France, 2004), an adaptation of Bataille's posthumous novel of the same title, in order to consider the impact of Bataille on the corpus of the new extremism. Looking at the ways in which *Ma mère* displaces, reworks and reframes its Bataillean intertext, Kendall reflects upon the problematic place of Bataille in the explicit sex formula of recent 'hard core' international art cinema. Of particular interest in this regard is Honoré's decision to re-imagine the backdrop against which Bataille's story of incest unfolds – transposing it from 1920s Paris to the seedy nightclubs and sexual tourism sites of the Canary Islands in the present day. In so doing, Kendall argues, Honoré seeks to interrogate and reposition Bataille, to render his message intelligible in the context of global consumer capitalism. Drawing on Martin Crowley's claim that the appeal of Bataille today arises from his 'tackiness', Kendall argues that what is most subversive about Honoré's film is the 'tacky spectatorship' it solicits – what she describes as the 'oh, please!' factor that comes from the film's more embarrassing and risible moments.

Rounding off this section on the new French extremism is Neil Archer's examination of Bruno Dumont's reworking of the American road movie, *Twentynine Palms* (France, 2003). Here, Archer identifies and critically explores one of the key aspects of a new European cinema of extremity – the manipulation of popular genre and generic motifs in a high art, philosophical context. In reconsidering the extent to which Dumont can be seen to subvert the values and conventions of the road movie, Archer sounds an important cautionary note about the latent Eurocentrism at work in *Twentynine Palms*, which 'veers at times toward an implicit endorsement of (European) high-cultural values'. At its most complex and engaging, however, Archer suggests that the 'cinematic particularity' of the images in Dumont's film call such cultural binaries into question, inviting us to contemplate issues of 'space and the violence of human presence' and, finally, perhaps, the very idea of ' "centrist" cultural models in general, and the human-centric assumptions of knowledge and truth in particular'.

This reference to a critique of a human-centric understanding of the world provides a useful transition to the next section of this volume, 'Becoming Animal: Posthumanism and the New Extremism'. In this section, the contributors explore the complex ways in which the films of the new extremism foreground, and seek to challenge, the cultural and political construction of divisions between the human and its multifarious 'others'. The contributors argue that by intensifying those divisions between human and non-human, filmmakers such as Philippe Grandrieux and Ulrich Seidl offer a means of thinking through current socio-economic and political realities and East/West polarities. Drawing on the work of Giorgio Agamben, Jenny Chamarette considers the way that Grandrieux's films, through their scantly composed narrative frameworks, evoke archetypal figures which, she argues, point past 'narrative and representational configuration[s] of the human' to disclose 'the non-human construction of the ethics of humanity' at the heart of his films and others associated with the new extremism. In her analysis of *Sombre* (France, 1998), Chamarette argues that it is precisely through the film's address to sensation and the corporeal over narration and figuration, and an approach to filmmaking that insists on the film body itself, that such an ethical appeal is premised. She argues that the presentation of human bodies in *Sombre* 'offers a starting point for thinking subjectivity outside the sphere of the human'. By attending to the 'bare life', or 'what is excluded when humanity [. . .] is no longer accorded', films such as *Sombre* construct an ethical address to the spectator.

Michael Goddard continues the discussion of Grandrieux through a fascinating comparison of his film, *La Vie nouvelle* (France, 2002), with Seidl's *Import/Export* (Austria, 2007). While both directors have been accused of recycling clichéd ideas about Eastern Europe, Goddard argues that in fact they radically destabilise ideas about Eastern European monstrosity 'by pushing them to a higher level of intensity'. It is through their evocation of extreme visceral sensation (something that leaves them open to charges of sensationalism) that Grandrieux and Seidl are able to evoke the 'political unconscious' of post-Cold War Europe, and to explore critically how the West is implicated in the emergent modes of life and biopolitical experiences of the 'new Europe'.

Catherine Wheatley offers a slightly different take on Seidl in her contribution, by zeroing in on the tension between documentary and fiction in his work and reflecting more broadly on the 'status of the "real"' in the cinema of the new extremism. Considering how reality is deployed in the films of the new extreme, Wheatley focuses on what she describes as one of the tropes of the new extremism: the real-life slaughter of animals on screen. Debates about the viewer's ambivalent, emotional response to the death of animals relates in intriguing ways to Seidl's treatment of human subjects in films such as *Import/Export*. While acknowledging the uneasiness generated by his films and the uncertainty regarding the issue of the consent of his performers, Wheatley ultimately draws a conclusion not dissimilar to Goddard's: namely, that Seidl's pushing at the limits of the real, as frightening as it may be, is also extraordinarily effective at bringing 'us into contact with realities of human suffering in a manner unprecedented in the other films of the new extreme'.

The third section of the book, 'Watching the Extreme: Cultural Reception', foregrounds the central issue of how audiences respond to the films of the new extremism. It begins with Martin Barker's provocatively titled chapter, 'Watching Rape, Enjoying Watching Rape ...: How Does a Study of Audience Cha(lle)nge Mainstream Film Studies Approaches?' This chapter emerges out of an important 2005 study Barker and his associates were invited to conduct by the British Board of Film Classification (BBFC), exploring how actual audiences 'make sense of and respond to watching images of sexual violence on screen' in extreme cinema. For Barker, such an endeavour is imperative because it challenges the widespread tendency to make general predictions regarding the 'ways in which films might affect audiences'. Looking at the different responses that Critics (those who reject the film) and Embracers (those who engage with it) had to the violent ending of Catherine Breillat's *À ma sœur!* (France, 2001), Barker concludes by arguing for the importance of heeding the 'rich and complex' ways that Embracers engage with films, noting that 'we need as film scholars to *learn how to learn from them*' rather than falling back onto generalised predictions about the figure of the 'spectator'.

Working in the same tradition of audience analysis as Barker, Daniel Hickin's chapter tracks the changing attitudes of the BBFC towards film censorship during the 1990s into the noughties, by examining how it dealt with the cinema of the new extremism, in particular that of *enfant terrible* Gaspar Noé. Through exploring the BBFC's response to Noé's *Seul contre tous* (France, 1998) and *Irréversible* (France, 2002), Hickin argues that the BBFC eventually 'distanced itself from the concept of "censorship" towards a policy based on "classification" and the principle that adults should be free to choose their own viewing (provided it does not contravene British law)'. Through a close analysis of BBFC decisions and journalists' reviews of the films, Hickin's chapter looks at what happened between the BBFC's cutting of images of explicit sex in *Seul contre tous*, a film that can be considered part of the 'first wave of the new extremism', and its decision to release *Irréversible* uncut just four years later. As Hickin concludes, 'The release of *Seul contre tous* and *Irréversible* heralded the emergence of a new form of provocative European cinema that coincided with the beginning of an increasingly open, accountable and liberalised form of British film censorship.'

The next chapter, by Leila Wimmer, is an important attempt to contextualise *Baise-moi* (France, 2000), one of the most notorious of the films of the new extremism. Released in 2000, *Baise-moi*, along with *Irréversible* is part of the 'second wave' of the new extremism identified by Hickin in the previous chapter. Drawing attention to the structuring absences of *Baise-moi* and analysing the media furore surrounding the film's release, Wimmer suggests that what ultimately unsettles is the film's 'exposure of difference', a strategy which calls into question the 'rhetoric of universalism' that is a staple part of French national identity, and reveals 'unresolved anxieties and concerns about ethnicity, citizenship, gender and sexuality' that are at the heart of contemporary French society. As Wimmer notes, the censorship of the film was ultimately a means of displacing these anxieties on to the more manageable category of 'pornography'.

Finally, Mariah Larsson's chapter relocates us from France to Sweden with her consideration of a filmmaker who may not have received as much analytical attention as other directors of the new extremism but whose work is none the less key to an understanding of a wider European turn towards the extreme – Lukas Moodysson. Larsson examines the reception of Moodysson's work in Sweden, where he has developed a reputation as a politically subversive filmmaker. In particular, she analyses his fifth feature film *A Hole in My Heart* (Sweden, 2004), which is notable for its controversial and sensationalist images, including close-up plastic surgery on labia. Larsson notes that *A Hole in my Heart* did not fare as well with audiences as some of Moodysson's earlier films, though critics were more favourable towards it and tended to read it as a scathing critique of the pornography industry. Considering the links between Moodysson's filmmaking and the Swedish feminist anti-porn movement, Larsson's central argument is that, despite his reputation as a radical, there is a much more conservative strain running through his work than is generally acknowledged.

One of the major themes of this book is the question of ethics and spectatorship, and it is to this topic that we turn our attention in the final section. Each of the contributors in this section explores the complex ways in which the films of the new extremism position spectators affectively and ethically. Nikolaj Lübecker's chapter on Lars von Trier's *Dogville* (Denmark, 2003) argues that the film is really all about the spectator; more precisely, it is a film that seeks to manipulate the spectator and 'the aim of these manipulations is to bring out "the beast" in us.' Arguing that the film puts a 'deadlock on catharsis' through use of a colliding Brechtian and surrealist aesthetic logic, Lübecker suggests that the 'feel-bad' experience of *Dogville* and other films of the new extremism are what, however perversely, lead us to ethical reflection. Indeed, he goes so far as to conclude that 'aggression and manipulation not only save the films from facile moralising, but also allow the spectator to engage with the "inner bastard" in a way more intimate than otherwise possible.'

The next chapter, by Tanya Horeck, is an attempt to consider what the idea of a new European extremism might mean in the context of contemporary British filmmaking through an address to the work of Andrea Arnold. While Arnold's work is seen to sit somewhere between British social realism and European art cinema, Horeck looks at how her emphasis on the sensory and the affective aligns her with the films of the new extremism. Focusing on the explicit sex scenes in her two feature films, *Red Road* (UK, 2006) and *Fish Tank* (UK, 2009), Horeck argues that these affective encounters make 'the viewer engage in an intimate' and '*ethical* way, with the bodies on display'. In looking at how Arnold's films invite spectators to watch the sexual encounters through an ethical optics, revising understandings about the relationship between viewer and viewed, Horeck observes that, 'despite the fact that the films of the new extremism are frequently viewed as amoral for their sensational content, there is more of an ethical dimension to many of these films than is generally credited.'

In the penultimate essay to this section, Lisa Coulthard continues the discussion of ethics and spectatorship through an important reconsideration of the role that violence plays in the films of Michael Haneke, specifically *The Piano Teacher* (Austria, 2001) and *The White Ribbon* (Austria, 2009). Arguing that Haneke's films 'do not address violence directly so much as they create an environment where one expects violence to erupt any second', Coulthard suggests that this idea of a violence 'lying in wait' is key to understanding how violence 'works as cinematic and ethical critique' in his work. What makes Haneke's films so unsettling for spectators is the way they 'trouble our certainty as to what we consider violence and what we exclude'. For Coulthard, 'Haneke's films explore and extend the parameters of violence itself' in ways that go beyond ideas of excess or the sensational more commonly associated with the films of the new extremism to reveal the 'obscenity of the everyday'.

In the final chapter of this section, Asbjørn Grønstad explores the notion of the 'unwatchable' in relation to a 'roughly decade-long cycle of art films that compel us to rethink the notions of spectatorship, desire and ethics'. The films of the new extremism are films that compel us to look away – that constitute a 'fork in the eye' – an intensive visual assault on the film audience. But the infliction of such brutality on the spectator is not necessarily just about sensationalism for sensationalism's sake, and Grønstad argues that the idea of the unwatchable is in fact a key theoretical and philosophical concept, which is crucial for thinking through the ethical terms of the relationship between spectator and screen. In elaborating the concept of the unwatchable, Grønstad focuses on two films notable for their prolonged and 'excessive' scenes of sexualised violence, and for their deliberate attempt to inflict pain on the spectator, Noé's *Irréversible* and von Trier's *Antichrist*. How do we account for the (unpleasurable) spectatorship of such films? Or, as Grønstad asks, in a question that we believe is fundamental to this book as a whole: 'How, with reference to the spectator, is one to make sense of this ostensibly masochistic penchant for unwatchable images, and how, with reference to the artist and the film, is one to make sense of a poetics which accentuates such an excess?' Exploring possible ways of answering this question, through close reference to the films themselves, as well as to the notion of a 'fantasy of self-destructive viewing', Grønstad concludes with the suggestion that we need to consider how the films themselves generate theories of spectatorship, and to acknowledge that 'sometimes a film opens up spaces of reflection that are more vital than the film itself.' Ultimately, argues Grønstad, the films of the new extremism do nothing less than require us to reconsider existing ways we have in film studies for thinking about the ethics and the phenomenology of watching images.

The contributions to this volume engage with some of the most important theoretical issues facing film and media studies today: including the 'affective' turn in cultural theory; the role of the senses in cinema; the kinds of ethical engagements that media forms can be understood to enable; insights about what audiences do with violent and sexually graphic images; posthumanism; the relation of aesthetics and politics; and the distinctive ways that fantasy and reality are entwined in contemporary cultural production. That these theoretical issues are often already embedded in the films themselves is part of what makes the study of the new extremism in contemporary European cinema such a captivating, if troubling, pursuit.

Finally, the question of whether the new extremism is still alive or whether it is a thing of the past (not so new any more, in other words), or to what extent it is useful to employ such a term, remains a matter for debate. For Quandt, who refers to the new extremism in his Afterword as a 'waning phenomenon', the pertinent question to ask now is, 'what *was* the new extremism'? We are not quite so confident about sounding the death knell for the films of the new extremism just yet, for it would appear that the desire to provoke and disturb the spectator cannot be easily quelled and is, indeed, what constitutes the very foundation of the philosophical reflection on the ethics of looking that we find so prevalent in contemporary European art cinema. Instead, we want to hold on to the ambiguities surrounding the idea of a new extremism in contemporary European filmmaking, which, despite debates regarding its meaning and provenance and the direction in which it is heading, retains its cultural currency as a rubric by which a specific body of contemporary films – and *auteurs* – are viewed and understood.

NOTES

1. For an example of the debate over *Antichrist* see Xan Brooks (2009).
2. Although there are a number of ways of approaching the terms 'affect' and 'affective', by far the most influential has been Brian Massumi's account. In *Parables for the Virtual: Affect, Movement, Sensation*, Massumi argues for the need to differentiate between affect and emotion. For Massumi, affect and emotion 'follow different logics and pertain to different orders' (2002: 27). Steven Shaviro provides a useful gloss on Massumi's understanding of

this distinction when he writes that '[f]or Massumi, affect is primary, non-conscious, asubjective or presubjective, asignifying, unqualified and intensive; while emotion is derivative, conscious, qualified and meaningful'. Emotion, Shaviro elaborates, 'is affect captured by a subject, or tamed and reduced to the extent that it becomes commensurate with that subject. Subjects are overwhelmed and traversed by affect, but they *have* or *possess* their own emotions' (2010: 3, italics in original).

3. See Blackman and Venn (2010).

CHAPTER 2

Flesh and Blood: Sex and Violence in Recent French Cinema[1]

James Quandt

The convulsive violence of Bruno Dumont's new film *Twentynine Palms* (2003) – a truck ramming and a savage male rape, a descent into madness followed by a frenzied knifing and suicide, all crammed into the movie's last half-hour after a long, somnolent buildup – has dismayed many, particularly those who greeted Dumont's first two features, *Life of Jesus* (1997) and *L'Humanité* (1999), as the work of a true heir to Bresson. Whether *Palms*' paroxysm of violation and death signals that Dumont is borrowing the codes of Hollywood horror films to further his exploration of body and landscape or whether it merely marks a natural intensification of the raw, dauntless corporeality of his previous films, it nevertheless elicits an unintentional anxiety: that Dumont, once imperiously impervious to fashion, has succumbed to the growing vogue for shock tactics in French cinema over the past decade.

The critic truffle-snuffing for trends might call it the New French Extremity, this recent tendency to the willfully transgressive by directors like François Ozon, Gaspar Noé, Catherine Breillat, Philippe Grandrieux – and now, alas, Dumont. Bava as much as Bataille, Salò no less than Sade seem the determinants of a cinema suddenly determined to break every taboo, to wade in rivers of viscera and spumes of sperm, to fill each frame with flesh, nubile or gnarled, and subject it to all manner of penetration, mutilation, and defilement. Images and subjects once the provenance of splatter films, exploitation flicks, and porn – gang rapes, bashings and slashings and blindings, hard-ons and vulvas, cannibalism, sadomasochism and incest, fucking and fisting, sluices of cum and gore – proliferate in the high-art environs of a national cinema whose provocations have historically been formal, political, or philosophical (Godard, Clouzot, Debord) or, at their most immoderate (Franju, Buñuel, Walerian Borowczyk, Andrzej Zulawski), at least assimilable as emanations of

---

[1] First published in *Artforum* in 2004.

an artistic movement (Surrealism mostly). Does a kind of irredentist spirit of incitement and confrontation, reviving the hallowed Gallic traditions of the *film maudit*, of *épater les bourgeois* and *amour fou*, account for the shock tactics employed in recent French cinema? Or do they bespeak a cultural crisis, forcing French filmmakers to respond to the death of the ineluctable (French identity, language, ideology, aesthetic forms) with desperate measures?

An outrider of French extremity, Ozon's first feature, the suspense thriller *See the Sea* (1997), alternates oblique terror with shock shots – of a toothbrush dipped in a shit-filled toilet or the subliminal suggestion of a sutured vagina. Ozon defended it and the *outré* nature of his *Criminal Lovers* (1999), a cross between *Natural Born Killers* and 'Hansel and Gretel,' steeped in sexual pathology and cannibalism, this way: 'What I am interested in is violence and sex, because there is a real challenge in rendering the strong and powerful, as opposed to the weak and trivial. I like something that asks moral questions.' Ozon has since matured – e.g., the classical, contained *Under the Sand* (2000), starring an exquisitely anguished Charlotte Rampling – but to the nascent enfant terrible whose every kink was calculated (especially in the screeching satire of *Sitcom* [1998]), morality seemed a canard, a pretext for provocation. Certainly, his films never approach the unsettling vision of his hero, Rainer Werner Fassbinder, who could traumatize audiences simply by confronting them with uncomfortable truths.

Fassbinder's painful verities about race and abasement also inspired Claire Denis, whose *Chocolat* (1988) and *No Fear, No Die* (1990) are distinguished by clear-eyed empathy and sociological insight. Denis disdains these traditional virtues in *Trouble Every Day* (2001), a horror show in which Béatrice Dalle is cast for her ravenous mouth as Coré, a cannibal sated only when she consumes the bodies of her hapless lovers. An enervated Denis barely musters a hint of narrative to contain or explain the orgiastic bloodletting; a shadow plot involving Vincent Gallo as an American doctor struggling with his own bloodlust while on honeymoon in Paris is both cursory and ludicrous. Denis's superb cinematographer Agnès Godard, responsible for the ravishing images of *Beau Travail* (1999), here trains her camera on landscapes of flayed flesh, on Dalle's tumid lips and hungry tongue aswim in crimson, and on walls artfully spattered with blood. (The Pat Steir-like sprays of incarnadine remind us that the French can never abandon their tendency to aestheticize even when aiming to appall; the paintings of Francis Bacon and Lucian Freud are invoked in Patrice Chéreau's *Intimacy* [2001] and Philippe Grandrieux's *La Vie nouvelle* [2002], and an eleven-second cum shot in Bertrand Bonello's *The Pornographer* [2001] is proudly described as having been inspired by 'Rothko at the Grand Palais'.)

Cannibalism and mutilation turn autoerotic in Marina de Van's debut film, *In My Skin* (*Dans ma peau*, 2002). De Van coscripted *See the Sea* and starred as its dead-eyed monster, a domestic intruder whose psychosis, according to director Ozon, 'confounds the anus and the vagina.' In *Peau*, de Van's ashen, impassive features become a Noh mask in her rendering of Esther, a young research analyst who accidentally slices her leg during a party and becomes increasingly obsessed with the pleasure she finds in her suppurating wounds. Compulsively cutting herself with knife or razor, Esther delects in her own flesh, mutilating and hungrily tasting an arm or tanning a swatch of epidermis in her quest to test the boundaries between self and world.

De Van's occasionally gruesome and unbearably intense work owes an obvious debt to both *Repulsion* and *Crash*, but it also stands with such recent French films as Catherine Breillat's *Romance* (1999) and Virginie Despentes and Coralie Trinh Thi's *Baise-moi* (2000) as an extreme vision of women driven to limits of compulsion, sexuality, or violence in their rejection of a world that attempts to constrain or degrade them. *Romance* chronicles a grimly narcissistic voyage into sexual oblivion by a schoolteacher who undergoes rape, sodomy, orgies, bondage, and childbirth in her pursuit of self-discovery. In this joyless update of *Belle de jour* and *Mademoiselle*, even a gynecological examination becomes a kind of debauch, a group of interns each taking a turn to thrust a hand into the supine *institutrice*. Breillat, who played the un-Bressonian Mouchette in *Last Tango in Paris*, has made a career of erotic provocation, her specialty being adolescent female sexuality (*A Real Young Girl* [1976], *36 Fillette* [1988], *Fat Girl* [2001]). She has just premiered *Anatomy of Hell*, starring Chanel model Amira Casar as a woman who meets her ambisexual lover by cutting her wrists. Set in what Breillat calls a 'pornocratie' – 'this fantastical and hideous realm of obscenity [that] obsesses me' – and intended to make *Romance* look like a *fête galante*, *Anatomy* films 'forbidden images, hackneyed from their overuse in the porn industry, as a reconsideration of the reality of those images as such.'

As bare and blunt as its title, *Baise-moi* (literally, Fuck Me, though known as *Rape Me*) explores the lower depths of the comparatively safe, bourgeois terrain of *Romance*; both films use actual porn stars – director Trinh Thi among them – and feature real penetration and 'money shots' for an extra frisson of erotic authenticity. Where *Romance*'s every image of abasement is lovingly lit and photographed by Yorgos Arvanitis, the long-take master of Angelopoulos's cinema, *Baise-moi* is grottily shot in handheld digital video, ideally raw for this tale of two women who go on a screwing and shooting rampage across France, taking their revenge for rape by blowing out the brains (or the assholes) of the men who don't satisfy them. Breillat mitigates her graphic sequences with pearly light and faux-profound philosophy – 'physical love is triviality dancing with the divine,' she proffers in mock-Durasian mode – but the pair of wantons who romp through the punk rock-propelled, blood- and sperm-smeared *Baise-moi* don't have much time for poetry: 'I leave nothing precious in my cunt for those jerks,' one of them declares after she is raped. Initially banned in France (and elsewhere, including Ontario), *Baise-moi* was, like *Romance*, championed by many feminists who found in its crude, violent vision an allegory of 'female empowerment'.

Baise-moi includes a clip from *I Stand Alone* (*Seul contre tous*, 1998) by the directors' friend Gaspar Noé, whose Lynch-like *Carne* (1991), a studiously repugnant short film about a horse butcher who takes revenge on a man he suspects of raping his autistic daughter, is perhaps the ur-text of the New French Extremity. The butcher reappears as the jobless and embittered protagonist of *I Stand Alone*, spewing hatred against immigrants, homosexuals, women, and blacks. Safely displaced as the rant of a mad meatman – Noé has the courage of few convictions – his harangues are subsumed by an aggressive style of abrupt cuts, extreme close-ups, and preposterous intertitles, of seismic sounds and hard-driving music whose effect Noé compared to an epileptic seizure. (No doubt young Alexandre Aja had Noé's hulking butcher in mind when he cast the same actor as a psycho killer in *Haute Tension* [2003], a grisly thriller that revels in human forms of *steak tartare*.) Noé merrily described his film as anti-French, suggesting that a waning sense of national power and identity informs its baleful vision. Ironically, his world-as-abattoir metaphor reminds one of a far more devastating film – Franju's epochal *Le Sang des bêtes* – proving perhaps that *I Stand Alone* incarnates the very decline Noé thinks he is critiquing.

Of the two kinds of *film maudit* – those that set out to scandalize and the guileless ones that sadly chance upon their disrepute – Noé's *Irréversible* (2002) is most flagrantly the former. The director suddenly finds philosophy (J. W. Dunne's 1927 treatise *An Experiment with Time*); 'time destroys all things,' his film announces, posturing as fearless vision of hell. A Bergson *de la boue*, Noé inverts his narrative, back to front, as the title suggests, so that we are forced to experience the tragic tow, and toll, of time. The film, shot in a series of faked long takes, begins in a squalid hotel room (with a brief appearance by the still-yelping butcher) and then woozily makes its way to a strobe-lit inferno – a gay fisting and fuck club delicately called the Rectum. Traveling backward to the moment when the film's heroine (Monica Bellucci) discovers she is pregnant by her boyfriend (Vincent Cassel), the film reveals in reverse order her departure for a party and (in a relentless, 'real-time' sequence lasting many minutes) her anal rape in an underpass by a gay pimp who then smashes her head in, leaving her comatose. Her boyfriend and his brainy pal search the city for her assailant, finally bashing the wrong man's brains to a pulp with a fire extinguisher amid a crowd of gawking gays, too insensate from poings and poppers to do anything but thrill to the kill. Hip nihilist Noé comes on as our Céline of the Monoprix, making sure it is the sensitive intellectual and not the primitive boyfriend who wields the weapon, proving, as the caterwauling press kit has it, that 'man is an animal, and the desire for vengeance is a natural impulse.'

Noé's noxious style and his primal theme of man as id or animal get a philosophical gloss in the work of Philippe Grandrieux. Serial killers, much like abattoirs, are pretty well exhausted as metaphor, but Grandrieux's *Sombre* (1998) attempts something new: a disorienting plunge into the consciousness of a compulsive rapist/murderer. The first half-hour of *Sombre* is taken up by a vertiginous transcription of a road tour of carnage, as the killer casually dispatches women in the French countryside. Underlit, indeterminate images, flickering, unfocused, and flash cut, summon a sense of menace and illegible dread, exaggerated by abrasive sound effects and roiling music by Alan Vega, of the protopunk band Suicide. Once the killer hooks up with a pair of sisters whose car has broken down, Grandrieux's attempt at a tour de force of Thanatos flattens into generic familiarity, and no amount of eerily liminal images and fetid sex can disguise his tired themes.

Grandrieux compares *Sombre* to a Grimm fairy tale; his follow-up, *La Vie nouvelle*, derives from the Orpheus and Eurydice myth. Orpheus in this case is Seymour, a young American soldier adrift in 'desolate, lawless Eastern Europe' – a handy signifier for existential chaos, much as Beirut once was for Volker Schlöndorff – who encounters a beautiful, defiled prostitute and follows her into an underworld of torture, sexual atrocity, and death. The performances veer between the catatonic and the histrionic, and again Grandrieux evokes the abyss with stygian, indecipherable images, each one tinged with hints of genocide and holocaust, of Chechnya and Bosnia; like Noé, he relies on a grinding sound track to accompany scenes of menace and barbarity. The bleary voyeurism of Grandrieux's style is deadening, then abhorrent; it arrogates political, social, and historical horror for a fashionista vision of the apocalypse – Salò as infernal rave. (The prostitute's green kohl-ringed eyes and chic Seberg bob suggest not ethnic cleansing but a St. Honoré catwalk.) Noé and Ozon seem earnest in comparison with Grandrieux, who fancies himself a *philosophe*: 'What do we seek, since the first traces of hands impressed in rock the long, hallucinated perambulation of man across time' – he once mused in the pages of *Cahiers du cinéma* – 'what do we try to reach so feverishly, with such obstinacy and suffering, through representation, through images, if not to open the body's night, its opaque mass, the flesh with which we think – and present it to the light, to our faces, the enigma of our lives?'

Standing at a tangent to these avatars of extremity is Bruno Dumont, whose trilogy about the despoliation of innocents began with *Life of Jesus*, set in a bleak northern French village. The teenage protagonist of Dumont's passion play is epileptic, inarticulate, and overwhelmed by the death of a friend's brother from AIDS. He searches for release from his dumb, monotonous life, first in animal sex with his bewildered girlfriend and then in a brutal attack on a young Arab. Dumont, influenced by the Bresson of *Au hasard Balthazar* and the Pialat of *Passe ton bac d'abord*, offhandedly shows us forbidden things

– an old woman's mottled body as she bathes, the ruddy boy penetrating his girlfriend in a meadow, their numbly thrusting flesh blanched by barren light – thereby inverting the expectation of spectacle that the film's CinemaScope format typically offers. That same expansive frame centers on the bloody genitals of a raped and murdered eleven-year-old girl at the beginning of Dumont's next film, *L'Humanité*. The camera contemplates her violated corpse with painterly dispassion, invoking both Courbet's *Origin of the World* and Duchamp's *Etant donnés*. The combination of carnality and Christianity, of Brueghel and Bresson found in *Life of Jesus* is both refined and expanded in *L'Humanité*. A film about the body in the landscape and the landscape of the body, it stares with naturalistic detachment at the brutish bouts of sex between a rawboned factory worker and her boyfriend and endows a seemingly unmotivated Scope close-up of a man's swimsuit-clad crotch with potent, appalling mystery.

Dumont's treatment of the flat Flemish landscape – muddy and rucked, with an imprisoning horizon – reminds us that the natural world is sublimely indifferent to *humanité*. In *Twentynine Palms*, Dumont's unerring eye similarly transforms the desert around California's Joshua Tree territory into a craggy, postlapsarian Eden in which to disport his New World Adam and Eve: an unhinged neurotic called Katia and her photographer boyfriend David. Drive, she said, and drive they do, scouting locations for his latest project in a new Hummer. She is prone to paroxysms of grief, joy, and jealousy; he mostly wants sex in various positions and various locations – a motel pool, on top of a remote boulder, even on a bed – and in a parody of *amour fou*, they fuck and fight, fight and fuck until the difference between the two F's dissolves into fullfrontal sulking. (The actress, Katia Golubeva, should be used to the ambience, having starred as the incestuous half-sister in Leos Carax's mopily hard-core *Pola X* [1999].)

Like Noé and Grandrieux, Dumont has succumbed to the elemental – and to the elementary. He treats as big news that man is an animal, reducing his characters to inarticulateness: The Eastern European Katia speaks hesitant, accented French, David a sort of guttural LA Esperanto. Blessed bouts of silence are punctuated by exchanges like this, as the two survey a field of wind machines:

'It's great.'
'It's fantastic.'
'It's perfect.'

Katia often collapses into mad laughter or tears; David shrieks when he comes, his Iggy Pop features screwed into a feral, teeth-baring squall of agony. Their every atavistic grunt and howl is exaggerated by a sound track that makes the breaking of a Chinese cracker resound like a rupture in the San Andreas Fault. Antonioni's *Zabriskie Point* and *The Passenger* are unavoidable references in *Twentynine Palms*, but the violence of the film's last half-hour erupts with signifiers from such American movies as *Deliverance* and *Psycho*, as if to emphasize that the very terrain and culture are born of and imbued with maiming and death. An auteurist case can be made for Dumont's foray into buggery and Humvees, horror-movie mutilation, and panting *Showgirls* pool sex; but where the extremity of Dumont's previous films was incorporated into both a moral vision and a coherent *mise-en-scène*, in *Twentynine Palms* it is imposed and escalated, the product of Dumont's slack, manufactured sense of American imbecility – Jerry Springer, artificial soft ice cream, oversize vehicles and ominous marines, rednecks snarling at strangers from their trucks, desert hillbillies with a taste for cornhole battery. Dumont surveys America as a toxic Tocqueville, deploying Hollywood methods, or so he thinks, against themselves. He has called his approach equal parts 'truth and poetry.' Absurd, false, and self-important, *Twentynine Palms* manifests instead a failure of both imagination and morality.

Asked why he set out to disturb his audience in *Twentynine Palms*, Dumont responded: 'Because people are way too set in their ways, they are asleep. They have to be woken up. . . . You can never definitely say you are human, you have to regularly be confronted by something, to remind you that you still have a lot to do as a human being, you have to be awakened.' Awakened, though, to what? What new or important truth does Dumont proffer that his audience needs to be slapped and slammed out of its sleepwalk into apprehending? In his sophistry, Dumont may place himself in the tradition of provocation, from Sade to Rimbaud to Pasolini, but *Twentynine Palms* has none of the power to shock an audience into consciousness evident in the elliptic violence of Bresson's *L'Argent*, the emotional evisceration of Eustache's *The Mother and the Whore*, or the bitter sexuality of Pialat's *À nos amours*.

The New French Extremity sometimes looks like a latter-day version of the hussards, those Céline-loving, right-wing anarchists of the '50s determined to rock the pieties of bourgeois culture; but for all their connections (shared actors, screenwriters, etc.), the recent provocateurs are too disparate in purpose and vision to be classified as a movement. Elsewhere, in the sclerotic shocks of Blier's *Les Côtelettes* (2003) and Brisseau's *Choses secrètes* (2002), the erotic fatigue of Bonello's *The Pornographer* and the charming jadedness of Nolot's old-fashioned *La Chatte à deux têtes* (aka *Porn Theater*, 2002), it appears to be the last gasp of Gallic libertinism. Some French commentators have dismissed the notion that there is any such trend; others have suggested that it marks a reconfiguration between aesthetics and the body in a dire, image-clotted culture; while still others that it is simply symptomatic of an international vogue for 'porno chic,' widely apparent in art-house films from Austria to Korea. More pragmatically, the drastic tactics of these directors could be an attempt to meet (and perchance defeat) Hollywood and Asian filmmaking on their own *Kill Bill* terms or to secure distributors and audiences in a market disinclined toward foreign films; and in fact many of these works have been bought in North America, while far worthier French films have gone wanting. But when Bruno Dumont, once championed as the standard-bearer of a revival of humanism – indeed, of classic neorealism – in French cinema, capitulates to this inimical approach, one begins to suspect a deeper impulse at work: a narcissistic response to the collapse of ideology in a society traditionally defined by political polarity and theoretical certitude, perhaps. The authentic, liberating outrage – political, social, sexual – that fueled such apocalyptic visions as *Salò* and *Weekend* now seems impossible, replaced by an aggressiveness that is really a grandiose form of passivity.

PART I

French Cinema and the New Extremism

CHAPTER 3

The Wounded Screen

Martine Beugnet

No facet of recent French cinema has created as much ambivalence and controversy as the so-called 'new extreme' phenomenon that came to prominence in the late 1990s.[1] The appellation itself may turn out to be somewhat misleading as it suggests the existence of a new genre or movement, where there is but a tendency, amongst a number of art directors with highly disparate stylistic and thematic interests, to draw on the kind of shock tactics usually associated with the 'genres of excess'.[2] Those films of Assayas, Breillat, Denis, De Van, Dumont, Grandrieux or Noé, to name but a few, which mingle the aesthetics and stylistic experimentation of art house and *auteur* film with those of horror, gore or pornographic cinema have, in turn, fascinated, repelled and irritated critics and film historians alike. For not only do these films' preoccupation with body horror and abjection test the spectator's capacity for forbearance, they also resist attempts at meaningful contextualisation. This chapter engages with such an effort of contextualisation, and in doing so, it endeavours to go beyond the recurrent critique of the new extreme as a typically postmodern exploitation of formal techniques and shock effects deployed merely to disguise the ideological void and artistic *cul de sac* that arguably characterised French film production at the end of the twentieth century.[3]

To this end, I connect the new extreme to the recurrence of a cinema that could be coined, in reference to Georges Bataille's writings, a 'cinema of expenditure'.[4] Although, as Elizabeth Ezra and I have argued elsewhere, this cinema finds some of its roots in the tradition of the Grand Guignol and the early serials of Louis Feuillade, in this chapter it is to the post-war period that I look for the establishment of those discursive and artistic practices that, I argue, remain as a pervasive backdrop against which the significance of French cinema's 'extreme' forms can be grasped. Hence in this chapter, even more than in my previous writing on the subject, the paradigm proposed by Kristin Ross in *Fast Cars, Clean Bodies* (1999) is key. In her classic study of post-war

France, Ross examines the profound shift that led French society to turn to the American model of intensive modernisation in order to dispel the ghosts of the recent past (World War II, the period of the German occupation and the Holocaust) and distance itself from the dramatic repercussions of the end of the colonial era. As Ross writes:

> Keeping the two stories apart is usually another name for forgetting one of the stories or for relegating it to a different time frame. This is in fact what has occurred. For, from this perspective (a prevalent one in France today), France's colonial history was nothing more than an 'exterior' experience that somehow came to an abrupt end, cleanly, in 1962. France then careened forward to new frontiers, modern autoroutes, the EEC, and all-electric kitchens [. . .] Modernization promises a perfect reconciliation of past and future in an endless present, a world where all sedimentation of social experience has been levelled or smoothed away, where poverty has been reabsorbed, and, most important, a world where class conflict is a thing of the past, the stains of contradiction washed out in a superhuman hygienic effort, by new levels of abundance and equitable distribution. (Ross 1999: 8, 10)

Writing in 1996, Ross emphasises the persistence of the dual history model in contemporary French culture. However, although this model has still not been overturned, by the end of the century it had, at least, become the topic of widespread critique. The end of the moratorium on the use of archives, the introduction of the Algerian war to the French school curriculum and the advent of the Papon trial in 1998 rekindled a debate now extended to the failure of countries such as France to prevent or respond ably to more recent conflicts. Current writings on the 'Vichy Syndrome' have highlighted the entangled legacy of the period of decolonisation and the years of occupation, and its lasting and potentially catastrophic influence. Emblematic of these ramifications is the appalling career of war criminal Marcel Papon, who not only participated in the campaign of repression and deportations orchestrated by the Vichy government, but also was later responsible, as the then chief of police, for the bloody repression of the peaceful demonstration in support of the Algerian FLN (the Algerian Liberation Front) in Paris in October 1961. Though he was convicted in 1998, the Papon affair came to prominence again in 2002 when, amidst heated controversy, Papon was released on the grounds of ill health. As historian Richard (Joseph) Golsan remarks in his study of French politics in *Vichy's Afterlife: History and Counterhistory in Postwar France*, it is perhaps appropriate that 'what has now come to be widely known as the "Vichy Syndrome" should evoke the same image of an ever-present, indisposable, living, growing corpse in order to describe a past that continues to haunt the French more than fifty years after the Second World War' (Golsan 2000: 2).[5]

The new extreme cinema emerged at a time when the corpse was stirring. Indeed, by then, the renewed questioning of France's role during the period of the occupation, as well as its colonial history and the '*guerre sans nom*', also informed attempts to come to terms with the contemporary catastrophes of war and genocide in the Balkans and Rwanda.[6] In French films, these burning issues would be addressed in more direct fashion and more classical cinematic styles through the resurgence, in the past fifteen years, of a social realist and political cinema in particular.[7] By contrast, the new extreme's foregrounding of a corporeal, embodied dimension offers a less immediately legible, more visceral connection to the historical context of production.

Compounded by the fact that many of the films overtly draw on the codes of the genres of excess, the partly retroactive nature of the public debates contemporary with the emergence of the new extremism makes it tempting to reduce it to a classic case of 'the return of the repressed' or to a radical example of a 'post-memory syndrome' (Hirsch 2008). But to offer such readings would amount to forgetting the recurrence of such extreme forms in French cinema, and to blank out the kind of critical vision – epitomised by the work of Georges Franju – that managed to express itself in spite of the censorship prevalent in the 1950s and 1960s.[8] It would also amount to overlooking the specificity of the cinema of the so-called new extremism: that is, its reliance on an 'aesthetic of sensation'[9] that pre-empts and exceeds the requirements of a restorative discourse.[10]

In other words, my aim here is not to assign a critical and historical value to this atypical corpus of films in order to try to explicate it within a framework of 'prescribed, pre-given theoretical discourses' (Hills 2005: 54) or to legitimate the visceral and disturbing nature of the works concerned. For the significance of this group of films emanates precisely from their resistance to be thus reduced to metaphorical readings in the conventional sense, just as the surplus of effects they offer makes it difficult to contain them within a functional aesthetic economy. The sensory overload that the viewing of these films elicits determines the way we conceptualise them – to paraphrase Brian Massumi in *Parables for the Virtual*, we have to *sense* before we can *make sense of these* works (Massumi 2002: 2, my italics).[11]

In this chapter I trace some of the motifs identified by Ross in relation to post-war French society in the recent new extreme corpus, where these motifs become part of a reversal, in evidence in the films' visceral aesthetics as well as in their diegetic or narrative details, of the paradigm established in *Fast Cars, Clean Bodies*. This reversal is further illustrated through an unlikely match: a comparison between Agnès Varda's *Cléo de 5 à 7* (1962) and Claire Denis's *Trouble Every Day* (2001).

BROKEN CARS, UNCLEAN BODIES

In the cinema of the 1950s and 1960s, modernisation, consumerism and the American model are ubiquitous elements of the diegesis, from fashion, consumer goods and the intensified presence of advertising, to cars and the celebration of speed, to the love of jazz. In the new extreme, such elements have become embedded in a brutally dystopian vision of exploitation, exclusion and abjection – the implicit realisation of the failure of the transition into a new era where the conflicts of the past, absorbed by mass consumerism on a global scale, would evaporate under 'new levels of abundance and equitable distribution' (Ross 1999: 11). Those categories identified by Ross as emblematic of the post-war cultural shift – the idealisation of a distant yet dominant American model, the reorganisation of urban and domestic spaces, the fixation on hygiene and cleanliness, the car and the home as safe, private and functional spaces, the emergence of the 'new man' in the form of the '*jeune cadre*' or young corporate manager – thus find their distorted echoes in the worlds that the films of the new extreme construct, as well as in the aesthetics of excess they flaunt. First consider Ross's description of the growing dominance of the new professional model in the shape of the aspiring corporate manager,[12] next to the disturbingly graphic vision of corporate normalisation offered in *Dans ma peau* (2002), whose main character Esther (by now, the '*jeune cadre*' can also be a young woman), like the protagonists of Georges Perec's 1965 novel *Les Choses*, works for a survey company. Then consider Ross's description of the car and the modern home as emblems not only of social achievement but also of a new individualism flourishing through consumerism next to the sinister humour with which Manu, the heroine of *Baise-moi* (Despentes and Trinh Thi, 2000) who is the victim of a rape, compares this brutal attack on her body to having one's car broken into. The sequence, shot in a derelict warehouse, bears the film's typically drab, low-definition video look (Beugnet 2007a: 54). Ross's contention that in France the car 'marked the advent of modernization [and] what came to be known as the society of consumption' (39), a new form of mobility that constituted drivers and passengers themselves as commodities, thus resonates uncannily with the definition of sexual assault offered by *Baise-moi*'s character (Manu, incidentally, works as a porn movie actress): 'If you park in the projects, you empty your car 'cause someone's going to break in. I leave nothing precious in my cunt for those jerks.'

In *Fast Cars, Clean Bodies*, Ross further compares the advent of the car with the growing dominance of American-style genre cinema, both of these characteristic cultural and economic shifts being underpinned by the ascendancy of the myth of the American way of life: 'In the late 1950s, young French film directors and moviegoers alike tended to prefer the American product, produced and distributed with assembly-line regularity in tight little genres'

(46). In the films of the new extreme, the fascination for the American model is still traceable in the way a number of the films play on and distort the conventions of all-American genres (*Baise-moi* and *Demonlover* [Assayas, 2002] with the thriller; *Trouble Every Day* with horror; and *Sombre* [Grandrieux, 1998] and *Twentynine Palms* [Dumont, 2003] with the road movie), as well as in the recurrence of American characters and the choice of location (*Trouble Every Day*, *Demonlover*, *La Vie nouvelle* [Grandrieux, 2002], *Twentynine Palms*). By the turn of the century, however, the fascination had turned into the evocation of the murky underbelly of global capitalism and the desacralisation of the old American myth. Ross comments that 'the combination of fantasies of technological sophistication and the wild nobility of wide open spaces is a combination that the car, and the "American way of life" predicated on the car, provided as well' (46), a claim which is striking in the context of Bruno Dumont's disturbing revisiting of such old myths and fantasies in *Twentynine Palms*.

One of the most striking connections between Ross's study and the phenomenon of the new extremism in cinema, however, is that of the filth/cleanliness polarity. Throughout her book, Ross links the need to consign to the past both the memory of World War II and of the colonial disaster to a 'national obsession with cleanliness' (74). She further underlines how women in particular 'as the primary victims and arbiters of social reproduction' (77) became the focus and the embodiment of this obsession. One of the distinctive features of the new extremism is the specific concern with the debunking of some feminine stereotyping, a concern in evidence in the work of certain female filmmakers. Alongside Despentes and Trinh Thi's *Baise-moi*, De Van's *Dans ma peau* (2002) and Denis's *Trouble Every Day*, Catherine Breillat's films are exemplary explorations of the feminine 'abject' set to generate, as Asbjørn Grønstad puts it, 'images of that which is culturally prohibited, the visually illicit'[13] so as to enact 'a decommodification of the body that in turn implies a liberating gesture vis-à-vis the reductive regimentation of the corporeal by the hegemony of spectacle' (Grønstad 2006: 161). The films of the aforementioned directors offer a vision of feminine corporeality that systematically offsets notions of purity, bourgeois order and medical sanitation both in their thematic and in their stylistic register. As such, the films create an embodied and discursive space where the paradigm described by Ross is explicitly overturned. Ross notes how the discourse of hygiene in advertisements directed at the post-war French woman emphasised shining, reflective surfaces in an effort to eschew the 'eroticism of boundary loss'. In particular, she remarks: 'there is no give to the surfaces, no tactile dimension, even an imagined one – just smooth shine' (84). In contrast, the new extreme cinema moves away from conventional filmmaking towards a more baroque, tactile aesthetic in an attempt, precisely, to disturb boundaries, to infiltrate surfaces, including that of the film image itself for, as Grønstad remarks, 'what can possibly be more remote from the pristine, impenetrable non-tactility of the film image than the hideous, all-too-tangible fluids of the human body?' (167). Here, the tactile gaze of the camera that probes the surface and lingers in the folds of matter animate and inanimate, the confrontation with the abject and the refusal of the visual ellipsis are means to engage with the teeming horror of materiality.[14] It is the variation, after a forty-year gap, of art cinema's take on the discourse of cleanness and filth, between the lure and reflective shininess of surface appearances and the attraction of the horror inside, that provides the context for revisiting and comparing two key films: *Cléo de 5 à 7* (1962) and *Trouble Every Day* (2001).

CLÉO AND CORÉ

Cléo de 5 à 7 and *Trouble Every Day*, Cléo and Coré: beyond the distant echoes created by their titles and the names of their heroines,[15] what could there be in common between Agnès Varda's celebrated, elegant, black and white[16] *Nouvelle Vague* feature and Claire Denis's controversial, blood-soaked gore opus, separated by almost forty years? Between Varda's smart, corseted heroine and the blood-thirsty, lurking female monster of Claire Denis's film? Though embedded in the study of post-war French society, Ross's argument resonates across the body of both films, in the respective play on suppression and exposition staged in *Cléo* and *Trouble Every Day*. In *Cléo*, modernisation and cleanliness are an unspoken yet persistent sub-text that permeates the images and soundtrack,[17] and is epitomised by Cléo's body, a body that may be ill with cancer, yet appears neat and perfectly contained. Forty years later, it is bodily contamination, the dangers of unchecked technological 'progress' and the prevalence of a capitalist model of profit-led scientific research that dominate as classic elements of *Trouble Every Day*'s horror plot. Both films speak of disease, and both make discrete yet recurrent references to the continuing legacy of France's colonial history, thus connecting the individual and the filmic body with the national body and history's festering wounds. Whereas *Cléo* is about appearances and (the failed) concealment of disease, in *Trouble Every Day* the horror can never be contained, it bursts out and is splattered across the screen in typically gore fashion. At the same time, in spite of their highly contrasting registers, the films betray a common, baroque-like sensibility, a comparable willingness to use film almost as a form of *vanitas*, to cultivate proximity with death and, by extension, to engage with historical time.

Cléo de 5 à 7 was shot in the summer of 1961 and released in 1962, at a time when the painful, bloody process of the disbandment of the French colonial empire was still unravelling.[18] As is well known, the French government had established a tight policy of censorship in connection with the wars of independence and the Algerian conflict in particular, a policy that strongly affected cinematic production.[19] In Varda's film, allusions to the political context are therefore indirect or discrete, yet they are ubiquitous. Varda's heroine is a fashionable pop singer initially portrayed as a self-absorbed young woman, intoxicated with the reflections of her own success and attractiveness, and enthused by what Ross describes as the new female consumer's 'appetite for frivolity, for changes of taste in clothing and dress' (79). But Cléo's existence is brought into crisis by her learning that she might have cancer. Together with the realisation of her own vulnerability comes an increased awareness of the broader reality, a reality that resonates with the echoes of not-so-distant wars. Most of the commentaries on Varda's classic feature have focused on the film as a ground-breaking, critical exploration of an emerging feminine consciousness, while acknowledging the film's indirect but recurring references to the political context – and the Algerian War in particular – as a significant backdrop for the depiction of a young woman's experience of growing self-awareness and self-assertion (Hayward 1992; Flitterman-Lewis 1996; Smith 1998; Mouton 2001).[20] The way references to the political context occur in the film, however, arguably emphasises the metaphorical significance of illness, opening the film to allegorical readings of the colonial wars as the cancer within the national body, hiding behind the apparently unchanged face of the sunny French capital city. As Florence Martin points out in her illuminating account of the film:

> Both Cléo's cancer and Antoine's going off to war are obscene in all senses of the term. Both point to a potential death which cannot be seen and which is repulsive [...] Like Cléo's cancer, the war is not so much hidden as still 'unseen' by France (and Cléo), but about to become very visible in the summer of 1961. (Martin 2006: 120)

Interestingly, Varda resorts to montage to show how an unwanted reality pierces through the surface of Cléo's self-centred existence. It is during the extended taxi ride that the young woman takes across Paris, early in the film, that the most intriguing references to the colonial context occur.[21] As the taxi passes in front of shop and gallery windows, Cléo's profile is outlined against a series of African masks. The young woman glances at the display and turns away. Tellingly, the presence of the masks is emphasised beyond the required eye line match and shot-counter-shot, through two close-ups that briefly but forcefully invade Cléo's and our field of vision. A few instants later, the taxi slows down in front of a small gallery, and again, African masks appear in the form of intrusive close-ups, images that burst on to the screen in spite of Cléo's attempt to avert her gaze. Almost immediately, the car is stopped by a group of young students – freshmen fooling around, dressed in fancy clothes. A black student fleetingly appears at Cléo's window and she recoils. In the remainder of the ride, it is through the soundtrack that references to the historical context force their way into the taxi's enclosed space and into the spectator's consciousness. The taxi driver switches on the radio, and following a series of adverts – including one for an American (whisky) shampoo – we hear a live news bulletin that talks of riots in Algeria and of a trial linked to the Algiers putsch. As Valerie Orpen notes, what makes these shreds of news stories – fleeting reminders that 'hundreds of miles away, people are dying every day' – so poignant is the contrast between the content of the live broadcast and the synchronised[22] images of Paris, 'sunny, beautiful, normal, with people going to work, going on and off buses, crossing roads' (Orpen 2007: 18).

Forty years later, Denis turns the bright, jazzy Paris of the *Nouvelle Vague* into a gothic city, reminiscent of Louis Feuillade and Georges Franju's Paris.[23] In *Trouble Every Day* the haunting, melancholy tune of the Tindersticks' music has taken the place of pop songs and shampoo adverts, and horror seeps through every image, it lurks through the streets, alongside the banks of the Seine and in the sleepy residential suburbs. In accordance with the classic parameters of the genre, Denis's horror tale is about scientific advancement gone wrong. Typical of Denis's approach, the film is loosely plotted, yet the elliptical storyline offers significant clues in the way it combines the lure of success and profit, a Franco-American connection, and a link to the former French colony of Guyana. It is in Guyana that the deadly virus that affects the two main characters, Shane and Coré, was first developed. It is apparently for reasons of greed and ambition that Shane, an American scientist, stole the discovery from a French colleague and became infested with the disease as a result, turning himself and Coré, the wife of the French scientist, into monsters that sexually prey on their victims before eating them alive.

The stylistic registers might be worlds apart, yet there is something akin to the art of the *vanitas* in both films in the presence of recurrent motifs that emphasise the futility of certain pursuits in the face of human mortality, and the deployment of filmmaking techniques that allow death's gaze to peer from the folds of the cinematic continuum. In *Trouble Every Day*, science, greed and love, are ineffectual counterparts to the progress of the disease and the inevitability of a gruesome death. In *Cléo*, the reality of illness and mortality is initially offset by a profusion of fashion items and an abundance of mirrors in which Cléo, like the young women in the paintings of sixteenth-century artist Hans Baldung Grien, whose work Varda cites as a key inspiration for the film, finds illusory comfort.

In the following comparison of sequences, however, it is a work from a different period of the history of painting that brings the two films together – Marcel Duchamp's famous *Nude Descending a Staircase* (1912). *Cléo* and

Trouble Every Day both feature a staircase sequence that functions as a significant moment of anticlimax and condensed evocation of their heroine's predicament, offering an intriguing contrast in their treatment of a feminine embodiment of mortality. Taking place at the beginning of the film, the oft-discussed staircase sequence of *Cléo de 5 à 7*, reminiscent of Duchamp in its cubist-like composition, is remarkable for its use of montage as metaphorical device. It comes at the end of an introductory sequence that shows Cléo seeking reassurance about her future from a Tarot reader. But it is the skeletal effigy of Death that comes out from the stack of cards, and Cléo leaves in a state of increased anxiety. In the following sequence, which shows the young woman descending the stairs after leaving the Tarot reader's place, the spatio-temporal continuity is undermined by a rapid succession of slightly overlapping shots and falls fleetingly but dramatically out of joint, as if hidden temporal folds were suddenly surfacing to disrupt the deceptive evenness of the cinematic take. The effect forms a striking visual evocation of death's grip making itself felt from under the smooth surface of daily reality's continuum. Yet the camera becomes Cléo's ally again as she attempts to deny the awareness of her own mortality and clings to deceptive appearances instead. The images show us a handsome young woman, carefully made up, wearing an elaborate blond wig and a close-fitting, American-style dress. A tumour may be growing within, the cancer may be spreading, infecting her cells, but on the surface there are no tell-tale signs yet; the contemplation of her reflection in the mirror, of her beautiful, unblemished face, allows Cléo to deny the existence of the illness within.

The staircase scene in *Trouble Every Day* takes place after a brutal, messy scene of carnage. A taxi ride takes Shane across a gloomy, deserted suburban district, to the villa where Coré has just performed a violent killing. The scene that greets Shane as he penetrates the house is one of utter chaos. Coré appears at the top of a staircase, a dark silhouette bathed in reddish light, loosely draped in a soiled tunic. As she slowly descends towards Shane, the gaze of the camera remains unmoving, letting the awfulness of the scene fill the screen. The young woman is literally covered in blood. In *Cléo*, the body – the body of the character, of the film, of the city – is the locus of a play on appearances, where, through virtuoso camera work and montage, the dreadfulness hidden within threatens to emerge, and fleetingly yet repeatedly pierces though the surface of things. The play on surface appearances and exposition is also a key motif of *Trouble Every Day*, emphasised through film citations and the use of generic clichés, as with the attentive description of the sanitised environment of scientific laboratories, the repeated bathroom scenes, the depiction of the chores performed by the American couple's hotel maid, and the insistence on certain gestures (the silent scene that shows Shane's wife helping the maid make the bed with starched white sheets, for instance). But the camera also loses itself in the blood-soaked folds of the sheet that cover the young woman's body in Shane's fantasy (Morrey 2002), an image later echoed by Coré's appearance on the staircase, where the image itself becomes suffused with the dark and red hues of blood. The sensuous camera work of *Trouble Every Day* unravels a sumptuous array of gore effects, alternating between the creeping gaze of the hidden observer, and a caressing closeness to the bodies, looking on as they are torn apart and turn into a mass of blood and viscera. The border between inside and outside collapses; bloody mess eventually prevails and, as the film's closing images emphasise, will not be washed away. Affecting the body of the film like the symptoms of the disease that is the subject of its loose plot, in *Trouble Every Day* genre itself functions, in Sébastien Chauvin's words, 'like a strange illness that infiltrates the story to the core' (Chauvin 2001: 77). Generic conventions allow Denis to construct a film world where different temporal layers co-exist, from pre-war Europe (a Paris of dark alleyways and prowling vampires) to 1950s America (Shane's beautiful, smartly dressed young wife seems to come straight out of a 1950s American magazine or a Hollywood film of the period) and back (to a postcolonial era of late capitalism and advanced scientific competition). Like the virus, genre circulates through cinema's transnational body, and the film thus forms a partial evocation of the horror genre's own history that implicitly reconnects those various histories whose connections, in Ross's account of modernisation, had been suppressed.

In her classic study of illness, Susan Sontag warns against metaphorical and allegorical uses of illnesses such as cancer, of the way metaphors can reduce pain to abstraction, and turn it into a mere element of ideological discourse (Sontag 1977a). Yet as recent writing and filmmaking have demonstrated, metaphors of illness that acknowledge and seek to address such pitfalls offer themselves as powerful means of anchoring works into a historical context, evoking undesirable, suppressed realities in an embodied, affecting way.[24] Kristin Ross emphasises the importance of metaphor in this sense. She casts a critical eye on a strand of artistic production of the 1950s and 1960s that seemingly mirrored the process of capitalist modernisation in the way it strove to 'clean' artistic expression, stripping away 'visceral adjectives, metaphors and any analogical and emphatic trope' (75). In particular, she quotes *Nouveau Roman* writer and theorist Alain Robbe-Grillet, who argued that it was through 'the cleansing power of the look' – that is, the distanced, purely objective practice of the uninvolved look – that language would be redeemed of 'the polluting propensities of the metaphor' (76). In contrast, in *Shocking Representation*, Adam Lowenstein emphasises the power of the visceral, in film in particular, to convey a vision of the past that cannot be dissociated from the present. Lowenstein's definition of what he calls the 'allegorical moment' thus resonates with the attempt at contextualising the new extreme offered in this chapter: the allegorical moment, Lowenstein argues, 'is a complex process of embodiment [. . .] a shocking collision of film, spectator and history where registers of bodily space and historical time are disrupted, confronted and intertwined' (Lowenstein 2005: 2).

Although many of the new French extreme films, in their exploration of the body (both the body of a character and actor and, by extension, the social body, and the body of the film itself) as a body that is diseased, dismembered or defiled, open themselves to metaphorical or allegorical readings, their deployment of an aesthetics of the *corporeal* reconnects the metaphorical to the realm of the affective. As such, it is the shock and the excess, embedded in the form of the films themselves, that actualise the past, showing how history's festering wounds contaminate the present. As Lowenstein remarks, 'To speak of history's horrors, or historical trauma, is to recognize events as wounds [. . .] wounds in the fabric of culture and history that bleed through conventional confines of time and space' (Lowenstein 2005: 1).

CONCLUSION: 'HISTORY [IS] A REALITY LIVED IN THE FLESH'

In a recent issue of *Cahiers du cinéma*, Cyril Neyrat compares recent films by Algerian and French directors, and concludes with a scathing dismissal of the work of the latter. Commenting on the work of Algerian directors Tariq Teguia and Rabah Ameur-Zaïmeche, Neyrat writes that their films 'come from countries where history is not an old, moribund idea, but a reality lived in the flesh. Will it take a historical upheaval for the cinema of our country to get out of its apathy?' (Neyrat 2009: 11). Given the entangled history of the two countries concerned, such a critical view of French cinema appears productive as well as provocative. Yet it is not entirely justified. In recent years, there has been a flurry of French art and mainstream films that attempt to bring to light those under-represented areas of France's history and politics, and to reconnect the conflicts of the past with their present implications.[25] Foreshadowing the re-emergence of such explicitly political cinema, the so-called new French extreme created a shock to the system, fascinating in the way it co-opted the formal possibilities of experimental films as well as of the genres of excess to refute the 'cleansing power of the look' in favour of a tactile, haptic regime of the gaze.

Indeed, appearing as a late twentieth-century, early twenty-first-century phenomenon, the new extreme suggests that the kind of paradigm deployed by Ross, though related to a precise historical context, retains a profound resonance in the context of the evolution of France's culture and society. Late twentieth-century modernisation brings with it its own drive to clean and forget. With new technologies, digitisation and the internet becoming part of everyday life in the Western world, the question of the obsolescence of the old corpo-reality and the rewriting of history that were at the core of Ross's argument takes on a new meaning. Arguably, in the posthuman era, the body can be freed from the limitations of its flesh and bone existence, just as the film body can be rid of the scoria and the signs of decay of the old analogue image. Like the post-war drive for perfect hygiene and the promotion of American shampoos and deodorants, the contemporary process of encoding now carries with it, to a very powerful degree, the promise of more than ultimate cleanliness – the possibility of endless self-reinvention. It is in this sense that the symptomatic, visceral aesthetic of the new extreme can also be envisaged: as an inchoate, chaotic and excessive reaction to the drive towards the 'dematerialisation of embodiment' (Hayles 1993: 148), it stands as a 'shocking' reminder of the lasting incorporation and inscription of stories and histories in our bodies as well as in the fabric of the present.

NOTES

1. See, for instance, Falcon (1999), Muray (2000), Williamson (2003) and Quandt (2004). On the emergence of extreme French genre cinema, see Ben McCann's illuminating article (2008).
2. As Linda Williams (1999) classically designates pornography and horror.
3. See, for instance, Muray's (2000) and Quandt's (2004) pessimistic assessments of French cinema's recent production.
4. In 'Traces of the Modern' (2010), Elizabeth Ezra and myself argue that French cinema's vision of modernity is expressed through the variations and overlap of two aesthetic poles: an 'aesthetic of restraint' and an 'aesthetic of excess' or 'expenditure'. The 'aesthetic of expenditure' refers to Georges Bataille's concept of the 'accursed share' – that portion of the human economy and culture that denies the logic of functionalism and caution that dominates bourgeois culture and economy. In contrast with the 'aesthetic of expenditure' characteristic of the films of Georges Franju and the directors of the new extreme, the 'aesthetic of restraint' of a Jacques Tati or Michael Haneke offers a critical vision of bourgeois culture from 'within', as it were.
5. Golsan quotes historian Henry Rousso, who resorts to a telling metaphor, comparing this chapter of French history to an open wound, and his work as a historian to that of a doctor: 'I thought sufficient time had passed to allow me to wield my scalpel. But the corpse was still warm. It was too soon for the pathologist to do an autopsy; what the case called for was a doctor qualified to treat the living, not the dead' (cited in Golsan 2000: 1). Similarly, journalist Eric Conan remarks: 'Vichy is a cadaver that continues to grow as we speak of it, a cadaver that invades everything, and that we no longer know how to get rid of' (ibid.).
6. The war in Algeria was called the 'nameless war' in reference to the tight policy of censorship that ensured maximum secrecy around the conflict while it raged. For the connections between the Vichy period and the recent conflicts see Golsan (2000: 101, 143 et passim).
7. As exemplified by the recent films of Nicholas Klotz. See Martin O'Shaughnessy (2010); Beugnet and Ezra (2010).

8. Interestingly, neither Georges Franju nor Georges Bataille features in Kristin Ross's study. Both Adam Lowenstein (2005) and Joan Hawkins (2000) look at Franju's work as a key example of a critical vision, close to Bataille's dark surrealism, of France's engagement with capitalist logic and historical amnesia. See also Beugnet and Ezra (2010: 22).
 9. See Beugnet (2007a).
10. In *The Pleasures of Horror*, Matt Hills (2005) complicates the notion of the uncanny on which classical studies of horror have been based to demonstrate both the usefulness and the limitations of the paradigm of the 'return of the repressed', as established in Robin Wood's ground-breaking work on horror in particular. Extending his critique to Barbara Creed's use of the concept of the abject in her psychoanalytical readings of horror films, Hills argues that contemporary horror is not so easily contained within existing theoretical discourses.
11. Massumi (2002) speaks of the passage from affect to emotion, from an as yet unmediated experience (affect) to an encoded one (emotion).
12. Ross describes how the 'centrality of the car in movies, novels, in the print consciousness of the [post-war] period' was surrounded by a discourse that hovered between fascination and anxiety (Ross 1999: 27).
13. Compare this with the discourses destined to accompany the post-war French woman in her mutation without provoking scandal: Ross takes her cue from Ménie Grégoire's 1959 article in *Esprit* in remarking that 'The French woman of 1959 was easily shocked, and shock was to be avoided at all cost' (cited in Ross 1999: 81).
14. For a discussion of *Trouble Every Day* in relation to the concept of the fold explored by Gilles Deleuze in his study of Leibniz see Douglas Morrey (2002); Deleuze (1988).
15. Both names have an Ancient Greek etymology. Both refer to the notion of filiation, but whereas Cléo's name (Cleopatra) has an association with the father, Coré's (Perséphone) refers to the daughter of Demeter, married against her will to the god of the Underworld.
16. *Cléo* is shot in black and white with the exception of its introductory sequence, which is in full colour.
17. On Varda's use of sound and the presence of adverts, see Orpen (2007: 11, 17).
18. Started in November 1954, the Algerian War officially ended with the Evian agreement in March 1962. The shooting of *Cléo* took place only a few months away from the October tragedy, when a demonstration of FLN supporters was brutally repressed by the French police, resulting in the death of hundreds of people. Some of the bodies, thrown in the Seine, were never found and identified.
19. As the fate of Jean-Luc Godard's *Le Petit Soldat* (1963) (in)famously attests. In a recent keynote lecture, Susan Hayward reminded us that political critique was also in evidence in the so-called '*cinéma de qualité*', and described the drastic problems of censorship encountered by Louis Daquin with his 1954 adaptation *Bel Ami*. Studies in French Cinema Conference, 27 March 2010.
20. For an alternative reading see Jill Forbes (2002), 'Gender and Space in *Cléo de 5 à 7*, *Studies in French Cinema* 2:2, pp. 83–9.
21. For an in-depth study of masks, colonial memory and commodification in *Cléo* and other films of the period see Elizabeth Ezra's article: 'Cléo's Masks: Regimes of Objectification in the French New Wave', forthcoming in *Yale French Studies*.
22. Orpen outlines the documentary nature of these images and the news that was recorded the same day as the soundtrack (Orpen 2006: 18).
23. In his review of the film, Jean-Marc Lalanne compares Denis's Paris to 'The Paris of Fantômas and Belphégor' (Lalanne, cited in Beugnet 2004a: 168).

24. See, in particular, Jean-Luc Nancy's *L'Intrus* (2000), which directly inspired Claire Denis's eponymous film (2004), as well as Nicolas Klotz's *La Blessure* (2005).
25. See Michael Haneke's *Caché* (2005), Nicolas Klotz's *La Question humaine* (2007), Philippe Faucon's *La Trahison* (2005), Laurent Herbier's *Mon colonel* (2006), Rachid Bouchared's *Indigènes* (2006) and Claire Denis's *White Material* (2010) as examples.

CHAPTER 4

Reframing Bataille: On Tacky Spectatorship in the New European Extremism

Tina Kendall

The promotional poster for Christophe Honoré's second feature film, *Ma mère* (2004), features a soft-focus, slightly blurry image of Isabelle Huppert, an actress known for her portrayal of sexually perverse, murderous or otherwise pathological characters. She is wearing a provocatively cut dress, and seems to gesture seductively to the viewer with an outstretched hand. Louis Garrel – equally associated with the sexual-transgression-with-a-hint-of-incest formula via his role in Bertolucci's *The Dreamers* (Italy, 2003) – appears in the background with his back to Huppert. He is shown stepping over a door's threshold into an obscure space beyond. At the top of the poster, the marketing tagline boldly announces, 'There are no boundaries to desire'. The poster clearly serves to market the idea of transgression, but it also conceals something of an irony: in the UK and French promotional material for this film, this image has been airbrushed to remove Huppert's cigarette, a detail which certainly calls into question the boundaryless nature of the kind of desire advertised here. What the poster amply foregrounds, then, is the contradictory status of transgression in our era of global consumer capitalism. For while the poster serves to advertise – and to endorse as truly subversive – the film's shocking and 'taboo-busting' portrayal of mother–son incest, sado-masochism and necrophilia, it does so in terms that are in keeping with market values, and promotes such transgression to an already carefully identified and differentiated target audience.

In the case of Honoré's film and other films that have been associated with the new extremism in Europe, this audience might be exemplified by the kind of spectator who is willing to pay for the vicarious thrills of such shocking content, so long as they are packaged in the reassuring context of an *auteur*-driven, European cinema with its high-art credentials intact. In his article entitled 'Every Cannes Needs its Scandal', Hampus Hagman (2007) considers how the films of the new extremism rely on the marketability of the controversies that such films generate on the international film festival circuit; reports of catcalls and mass walkouts, or of people fainting and vomiting in the aisles help to consolidate and to market the experience of watching these films as inherently transgressive and profoundly – even uncontrollably – visceral. Of course, Cannes also carries connotations of cultural respectability and intellectual refinement, and these terms, no less than the reports of scandal help to construct and market such films to global cinema audiences. Together, these terms help to define the new extremism as a distinctive experience of spectatorship that negotiates between the intellectual and the visceral. In the case of *Ma mère*, both the cultural imprint of Georges Bataille and the star presence of Isabelle Huppert also lend legitimacy to the sensational subject matter by situating it within what Nick Rees-Roberts calls the 'much lauded cultural package of transcendence through perverse sexuality that is now a staple ingredient of the high French philosophical and literary canon' (2008: 97).

Scholarship on the new extremism in French and European cinema has foregrounded the critical legacy of Georges Bataille as a key influence on the depiction of explicit sex and violence in the work of Catherine Breillat, Gaspar Noé, Lars von Trier, Michael Haneke and others (McNair 2002; Best and Crowley 2007; Beugnet 2007a; Vincendeau 2007; Lawrence 2010; Angelo 2010). Bataille's elaboration of a base materialism, with its emphasis on the subversive potential of erotic transgression, and the sovereign character of violence and torture, would seem to provide a relevant critical framework for a cinema of explicit and perverse sex and graphic violence. And yet, as Victoria Best and Martin Crowley have argued, one of the defining features of such extreme filmmaking in France is the awkward relationship it establishes with genre norms and with literary and intellectual culture more generally. They note that the emphasis on explicit sexuality in these films 'often fits with difficulty into the progressive political and aesthetic narratives – including this tradition of sexuality as supposedly "subversive" – by which the culture is largely, if uncertainly sustained' (2007: 6).

Such difficulties of harnessing sex to radical political aims today are well documented, and spring from the context of what Linda Williams has called the 'discursive explosion' of sex since the period of countercultural and sexual revolution in the 1960s and 1970s (1999: 283). Where Bataille's literary and philosophical writings emphasised the transgressive, sovereign potential of eroticism, the ubiquity of pornographic reference in today's era of global consumer capitalism can hardly be seen as anything other than the 'triumph of niche marketing' (Shaviro 2006). Williams's notion of 'on/scenity' is relevant here – a term which 'marks both the controversy and scandal of sexual representation *and* the fact that its details have become unprecedentedly available to the public at large' (1999: 282). This discursive explosion of sexuality does not, as Williams argues, lay bare the 'truth' of sexuality so much as it works to create a persistent compulsion for 'telling all, showing all, seeing all' that is just as likely to sustain the interests of global consumer capitalism and dominant ideological norms as it is to disrupt them (ibid.: 283). As Steven Shaviro points out, those discourses of 'sex and transgression' once championed by Bataille and other avant-garde cultural dissidents are now central to the functioning of the global capitalist marketplace, where they hold out the 'shiny allure of transgression and taboo' but only 'stimulate consumer demand for porn-as-commodity, and sex-as-commodity' (Shaviro 2006). As a result, he notes, 'transgression has lost its sting,' and he concludes, 'it's hard to know what sense [Bataille's taste for the luridly pornographic] can have for us today' (Shaviro 2005).

Christophe Honoré's 2004 adaptation of Bataille's posthumously published pornographic novella *Ma mère* takes up this challenge. Found amongst the author's papers upon his death in 1962, Bataille's novel tells the story of the sexual initiation of 17-year-old Pierre under the guidance of his mother Hélène, through the relay of his mother's lovers Réa and Hansi. Although unfinished at the time of Bataille's death, the novella culminates in the suggested consummation of their incestuous bond, followed by the mother's suicide. Honoré's adaptation remains faithful to the structure of the novella, but introduces several notable alterations, including changing the lesbian sex-slave character Loulou into a man, making the suggested sexual contact between mother and son shockingly explicit, and adding on an entirely new ending. Crucially, Honoré also re-imagines the backdrop against which Bataille's story of incestuous desire unfolds, transposing it from early twentieth-century Paris to the Canary Islands in the present day. As Honoré acknowledges in interviews given for this film, his intention was to consider whether Bataille's ideas still resonate today, and to 'take stock of the state of sexuality through the cinema' (Revolver Entertainment, 2004). The Canary Islands setting, he says, offers a way of thinking about how contemporary society 'manages its relationship to the body, to sexuality, and to the other' (ibid.). However, like many of the films associated with the new extremism, *Ma mère* does not harness its images of explicit sexuality to a transparent political agenda. In this respect, the film is not simply nostalgic for a time when transgression really seemed to mean something; it does not simply look back at Bataille's legacy, but brings it – for better or worse – into close and often jarring contact with the 'real' of modern sexual tourism and its watered-down transgressions. Largely written off in the US and the UK for the awkward ways that it weaves together these two contexts, Honoré's film, I will argue, is interesting precisely for the ways in which it both draws from, and troubles, the by now culturally institutionalised and endlessly marketed notion of 'transcendence through perverse sexuality' that remains a kind of easy shorthand for Bataille's extensive and challenging philosophical and literary output (Rees-Roberts 2008: 97). This chapter will consider some of the ways in which Honoré's film both foregrounds and subverts this cultural legacy, and will argue that the film ultimately reframes its Batallean intertext in much more challenging and uncomfortable ways than have hitherto been acknowledged.

In making this argument, I will draw from Martin Crowley's claim in an article called 'Bataille's Tacky Touch', that the appeal of Bataille today springs from his 'tackiness', understood at once as the risible, cringingly formulaic, or even embarrassing aspects of his writing *and* the kind of sticky, contagious contact that is effected by his work as a result (Crowley 2004). I will argue that the subversive force of Honoré's film springs from something similarly tacky: from its sense of jarring incongruity, and from the aspects of the film that seem most hopelessly out of step, pompous or even eye-rollingly embarrassing – what we might call the 'oh, please!' effect – rather than from the presentation of sex as inherently transgressive. The critical and aesthetic interest of the film, this chapter will argue, does not hinge on the question of its representational fidelity to the 'taboo-busting' world of explicit sex depicted in Bataille's novel, but is derived from the grating encounters that the film stages between a literary-philosophical Batallean elsewhere and the 'real' of global sexual tourism. To the extent precisely that these encounters grate, they produce an affective excess that may work to pervert, and hence to subvert, the more culturally endorsed legacy of Batallean transgression which has proven all too compliant with the logic of the global sexual marketplace. The larger aim of the chapter, then, will be to consider how we can adapt Crowley's notion of tackiness and the kind of 'sticky subjectivity' it implies as a model for thinking about a distinctive – but less commonly theorised – type of spectatorship associated with the new extremism in European cinema.[1] Whereas much of the scholarly work on the new extremism has focused on the experiences of shock, outrage or bodily upheaval solicited by these films, the notion of 'tacky spectatorship' I develop here describes a more ambivalent response that, I argue, is less readily recuperated by discourses that would market the idea of the new French and European extremism as a saleable commodity.

Given its exorbitant and taboo subject matter, *Ma mère* was destined from the start to stir up controversy, and as with other films of the new extremism, critical opinion on the film was decidedly mixed. However, unlike with some of those films, the media furore surrounding *Ma mère* did not tend to focus on its troublingly explicit portrayals of sex and violence. Instead, much of the critical backlash levelled at the film focused on the incongruities generated as a result of Honoré's transposition of Bataille's philosophical musings to the Canary Islands setting, or on its soaring pretentiousness, or both. In his review for *The Guardian*, Peter Bradshaw castigates the film for its 'persistent and inescapable [. . .] absurdity' (2005a), while *New York Times* columnist

Stephen Holden writes in more measured terms, '[a]vid sensation-seeking in *Ma Mère* is such a grim affair that after a short while, the spectacle of its aimless characters bending themselves out of shape for the sake of alleged pleasure mutates from titillating to pathetic to laughable' (2005). Kevin Thomas of the *LA Times* dismisses the film as 'pretentious Eurotrash' (2005). Finally, Nick Rees-Roberts argues that 'even distanced by 1980s pop music, the overwrought Catholic interjections are alienating for the (assumed secular) twenty-first century audience, who might easily find such overtones outdated or irrelevant,' adding that 'Bataille's religious preoccupations are incongruous in the context of mass tourism and sexual consumption' (2008: 98). Many of these critics dismiss *Ma mère* on the basis of what they take to be Honoré's naïve approach to his subject matter, with the implicit assumption that those 'outdated' and 'irrelevant' overtones are simply misjudged moments. In interviews, however, Honoré suggests that the effect of incongruity generated in his film is more carefully calculated than it may appear. He notes that his intention was to cultivate what he calls an 'aesthetic of impurity', of mixing things that do not go together, and allowing for a modicum of experimentation that might take French cinema outside of its 'hermetic' and highly regulated enclave (Revolver Entertainment, 2004).[2]

Honoré's aesthetic of impurity is amply demonstrated in this film's promiscuous mixing of settings, its jarring use of music, its ubiquitous, oddly out-of-place zooms and, perhaps most notably, its uncomfortable amalgamation of documentary and fictional registers. The early sequences of the film, set in the hilltop villa overlooking the ocean, or those set amidst seemingly endless sand dunes, conjure a mythic placelessness that seems in keeping with the idea of transcendence – as if the characters' sexual transgressions were enough to remove them from the tedium of needing to belong anywhere in particular. The casting of Huppert helps to underscore this; her star image evokes a similar ethereal timelessness that helps to differentiate these characters and their relationship to sex. Huppert is also given most of the novel's dialogue, delivered with such characteristic cold distance that it sometimes seems as though she has walked into the film directly from the pages of Bataille's novel. The sequences where she and Pierre deliver Bataille's lines draw most closely from the atmosphere and from the 'philosophical porn' sensibility of the novella, and although in keeping with the mythic settings, there is something very odd and incompatible about hearing Bataille's dialogue spoken in this way; something in the transition from page to screen, and from an early twentieth-century Parisian bourgeois milieu to our own that has the effect of transforming Bataille's philosophical eloquence into so much 'highfalutin verbiage' (Holden 2005).

Indeed, part of the challenge of adapting Bataille involves the question of how to render his elusive, heavily metaphoric prose in visual terms without simply catering to on/scenity's compulsion 'to show all, tell all, see all' (Williams 1999: 283). As Honoré notes:

> [T]he problem of Bataille's book is that he says a lot that [the characters] do 'the worst things that can be done'. [. . .] But in cinema, what does this mean, 'the worst things that can be done'? That depends on one's sexuality, on what a person esteems to be acceptable or not. Very quickly I realized that this was slippery ground and not very interesting. (Honoré in Amour Fou 2007)

Rather than try to film bodies in a radically new or extreme way, Honoré shifts the focus away from the spectacle of sex as the primary conduit through which transgression might operate. Though he does suggest that he wanted the film to provoke an 'inner experience' for the spectator, he maintains that this is not to be found in the spectacle of the erotic encounter; the sex is a decoy that leads the spectator somewhere else (ibid.). Honoré develops a clinical style that results in a series of sexual episodes that are oddly flat, distanced and abstracted. Even those scenes that are most patently shocking in terms of their violation of sexual taboo are clearly not presented in order to titillate, even if they are meant to gesture towards the shattering experience of self-loss and transcendence that Bataille located in the erotic encounter.

In one pivotal scene, for instance, Pierre and his mother return home at dawn with an entourage of lovers, including Réa and Hansi. Although the suggested orgy that ensues is elided, the sequence that follows it pictures a panoply of naked or scantily clad bodies strewn about a white room with a large bed at its centre. The mood is one of languorous, post-coital exhaustion, until eventually Pierre enters Réa from behind to have sex with her. As he does so, he is shown looking out of frame in the direction of his mother, whose feet and legs are visible in the shot. As he continues having sex with Réa, Pierre creeps over toward his mother, licking and passionately kissing her leg. She visibly recoils, and props herself upright on her elbow. This shot, held for some considerable time, shows Huppert framed in a statuesque pose, turned away from Pierre and framed by gauzy white billowing curtains and wearing a pink negligee, staring off into an unseen distance. These details transmit something of the ethereal placelessness that seems in keeping with the atmosphere of Bataille's novel. However, like the other erotic encounters in this film, the approach to filming sex is neither unprecedentedly explicit, driven by the urge to show everything, nor aestheticised in the manner of more mainstream representations of sex. Rather, it is very descriptive, matter-of-fact and plain in its presentation of sex as 'what happens next'. After this initial encounter between Pierre and his mother, the sequence cuts to a shot of Réa and Hélène curled up next to one another on the bed; Réa is naked, and Hélène gently caresses her stomach and thigh. Pierre, meanwhile, is on the edge of the bed, and watches the pair with an air of slight confusion or disturbance. Hélène turns toward Pierre, then turns away; the camera comes in tighter, and we see her lift up her negligee to reveal her naked body to Pierre (but not to us) as she strokes her own skin lightly. We hear the faint sound of rain in the background. Meanwhile, Hansi, who has been watching all of this from the edge of the room, rises and walks toward Pierre, covering his eyes with her hands. Narratively, this is an important sequence, because it depicts the moment at which the mother's sexual initiation of Pierre crosses the line, and in the aftermath of this encounter, Pierre's mother decides to leave, telling him that 'what happened between us can never happen again.' Honoré maintains that he wanted to develop sex scenes that would convey plot details and characterisation rather than scenes that would act as privileged moments of spectacle. This scene's matter-of-fact approach to sex inverts the distinction between narrative and spectacle that is central to pornographic representation. As a result, although the sexual encounters are central to the way that Bataille's text characterises transgression and brings it into play for his readers, the sex scenes in Honoré's film are not charged with the role of enacting that inner experience for spectators. The sex is too bound up with narration, too oddly flat and distanced to produce much of a fuss.

These settings contrast visually and stylistically with the scenes in the Canary Island nightclub locations, where Honoré films his characters in 'real' settings, interacting with 'real' tourists. In one such sequence, Pierre and Réa wander into the Yumbo shopping complex, wandering past its strange amalgamation of cafés, children's amusement areas, nightclubs, and other venues whose reputation on the sexual tourism circuit are well known. In contrast to the earlier settings, this world of global sexual tourism is much more fully realised. Honoré develops a shooting style that borrows from documentary techniques, which makes this milieu seem like some kind of sex theme park, an X-rated Disneyland – a global capitalist non-place that is similarly bracketed off from 'normal' daily life, and yet deeply marked by the immediacy of the contemporary setting. In contrast to Bataille's characters, who exist literally and metaphorically above the marketplace, these sex tourists are undeniably part of the immediate reality (or hyper-reality) of global consumption, marked by a cloying contact with the mundane textures, sounds and atmospherics of the contemporary world of capital. The contrasting sonic registers employed here are also key to this effect; while the world of sexual tourism is encapsulated by the crowd's raucous murmur, the clinking of glasses, and the throbs and pulses of techno music coming from the nightclubs, Pierre and Réa's experience of it is filtered through, and distanced by, the faint strains of Samuel Barber's 'Adagio for Strings', which is just audible on the soundtrack. Once again, this technique has the effect of differentiating these characters and their relationship to the world of sexual tourism that is on display so palpably here. This sequence brings these two worlds into contact, and insists on their relationship as one of discrepancy and discordance.

On the surface of things, these sequences seem to reproduce some fairly obvious and troubling visual and ontological contrasts between Bataille's world of 'authentic' sexual transgression and our own degraded and demeaning context of sex-as-commodity. Critic Ginette Vincendeau takes issue with what she sees as the 'facile snobbery' of these shots and the film's 'contempt for "ordinary" tourists' (2005: 3). Similarly, Nick Rees-Roberts points out that there is something ethically dubious about juxtaposing 'an elegant established star, an up-and-coming leading man and an underground fashion icon' with 'documentary shots of supposedly less real, less physically appealing tourists', arguing that these shots are designed to 'expose the perceived tackiness of the ambient mass tourism' (2008: 99). While I agree that we should approach these images with some degree of ethical unease, I wonder whether the division between the 'real' characters of Bataille's fiction and the 'less real' tourists in the documentary sequences is as facile and clear-cut as Vincendeau or Rees-Roberts take them to be. What I think these sequences foreground, rather, is the spectator's place within that economy of images, and hence also within the sexual economy designated by these shots. In the aforementioned Yumbo sequence, the handheld camera positions us firmly in the thick of things, using subjective shots that figure the spectator unambiguously as part of this world of mass sexual tourism. The camera pauses to disclose images that are striking for their banality and familiarity: children jumping on bungee trampolines, rows of shops and restaurants with crowds milling past, waitresses busy clearing off tables. The immediacy and contemporaneity of these shots implicate the spectator to a much higher degree, and dispel any illusions that the spectator might have about the possibility of bracketing sexuality off into a literary-philosophical Bataillean 'elsewhere', where sex retains its transcendent allure. These shots insist, rather, on the queasy but ineluctable creep of mundanity into that legacy of transgression, effecting a mutual, and indeed tacky, contamination of both registers.

This affective contamination works, I think, largely because of the sudden collapse of mediating distance that we get in these documentary-style sequences, and I want to relate this to an argument that Frances Ferguson makes in her work on literary pornography. In *Pornography, the Theory*, Ferguson considers works of literature that have been decried for their excesses, including the work of Sade, Flaubert and Lawrence. She is interested in the shift that happens in the period between when those works are considered scandalously violent or pornographic, and when they are upheld as works of art. In her afterword, she considers the case of Bret Easton Ellis's *American Psycho*, and argues that while *American Psycho* undoubtedly engages with shockingly violent material, what was most shocking about it is not what is represented, but (as she notes in a subsequent essay) 'the feeling of intense contemporaneity it temporarily establishes – its making us feel as though we share the time and place of its represented world to such a degree that our detachment is compromised' (2006: 119).[3] This affective response – the confounding of reading (or viewing) subject and text in a moment of compromising closeness – is central to the classification and rejection of certain texts as pornographic. Ferguson notes: 'the things we treat as pornography represent a genre not simply because of their content – their sexual explicitness or their sadism – but also because they feel closer to us than other texts or images' (ibid.).

I think such questions of distance and proximity are also helpful in thinking about what is at stake in Honoré's technique of juxtaposing this abstracted Bataillean elsewhere with the cloyingly present world of sex-as-commodity. Much depends on the question of whether the film pitches one against the other ultimately as part of an 'elitist project', and more significantly, the extent to which it asks contemporary audiences to find Bataille's libertine characters more believable, more authentic and desirable in their transgressions (Vincendeau 2005: 3). I am not so sure that it does. Rather, I am interested in the way that Honoré seeks to foreground, juxtapose and hold in tension both the clichéd tackiness of sex-as-transgression and the clichéd tackiness of sex-as-commodity. The formal oppositions between the tourists and the libertines, between the now of global tourism and the elsewhere of Bataillean transgression, may also perform a mutual critique, exposing both as ultimately vacuous, hollow or irrelevant. The film's unsettling contemporaneity – and the handheld, quasi-documentary shooting style is key here – sits awkwardly next to the neatly abstracted and remote cultural legacy of Bataille, and this sense of incongruity means that we cannot find protection and reassurance in either register. By holding them in tension, the film might be said to pervert both registers, but, like *American Psycho*, it does so with a level of indifference that seems to foreclose any kind of critical commentary. It brings them into jarring contact, but in my opinion does not propose Bataillean transcendence as a nifty way out. If the film is not trying to salvage something from Bataille's 'much lauded cultural package' that equates sex with transgression, but only exposing it equally as a sham, then what are spectators left with (Rees-Roberts 2008: 97)? What is the point? Following Crowley, I would argue that what matters here 'is not interpretation but contact' (2004: 778). This is to say that the critical, ethical and aesthetic value of the film consists in its appeal to affect over and above interpretation or analysis. It is in its creation of an affective residue generated, as I have attempted to demonstrate, through the grating contact between the elsewhere and the now, the encounter between the film and the spectator, that the film's critical interest might lie.

If the film insists throughout on dissonance, disjunction and disparity in its adaptation of Bataille's novel, the final sequence of the film ratchets these strategies up to a new level of intensity. Whereas Bataille's text ends with a suggested sexual liaison between mother and son, and with a monologue in which the mother explains to Pierre why she must die, the film version pictures both the erotic encounter and the mother's auto-mutilation (using a Stanley knife) in a chiaroscuro style that nevertheless leaves very little to the imagination. Following this scene, Honoré adds a brief coda in which Pierre is asked to identify his mother's body. In this sequence, Pierre is shown first weeping uncontrollably, and then masturbating furiously over his mother's dead corpse. The whole sequence is set to the Turtles' 'Happy Together' – a song that seems cinematically destined to underscore such moments of achingly arch anomie – before an abrupt cut to a vacant and silent white screen. This sequence offers a particularly exaggerated example of Honoré's aesthetic of impurity which, I would argue, leaves us reeling less from the shock of the range of taboos transgressed as from the preposterousness of the entire setup. Why, we might ask, does Honoré decide to end the film in this way? Is Bataille's incestuous tale no longer shocking enough in itself? And what is the point of setting this scene to a song that wears its mocking, postmodern intentions on its sleeve? Can Honoré really be serious? Is he poking fun at the world of sexual tourism here, or at Bataille's enduring legacy, or at us – our desire to participate in the latter while distancing ourselves from the former? Whatever the case may be, the cumulative affective impact of this sequence is, I think, as difficult to shake off as it is to take seriously as an 'authentic' account of Bataillean transgression. And this is precisely the point: in Crowley's terms, such moments are doubly tacky, 'sticking to us', but also 'embarrassing, inadmissible' (2004: 776). The mark of this contact, as Crowley sees it, is precisely our 'exasperation' at the tackiness, the 'quasi-pornographic' encounter that leaves us with 'precious little to say' (ibid.: 775). I have been describing this 'precious little' in terms of what I have called the 'oh, please!' effect; it is ultimately this 'contact with no content', the affective force of being left with nothing more to say than 'oh, please!' that might most effectively undermine the contemporary presentation of sex-as-commodity (ibid.). And as Crowley notes, it is through precisely this 'channel opened up that the real sticks to the text [. . .] the real as the unlocatable touch of Bataillean communication' (ibid.: 776). At stake in what I have been calling 'tacky spectatorship' is a type of contact that is effective precisely to the extent that its sticky but uncertain touch is something *other* than what we expect of it, something antithetical to the fantasy of immediacy offered up by the discourses that have been able to market the idea of the new French extremism as an uncontrollably visceral, and ultimately cathartic or desirable experience of transgression.

    This preoccupation with the real, with touch and affect, meanwhile, is in keeping with the 'affective' or 'bodily turn' in recent film theory, and theorists such as Steven Shaviro and Martine Beugnet have drawn from the work of Bataille to theorise spectatorship in terms of an intimate, contagious contact between film and viewer. In *The Cinematic Body*, for instance, Shaviro contends that film, by its very nature, offers viewers 'a Bataillean ecstasy of expenditure, of automutilation and self-abandonment' leading to the 'blinding intoxication of contact with the real' (1993: 54). And, as he goes on to argue, it is precisely that 'very loss of control, that abjection, and subversion of self-identity' (ibid.: 57) that animate the spectator's desire for certain types of cinematic experience. As Beugnet has demonstrated, the films of the new extremism, renowned for their emphasis on the visceral and affective, and for their problematic refusal of the kind of distance that might allow for easy critical evaluation, would appear to offer such an opening on to Bataillean expenditure. However, I think it is important to note a qualitative distinction at work here, between the type of 'blinding intoxication' that Shaviro writes about, and the more risible, eye-rolling and ultimately less desirable response that I have attempted to account for through the notion of 'tacky spectatorship'. Such an experience sits much less comfortably both with the alluring cultural legacy of Bataillean transgression, and with the ways in which the films of the new extremism are increasingly marketed. As I have argued in this chapter, if Bataille remains, it is certainly not in the reassuring places we would expect to find him: not in the treatment of sex and violence as inherently transgressive, and not in the critically endorsed notion of transcendence through transgression, but in the grating distance between *this* revered Bataille and the embarrassing, awkward or inadmissible one who insists on the value of communication, and hence spectatorship, as a sullying, embarrassing and ultimately vacuous contact. Ultimately, then, if we can reclaim something of Bataille's legacy in the films of the new extremism, it may be that Crowley is right in saying 'we have no other option [but] to embrace the tackiness' (2004: 779).

NOTES

1. Although it is outside of the scope of this chapter to explore them here, the spectatorial response I develop in relation to *Ma mère* can be attributed to other films associated with the new extremism, such as Lars von Trier's *Antichrist*, widely scoffed at for its Tarkovskian ambitions, its talking fox, and its 'ludicrous excesses' (Linda Ruth Williams 2009). Similarly, Bruno Dumont's *L'Humanité*, which Jonathan Romney describes as comic for its 'overwhelming portentousness', seems to elicit similar responses; in his review of the film, Romney takes issue with the film's overt 'metaphysical ambitions', claiming that they create an effect of comedy that 'feels [so] embarrassing' that 'sniggering seems the only healthy response' (Romney 2000: 24–5).
2. Notably, these comments come in the context of the question of whether Christophe

Honoré feels that he is part of a 'new wave of extreme French cinema' (Revolver Entertainment, 2004). In his response, he says that he sees a shared affinity between his work and that of filmmakers such as Bruno Dumont, Philippe Grandrieux, Gaël Morel and Catherine Breillat, and describes this common ground in terms of a shared willingness to 'dismantle' French cinema, and to return it to a state of adolescence (ibid.).

3. This quotation comes from an essay in Texte zur Kunst where Ferguson reflects on her findings in *Pornography, the Theory*. It is worth noting that Honoré cites Bret Easton Ellis, Dennis Cooper and Sarah Kane as influences for this film. Similarly, Best and Crowley note that *American Psycho* is a key influence on the new French extremism (Honoré in Amour Fou 2007; Best and Crowley 2007: 13).

CHAPTER 5

Beyond Anti-Americanism, Beyond Euro-Centrism: Locating Bruno Dumont's *Twentynine Palms* in the Context of European Cinematic Extremism

Neil Archer

A man is at the wheel of a car. Before him, through the windscreen, we see a highway of moving traffic. The opening strains of a song play on the car stereo: a Japanese voice singing to a country-style guitar backing. As the man drives, we watch him spool red tape around the high point of the steering wheel. This, it seems, shows him the way to go. The sequence shot is interrupted, revealing a pallid woman sleeping on the rear seat. A mobile phone rings. Cut back to the driver, now viewed from the side. He answers in English: 'I'm driving. Driving to Twentynine Palms.' So begins Bruno Dumont's third feature film, *Twentynine Palms* (2003). As the opening indicates, this is a road movie with a stated destination; and by its own nature, viewing and interpreting the film involve questions of location. In geographical terms, the film's titular destination is not a mystery; it is an actual place in California, where Dumont's film is shot. Like many road movies, the destination serves more as a pretext: in this case, for a meditation on the journey itself, and the experience of its viewing. As I will argue in this chapter, location is here a discursive category relating to the film's 'identity'. Many of those coming to the film through its cinematic or DVD release would have been aware of Dumont's status as the director of two critically lauded French-set films, *La Vie de Jésus* (1997) and *L'Humanité* (1999) – the latter receiving the Jury Prize at Cannes. From an auteurist perspective, this shift in geographical focus, from the rural Pas-de-Calais of his previous films towards the Californian desert, is a marked one. The journey towards Twentynine Palms, in other words, will come to embody its own exploration of this transition.

Dumont's choice to make an American-set road movie is notable, given the positioning of both American cinema and cinematic genre within certain theorisations of a European cinema of extremity. Martine Beugnet has emphasised the way filmmakers generally associated with the new extremism have often appropriated generic forms and motifs, in a notional effort to 'subvert' such generic elements (Beugnet 2007a: 34). Exactly how we might understand this notion of subversion is a key question. Beugnet addresses this by reference to qualities of generic 'excess', which at once defamiliarise and revitalise those cinematic characteristics which (as the term generic implies) may have become formulaic, stripped of the affective dimension they might once have possessed (ibid.: 125–6). Philosophical questions of affect and representation are at the same time paralleled at the industrial level, in terms of the fight for cinematic terrain, and those strategies required, within a cinematic landscape dominated by American cultural product (Hagman 2007); to this extent, as Jonathan Romney argues, there is always 'a professional bottom line' to extremism as a practice (Romney 2004).

We can put these two ideas together in trying to situate *Twentynine Palms*. Dumont's 'American' film engages with some of the motifs of a hegemonic cinema and culture. This hegemony can be understood in terms of the economic models of production and distribution, but also at the level of image culture, through what is arguably the internalisation of this model at the broader level of national production across the world. To this extent, the assertion of authorship has political implications relating to both industry and identity, as well as constituting a discursive location above and beyond the work's actual location. Dumont's film therefore bears similarities with other 'European' visions of the American West such as *Model Shop* (Jacques Demy, 1969), *Zabriskie Point* (Michelangelo Antonioni, 1970) and *Paris, Texas* (Wim Wenders, 1984). Moreover, this situating of the author as a marker of difference or opposition within the text is backed up discursively in the form of Dumont's own comments accompanying the release of *Twentynine Palms*: in particular, those regarding his antipathy towards American culture, and his wish to carry out a cinematic 'terrorist attack' (cited in Matheou 2005: 17).

Authorship is, of course, not just a marketing brand, but a series of textual markers, within which the manipulation of generic motifs plays a key role. The opening sequence sketched above clues us toward Dumont's stylistic approaches: sequence shots, the amplification of diegetic sound, and a focus on unexpected and enigmatic detail. The majority of the action consists of point-of-view shots from the car, shots of the car's interior, or of events that take place around the vehicle en route towards Twentynine Palms. Yet, for what is putatively a road movie, there is very little narrative movement, but rather a kind of narrative stasis (Beugnet 2007a: 94). Besides this deliberate undermining of the generic potential for speed or action, Dumont introduces tropes which, by their very exceptional nature, resist easy assimilation within mainstream generic categories: in this instance, explicit and often violent sex, actual sexual violence (towards the film's conclusion, the driver is anally raped by men who ram his car off the road) and brutal physical violence (the film ends with the driver stabbing his girlfriend to death in a motel room).

To assume that such representations necessarily connote a meaningful critique of, or an oppositional alternative to, mainstream American representation is nevertheless questionable. James Quandt's critique of the extremist turn, which targets Dumont's film in particular, raises the issue of exactly what such aesthetic tactics are supposed to demonstrate beyond their own visible excess (Quandt 2004). Beugnet also (quoting Philippe Muray) points to the possibility of extremism as merely recycling avant-garde aesthetics which once connoted a genuine sense of opposition, but now simply amount to 'a new form of academism' (Beugnet 2007a: 35). Where, in this sense, does a film like *Twentynine Palms* move beyond the postmodern play of surfaces which extremism, with its interest in affect and realism, might be assumed to challenge? Dumont's brand of cinephobia, moreover, is essentially ambiguous, freely re-employing some of its tropes from John Boorman's *Deliverance* (1971), and Alfred Hitchcock's *Psycho* (1960). As a road movie, moreover, the film draws on the representational motifs of a genre frequently inscribed historically as American, though itself an oppositional genre in the American context (see Krämer 1998; Laderman 2002). The fact that Dumont's film takes place in America and, following the codes of the road movie, makes such use of its physical landscape, indicates the importance and also the potential power of a particular American imaginary within the film. This ambiguity at the level of representation is further heightened by our knowledge that *Twentynine Palms* was something of a stop-gap film, made by Dumont while he sought funding for an unrealised English-language project (Matheou 2005: 16). In this sense, and to reiterate previous points, *Twentynine Palms* could be seen to move even further away from its notional European centre, in the professional and economic terms of a cinematic calling card to larger-scale production and wider distribution (Hagman 2007).

As I am suggesting in this chapter, then, the kind of anti-American (and implicitly pro-European) discourse that may coalesce both semantically and linguistically around an idea of 'European extremism', and which is often supported by the pronouncements of filmmakers themselves and the critical media that disseminate them, needs to be thought through in a more nuanced fashion.[1] Any critical understanding of such a politics of opposition has, in any case, to deal with the fact that any idea of European specificity risks a potential drift towards Eurocentrism; which, to follow the historical understanding of that term and its substantial criticism, positions a European Enlightenment model as central to imperialist adventure and its mythologizing in culture (Shohat and Stam 1994: 87–8). It is also the travel film in particular, as Bill Nichols points out, whose documentary qualities have provided 'a buttress for rationalism' since cinema's invention (1991: 167). In other words, a defence of European specificity, especially through the form of a travel film like *Twentynine Palms*, risks doubly re-inscribing that to which it might stand in notional opposition. How we reconcile these various tensions in *Twentynine Palms* is therefore the task of this chapter.

For example, an analysis of the film's initial treatment of its Californian setting indicates the complexity of the film's positioning, at once reiterating its own markers of authorship, yet in the same gesture attempting a renewed perspective on its subject. The kind of blank style favoured by Dumont employs as one of its typical features sustained shot-reverse shots between a protagonist's viewpoint and the object of vision (Bowles 2004): most often, both here and elsewhere, in the form of landscape. In their duration and focus, these images offer an unusually detailed view of geographical location. If the deserts of the American West are so steeped in cinematic image-history that cliché and generic connotations are hard to avoid, then the film's opening sequences, in their eschewal of dynamic montage, dialogue and extra-diegetic soundtrack, aim to look anew at this territory. If the film aims to defamiliarise and hence return to us the mythologised spaces and images of this territory – goods trains, gas stations, truck stops or motels – this return is at the same time an inherently outsider vision. *Twentynine Palms*, following the road movie's generic trope of discovery, linked to its interest in a mobile, replenishing vision, distinguishes itself from the more naturalised, 'national' comprehension of space often associated with classical continuity narrative. It forms part of a continuity within a European (and more specifically French) tradition that has looked towards the Pacific coast as a site of both optimism and anxiety. Twentynine Palms itself is one of the destinations to be found in Jean Baudrillard's *Amérique* (1986), a work which continued the westward direction of French post-structuralist and postmodern thinking in the 1970s (Starr 1995: 124–8; Weiner 2001). In their identity as outsider perspectives, Dumont's film and Baudrillard's book share similarities. Looking at *Twentynine Palms* in comparison with *Amérique* enables us to see not only how this self-distancing functions in the travel narrative, but also how the cinematic travelogue differs from the literary one.

Whatever Baudrillard's book may notionally describe, its actual subject remains imprecise. Is it the titular subject, an America 'out there' to be recorded, or is it about the author himself? Is it possible, in other words, to distinguish the observations in *Amérique* from its author's own alienated perspective? This is a relevant question, in so far as Baudrillard in *Amérique* is uninterested in eliciting anyone's thoughts apart from his own: as he admits, his interest is not in the social and cultural aspects of the country, but in '*astral* America [*l'Amérique sidérale*] . . . the America of the empty, absolute freedom of the freeways' (1988: 5). As Feroza Basu has pointed out, this compulsion to escape the confines of the centre and of culture reflects a specifically European rejection of tourism in favour of what, notionally, is its opposite: travel and discovery (2006: 143–4). In turn, though, in becoming an over-determined (and narcissistic) search, this risks an evasion of the subject with which travel putatively engages. As a film whose specificity traditionally resides in its indexical quality, we might expect *Twentynine Palms* to bypass the problem of mediation inherent to the literary travelogue. Yet it becomes difficult to make such clear distinctions as in Dumont's film; vision is very often allied to the point of view of its two protagonists, and to a large extent to their own spatial constraint within the automobile. Not dissimilarly to Baudrillard's travelogue, meanwhile, the supporting cast of actual Americans are reduced until the very end to mere background detail.

Nevertheless, an amount of self-reflexivity (intentional or otherwise) with regard to this mediated nature of cinematic images can be inferred from Dumont's film. There is little background to establish or account for the presence of the driver (whose name we learn to be David) in this desert. Yet this arbitrariness can by extension be applied to the overall intelligibility or significance of the film itself, especially as David, it appears, is a photographer, and that consequently his actions here in the desert reiterate those of the film itself. From these frames of image production it is only a small step to the subjects of consumption – we the viewers – whose own absorption in the production of images comes under subsequent scrutiny. In the absence of any other obvious direction in the film beyond the reiteration of its own construction, *Twentynine Palms* takes up this idea as its content, making the search for meaning the nearest thing to a narrative drive. Yet the possibility that this search is a fruitless one cannot be ruled out. *Twentynine Palms*, in a similar way to *La Vie de Jésus*, figures movement as an action without specific aims or goals; this is suggestive of the way that, for Dumont, movement is related to the possibility, or the impossibility, of action and meaning. Failure is central to his films' vision; in this film, the road trip becomes a road to nowhere.

The groundlessness of image production highlighted by *Twentynine Palms*, the way it becomes a text in search of its own motivation, draws attention to ethical issues at the heart of the photographic discourse. In particular, the desire to produce images, especially in its connection to travel and the encounter with difference, has been seen to intervene almost pathologically between the image-maker and real contact (Sontag 1977b: 14–15), to the extent that the photographic image even replaces experience (or at least displaces it, to use a Baudrillardian formulation, to the realm of the simulacral). The events and recordings of *Twentynine Palms*' aimless movement, in their context as part of a travel film, assume significance only within a closed circuit. The photograph within travel, to paraphrase Sontag, no longer records something significant; something becomes significant only because it is photographed. We see an example of this early on in the film. The initial driving sequence sketched above culminates in an utterance by David's companion, Katia: *'Regarde'* – an injunction to look directed at ourselves as much as the driver. But what is it that we are looking at, and why? A sequence shot shows a passing freight train, the field of wind turbines glimpsed in the flashing gaps between loads. We then return to the watching couple, who have nothing to say, but whose fixated attention seems to imply that the object of their vision is *supposed* to mean something. Following this, a fixed long shot displays the turbines in and against the desert backdrop; depth of field and bright light create a dazzling impression of the landscape into which the protagonists almost disappear, overwhelmed by the desert expanse and the hypnotic movement of the turbine blades. Time and again the film, as is the case in *Jésus*, will invite us to look via the diegetic shot-reverse shot, though without offering anything so obvious to connote as 'meaning' (Bowles 2004: 38). The excessive duration of the sequence shot, moreover, asks us to consider what, if anything, is intelligible in the image itself.

As suggested previously, a deliberate cessation of speed in both camera movement and montage, in favour of slowness and the duration of the sequence shot, can be seen as a way of revitalising generic motifs. An important implication for our understanding of the film is that this putative return of the real invoked through a real-time road movie aesthetic is suffused with unease, as if the elements of speed and distraction within more mainstream editing and composition were a way of obviating violence, rather than generating it. Chris Petit, who from *Radio On* (1979) to *Content* (2010) has made the road movie his own form of film-essay, suggests that the mobility of driving (and in turn the road movie) is less an expression of excitement than the product, or even practice, of boredom: a boredom that 'underpins consumerism' in its inevitable drift towards alleviation through consumption, but a boredom that also 'invites terror (as its only cure)' (Petit 2008: 40). Petit could be describing Dumont's film here, in its slow trajectory towards terror and bloodshed. The 'migratory drift' (ibid.: 40) of both travel and the road movie was once rooted in human necessity, the human traffic of John Ford's *The Grapes of Wrath* (1940) being an appropriate case in point. For many travellers and consumers of the developed West, however, travel – and travel photography – are not so much necessities as a symptom of boredom and of boredom's corollary, which is leisure: the by-products of a world of surfeit and surplus, where nothing is necessary. If a certain dialectic of Enlightenment sees the latter's logical culmination in the violence of colonisation, we can identify a similarly negative evolution of mobility in Dumont's œuvre more generally: from the wanderers, mopeds and trains of *Jésus* and *L'Humanité*, to the all-terrain automobile of *Twentynine Palms*, to its logical but regressive extension in the armoured vehicles of *Flandres* (2006). One review of *Twentynine Palms* notes that the protagonists' choice of car is a Hummer, the vehicle commonly used by the

US military in Iraq and Afghanistan (Falcon 2005: 76). In its connections to the film's opening shot, where the red tape forms a kind of sight or targeting device, this invokes an even clearer link between the practices of vision and its inherent connections to warfare (Virilio 1989).

Whilst initially embodying a discursively European turn from the touristic toward the sidereal, then, the protagonists of *Twentynine Palms* can be seen to exemplify the problems inherent to the mutually informing acts of travelling and viewing. The effect of this ambiguity is to deflect potentially reductive readings of the film's conclusion and, in particular, the eruption of violence from outside upon the bodies of David and Katia. Instead of situating the film's travellers within a 'hostile' landscape, which in itself is both relativist and generic, the film works to reveal the travellers' own participation in this violence through their very presence. Within the terms of a European cinematic discourse that would see itself in an oppositional relationship, say, to an American cultural hegemony, markers of the latter's ideology or violence would be the target of attack. Yet in *Twentynine Palms*, we can see the tension between this notional target of attack and the way the film replicates structures of representational violence. As previously discussed, the film's form, in relation to its content and geographical context, appears to counter the more generic connotations associated with it, the western most notably. The western, the most American of genres, is in fact essentially both colonial and Eurocentric, with its naturalisation of white manifest destiny and of Darwinian mobility and struggle (Shohat and Stam 1994: 116–19). Yet if the western in its classical mode leaves us asking where the natives are, the same question, as already seen, can be asked of Dumont's film. The all-terrain vehicle used by David and Katia barricades them against the intrusion of the outside, an expression of their general avoidance of other human contact. Any inclination to perceive the couple in Edenic terms – suggested at one point by their climbing a desert outcrop in order to have sex, and their subsequent naked dissolution into the bleached desert rocks – should be followed with caution, in so far as their general search for solitude is only achieved at the cost of a symbolic violence.

The trajectory of the two protagonists within the film oscillates between extremes: on one side, that which can be absorbed into a discursive notion of the 'wild' or the 'natural' (the desert, picturesque goods trains or the ecologically aesthetic field of wind turbines); on the other, the specifically cultural or urban, that which imposes itself violently upon the protagonists (a group of boys 'invading' their motel swimming pool, deranged and eventually violent drivers, featureless motel rooms and trash TV). The utilisation of the desert, its appeal to an untainted wilderness as a form of *tabula rasa*, makes sense within an economy of extreme representation. Yet the film's violent opposition of ideas, and the way that its search constitutes itself a form of violence, illustrate that the idealisation of wilderness either as the sublime or as pastoral return betrays its own cultural, anthropocentric constructed-ness. As in any artwork attempting to express 'nature', there exists a tension between the form of 'contact' desired and the work's own cultural framing (Garrard 2004: 74). This, as David Laderman points out, is a problem in the road movie. As a genre about freedom and discovery, which frequently opposes the open road to the city, it implicitly connotes culture and technology as that from which it takes flight, only to naturalise both in the medium and genre themselves. Not only do the transparency and indexicality of the cinematic image itself disguise its reality as a machine of technological reproduction, but the genre also paradoxically endorses the machine that permits this 'pastoral' return (Laderman 2002: 18).

In the ubiquity of the automobile and its windscreen as itself a form of camera, but one that is slow and unwieldy in this geographical context, *Twentynine Palms* inscribes its cultural framing at every turn. Throughout the film there is an attention to the surface textures of the car, and through Dumont's use of fixed cameras and amplified diegetic sound, a privileging of the jolts and noises of travel that all-terrain vehicles try to mollify in their design. By foregrounding the contradictions in its own diegetic and pro-filmic project, it exposes the limitations of its own vision of a fallen Eden. To reiterate the above point, the kind of pastoral described by Leo Marx as 'popular and sentimental' (Marx 1964: 5) is itself an inherently European vision: a legacy of Romanticism and its view of 'the present [as] a shadow of the spiritually richer and deeper life of the past' and of the wilderness as 'a measure of the fall from grace' (Short 1991: 6). Indeed, *Twentynine Palms* veers at times toward an implicit endorsement of (European) high-cultural values. One striking image, in a fixed and sustained long shot, shows a one-street desert town lined with motionless palm trees against a blue sky: a living postcard image. A piece of classical music – Bach – is discerned faintly, and it seems diegetically, within the image. A subsequent backward tracking shot of David and Katia walking down this consumer strip confirms the music as muzak, sourced from an unseen location. The collision of registers within the audio-visual image suggests the mutation experienced by such markers of culture in their postmodern process of signification: the static, antiseptic perfection of the desert town, and the abundance it offers as a consumerist haven, render the classical music a motif of an anachronistic culture now merely reducible to another commodity. In an earlier film which plays overtly with the ethnographic register of the travel film – Luis Buñuel's *Land Without Bread* (1932) – there is a similar use of music to set up disparities between sound and visual references: in this case, the use of Brahms to underscore images of Las Hurdes, then one of Spain's most impoverished and under-developed regions. Buñuel, however, uses music to draw attention to its insufficiency – and, ultimately, to the assumed cultural hierarchies of its privileged audiences, to whom such ethnographically inflected images are taken as given. In *Twentynine Palms*, contrastingly, the music by juxtaposition implies loss, which in turn works to reinforce, rather than confront, cultural status or distinction (besides, just as problematically, aligning the film itself within this same high-cultural context).

When read within the overall context of the film, however, such sequences may be less the signifiers of implied cultural hierarchies than juxtapositions which call into question the categories and meaning of culture at a fundamental level. As Baudrillard remarks, the desert renders such categories indeterminate; it is a kind of 'mental frontier where the projects of civilization run into the ground' (1988: 63). Baudrillard's implicit appeal throughout *Amérique* to vision, to the blinding light and formlessness of the desert, draws attention to what is ultimately most significant in *Twentynine Palms* and in Dumont's work in general: the minimal, *cinematic* particularity of his images, their reduction to pure sight, and in turn their resistance to some of the categorisation and cultural framing at work in travel *writing*. It is in this sense that Dumont's film undermines the possibility of its co-option within the discourses of pastoral return it also invites. The naked protagonists on the rock, as described above, are given a point-of-view shot of potential mastery: one which, for the most part, accords with their status as driver-protagonists, and hence the bearers of the look. Yet it is notable in this scene that the principal image is of the protagonists themselves, seen once more in extreme long shot, and therefore subsumed visually into the immense rock formation (a framing that is replicated in both the wind turbine long shot and the initial consumer strip sequence shot). Any abstract connotations the image might encourage – hostility, the sublime – have no basis in the image's construction but, again, can only be added on by the viewer. If this reinforces the validity of cinematic duration and stillness as effective tools for invoking the real or the tangible, it nevertheless does so through an undermining and decentring of the human as the governing figure within this world, to the extent that oppositional or identitarian discourses – be they of anti-Americanism or European cultural exception – are no longer just irrelevant, but actually constitute part of the problem.

The main (and possibly unintended) achievement of *Twentynine Palms*, then, may be the way it reorients an understanding of cinematic extremism away from divisive and potentially problematic questions of cultural binaries, and towards a more transnational dialogue with space and the violence of human presence. To return briefly to *Amérique*, Baudrillard's anxious sense of the desert as absence of culture acknowledges his own European perspective and the mental shock provoked by such geophysical indifference (1988: 123). As I have argued, it is useful to move away from Baudrillard's co-opting of the desert as a metaphor for moral and aesthetic absence, as his subtle shifting of the material presence of the desert to a figure for ontological malaise suggests how much a Eurocentric view persists in his vision. Baudrillard's view of the desert can again be read in terms of a European continuity of thought, in which the mutual fear and awe that its emptiness inspires are both confronted and obviated through discourse: be it religious, in the case, say, of Chateaubriand (Scott 2004: 159), or in the form of critical discourse such as the 'hyperreal' or 'simulacral' (ibid.: 160). The blank 'look' of the landscape in *Twentynine Palms*, interrogating the observer with its own resistance to signification, comes to suggest less an image of malaise than a deconstruction of the individual's bid to interpret and make meaning in their own image.

Such a reading has implications for our understanding of the film's conclusion. After David's symbolic emasculation in the form of a rape, he murders Katia in an overtly phallic stabbing (itself resituating, parodically, the male traveller-protagonist within a gendered economy of mobility, mastery and violence). A subsequent and final long shot shows a naked body, which we presume to be David's, lying face down in the desert, whilst a distressed police officer yells on his radio for assistance. If such a drifting narrative as this one can be said to have any logic, then the film's eventual violence, and David's own subsequent death, would seem interpretable in some form of sacrificial mode:[2] either in terms of the victim of a violent and hostile culture (a reading I suggest we should resist) or, to follow Petit's observations, in terms of the journey's own destructive inevitability. Yet it remains tricky to divorce the film's final image from essentially theological discourses of the fall (and consequently redemption), especially in terms of its location (the wilderness, within Judeo-Christian tradition, being a symbol of lost Eden, but in turn a site of spiritual return and transformation).

Our understanding of Dumont's work within the context of contemporary cinema may therefore benefit from some concluding thoughts as to what 'redemptive' might mean. As the conclusion to *Twentynine Palms* suggests, redemption should be considered less at the potentially self-serving level of the subject and its spiritual renewal than in terms of an abnegation of the subject itself. This is inevitably to open up another, and in this case ecocritical, line of enquiry; yet it is one to which Dumont's work, with its focus on landscape, inevitably directs us. In *Twentynine Palms*, far from mastering space, the film's protagonists, and in turn the viewer-as-protagonist, are situated as themselves the objects of vision. If, as I suggested at the beginning of this chapter, identity is already ambiguous in Dumont's film, it consolidates this ambiguous status in terms of a narrative that eschews the iconic trappings of its geographical location, but also questions the logic of a 'European' re-conquest of the West: one which would, in its imposition of a new ideology of opposition, risk reiterating the violent displacement of the 'savages' at the heart of the American pioneers' original gesture. At the same time, this idea of self-othering in Dumont's work enables us to think about the discursive category of cinematic extremism in terms of a broader – and in our world of precarious natural balance and increasingly porous borders, vital – questioning of 'centrist' cultural models in general, and the human-centric assumptions of knowledge and truth in particular.

NOTES

1. The edition of *Sight & Sound* in which Demetrios Matheou's interview with Dumont appeared (August 2005) had on its cover the rather sensationalist subheading: 'Béatrice Dalle, Bruno Dumont: Anti-Hollywood with Attitude'. The main cover image, ironically, showed a publicity shot of Johnny Depp in Tim Burton's *Charlie and the Chocolate Factory* (2005).
2. My thanks to Catherine Wheatley for this suggestion.

PART II

Becoming Animal: Posthumanism and the New Extremism

CHAPTER 6

Shadows of Being in *Sombre*: Archetypes, Wolf-men and Bare Life

Jenny Chamarette

Philippe Grandrieux's feature films, *Sombre* (1998), *La Vie nouvelle* (2002) and, more recently, *Un Lac* (2008), have generated critical acclaim and controversy in metropolitan France and beyond. At their release, both *Sombre* and *La Vie nouvelle* incited critical responses of the type frequently invoked in the face of aesthetically, ethically or politically provocative filmmaking, and in this respect the reception of these films is not unusual. Particularly since censorship has become a less pressing issue in global filmmaking and in the aftermath of the lifting or diffusing of anti-obscenity laws across the globe in the 1970s and 1980s, critical discourses on sexually or violently explicit and extreme filmmaking have left the courthouses and locations of institutional decision-making, and proliferated in the public arena.[1] The work of academic criticism in this area has done much to explore the discursive possibilities of extreme cinema, just as Pascal Bonitzer did in 1976 when he wrote 'L'Essence du pire', a careful critical response to the profoundly anti-voyeuristic aspect of total sexual display in *Aï no Corrida/In the Realm of the Senses* (Ôshima, 1976). Similarly in the case of Philippe Grandrieux's films, critics such as Nicole Brenez, Raymond Bellour, Martine Beugnet and Greg Hainge have fought against the tide of condemnation that accompanied the release of both *Sombre* and *La Vie nouvelle*.[2]

This chapter will not rehearse the vital critical work done already by these Anglophone and Francophone writers, but rather extends and develops the ethical questions that are raised by a deep, reflective engagement with films such as *Sombre* (Brenez 2005; Beugnet 2005; Hainge 2007; Beugnet 2007a). In particular, I will approach two key aspects of the film that have emerged both in Grandrieux's own responses and in the popular and academic critical reception of his works: namely, the scant traces of narrative available to the viewer in *Sombre*, and the ethical implications of these narrative traces in the penumbral archetypes that sparsely populate the film. This chapter concentrates on the archetypal figure of the wolf-man in *Sombre* that lies beyond a simply narrative and representational configuration of the human, but not so far from it that the formal innovation of the film totally obscures any possible relationship to Ur-narratives such as the archetype. The chapter explores the archetypal 'wolf-man' figure of the protagonist, Jean, in light of Giorgio Agamben's wargus, to envisage how such trace narrative configurations can traverse both cinematic reception and cinematic production, in order to rethink the subjectivity of the non-human. The shadows of being of the title of this chapter refer to precisely this: the non-human construction of an ethics of humanity at the heart of *Sombre*, and of many of the contemporary cinematic works that are in the process of being collectively annotated as 'the new extremism'.

IMMATERIAL BODIES AND MATERIAL NARRATIVES

In a radically violent way, Grandrieux's films extend notions of cinematic corporeality, exceeding the boundaries of representation.[3] A refutation of linear narrative or, indeed, of dialogue as a driving force of this narrative is a central feature of this film and others of this epoch.[4] Certainly in the case of Grandrieux's films, the movements of the camera and the movements of filmed bodies, human or inhuman, exceed the formal notions of a filmed 'text' that would involve structured dialogue as a constituent part of the diegesis. Grandrieux argues instead that the filmic images of *Sombre* and *La Vie nouvelle* are bodies, not narrative constructs:

> Cinema indissociably knits together the image and the body – the very fabric of our affective relationships to the world – by placing us under the threat of the stupefying and sudden appearance of what can neither be seen nor heard. (Grandrieux 2000: 92, translation mine)

Grandrieux's eloquence about his filmmaking espouses one extreme of philosophical materiality: the notion that the image is a body, it exudes bodiliness, and to ignore this is to ignore what is at the crux of his cinematic intimacy. None the less, Grandrieux's articulacy and philosophical approach are also precisely what found so much criticism in James Quandt's scathing critique of French filmmaking of this epoch. Although he reserves his more caustic criticism for *La Vie nouvelle*, Quandt ultimately dismisses *Sombre*'s 'disorienting plunge into the consciousness of a compulsive rapist/serial murderer' as so much 'philosophical gloss' (Quandt 2004). *Sombre* and *La Vie nouvelle* have tended to attract condemnation wherever they go.[5] Martine Beugnet (2007a) has substantially engaged with this type of critique of Grandrieux's work in order to interrogate its limitations, as has Greg Hainge (2007). As both Beugnet and Hainge have argued, accusations of misogyny and of dehumanisation on the part of the director belie the potential for a deeper and more sophisticated enquiry into the status of dehumanisation within the film, and the possibilities of thinking this dehumanisation critically. As an alternative to Quandt's polemic against flesh and blood in contemporary French cinema, Beugnet points out the precarious interstices between the sensory transformations of *Sombre* and its narrative drives. As she puts it:

> *Sombre* [. . .] speak[s] of darkness and, in effect, [. . .] works by foregrounding the sensual affect of film over representational and narrative functions, deviat[ing] from the custom of constructing a feature film as a process of progressive clarification. [It] develop[s] a story line, albeit an elliptical one [. . .] Grandrieux's experimental portrait of a killer adopt[s] a loose road-movie format and include[s] characters or figures with which identification is at least partially possible. A spectator's involvement with the film, however, is likely to take place pre-dominantly at a 'primary' level of identification – identification with the material aspect and transformations of the film body itself above identification with its figurative and narrative content. (Beugnet 2007a: 6)

It would be difficult to argue for a total evacuation of narrative in *Sombre*, particularly given the manner in which the visual tropes of archetypal storytelling emerge and erupt throughout the film. None the less, Hainge lays much upon the supposition that the extreme corporealities of *Sombre* and *La Vie nouvelle* exist at the very limit of narrative and hence representation, so much so that to perceive the geographical locations of the films as in some way participating in a symbolic or representational logic is to misapprehend the pure materiality of the images as something other than unsignified, persistent, aesthetic objects:

> [. . .] to try and apprehend this other logic [. . .] requires, for instance, that we should regard the Eastern European landscapes in which the apparently corrupt and inhuman exchanges of *La vie nouvelle* take place not as a commentary on the political state of countries destroyed by years of war and that have returned to an almost feudal state in a post-apocalyptic vision of an actual Realpolitik, nor as 'la plus profonde des fictions jamais données à voir sur la Shoah et tous les génocides du cœur de l'Europe', but, rather, as an aesthetic element. (Hainge 2007: 167)[6]

Hainge describes 'this other logic' as a mode of viewing Grandrieux's films, in particular *La Vie nouvelle*, as if one co-existed within the form, structure and images of the film, as if in fact, the spectator always viewed the film's aesthetic elements in a pre-oedipal, pre-cognitive, pre-worldly way of the kind Beugnet suggests or as if every spectator were a pre-cognate in the intimate, terrifying womb of Grandrieux's film. However, such a commentary paradoxically supposes that there are rules of viewing for Grandrieux's work – that in order to apprehend fully what is at work in the films, one must watch in a manner that assumes no a priori social subjectification, nor any awareness of the historical significance of, for example, an Eastern European setting in *La Vie nouvelle*, or indeed a setting in the heart of France in *Sombre*. The spectator must sense Grandrieux's world but without the spaces of their own. This intimate, dystopian, otherworldly mode of viewing seems perhaps unexpectedly prescriptive, given that the films themselves offer up no easy interpretation. Furthermore, such a consistently immersive viewing mode potentially distances the possibility of a more ambivalent ethical critique both of the film and with the film.

In contrast with *La Vie nouvelle*'s almost untraceable narrative, in *Sombre* there is a diegesis, in spite of the low level of dialogue and faint narrative flow. Events happen, although what kind of an order they form is unknown prior to their unfurling. Certainly the six murders of women take place throughout the film at rhythmic intervals, punctuating the cavernous impenetrability of the film with violence. However faint the narrative, there is a stuttering diegetic passage from the first dark travelling shot behind a car on a dark mountain road, to the last, mute tracking shot of the Tour de France. As Grandrieux himself admits, *Sombre* may not have a narrative, but it is a story – a fable of sorts, as ancient as oral history itself:

> [. . .] the film [*Sombre*] is a fairy tale. The character of Jean, who is archetypal, has no psychological refinement: he is presented as a block of childhood, a block of sensations cut off from other men. From this point onward, it is no longer a question of morality. Is there a question of morality in *Red Riding Hood* or *Bluebeard*? As a human being I carry with me a definitive social condemnation of murder. But I didn't place this film within a social framework, but rather on the level of the unconscious. *Sombre* invokes the most archaic of impulses. Hearing and sight, two senses which ground us from the very first moments. The film combines the question of form and ground through these senses, and only through these senses. (Grandrieux et al. 1999: 39, translation mine)

Sombre seems to appeal to the most primitive of storytelling desires. By calling upon the fairy tale, with its avatars and archetypes, Grandrieux places his work on the diegetic level of the dream, the unconscious and the mythical. However, emphasis upon the archetype and the fable also reframes narrative, not as a structuring device for the comprehension of a film in its totality, but in relation to the very storytelling modes that precede the social functioning of humanity. In a blurring of form and ground, narrative becomes the grounds for ambivalent inhumanity at work in *Sombre*, rather than the form of its development.[7] Even if deep narrative structures such as the archetype do emerge as grounds, and not forms, in *Sombre*, narrative and storytelling are key aspects of what representational signification can be gleaned from the film. In spite of the difficulties in extracting a meaningful diegesis from the scenes in *Sombre*, these tropes of narrative, storytelling and archetype work in concert with, rather than separate from, the overwhelming sensory apprehension of light, dark, skin and sound.

In particular, there are three scenes that appear to capture Jean, the central protagonist, in the act of practising or performing his craft as a puppeteer, a perambulating storyteller by trade. In the first instance, (the second scene of the film), the primeval screams of the child audience are accompanied by the children's faces, shot in close-up and at 6 to 8 frames per second instead of the usual 24 in order to make the image oscillate uncannily (Beugnet 2005: 181). These infant faces, caught between ecstasy and terror, reveal nothing of Jean but a prosthesis – an out-of-focus medium close-up of a hand puppet of a wolf, glimpsed only for a few seconds. In a slightly later scene following on directly from Jean's second murder, close-miked breath on the soundtrack accompanies close-up shots of the physical contortions and sharp movements of Jean, moving in almost darkness, gazing upward, his body shielded from his screaming young audience's gaze by a dark screen, with occasional cuts to deeply out-of-focus shots of the wolf and virgin puppets, and the muted screams of children clinging to the off-screen soundtrack. Later still, after the third murder, and withdrawn from the invisible theatre of the puppet show, Jean performs the balletic movements of puppetry, stripped to the waist in an empty neon-lit hotel room, whilst his sweating body suffers the contortions and weakness of age, injury and physical exertion.

The figure of Jean is the archetype of the predator, the traveller, carrying with him a wolf costume that we never see him wearing (only the gestures of the puppeteer are visible, not the bodily connection to the puppet); he appears to be not a person so much as a figure in a dark fable. He is more a figure at the heart of darkness than a murderous individual in the heartlands of France.[8] If this is the case, *Sombre* does not reveal the opaque shadow of Jean as some kind of visible, human consciousness, but rather configures him as a terrifying incarnation of the non-human, a shadow of being, clothed almost successfully in what we might understand to be a narratively illuminated, psychologically transparent human form.

In this respect, the presentation of human bodies in *Sombre* is, as such, not human, but rather symbolic of a structuring device in thinking what it is to be human – the archetype. Thinking through the archetype in *Sombre* offers a starting point for thinking subjectivity outside the sphere of the human or, rather, within the sphere of the human but attending to what is excluded when humanity, or the rights of humanness, is no longer accorded. There may not be a question of morality in a dark fairy tale, but there is certainly a question of good and evil. The most primeval of fables, legends and tales all pertain to the archetype, the 'block of sensations cut off from other men' in Grandrieux's terms: the hero, the wolf, the virgin – figural characters with no absolute or stable appurtenance to the realm of the human, but which are carried by the performance of a story. If *Sombre* is a film about the darkness of the human soul, where there are no heroes, then this is a very contemporary fable, whose darkness is a most pressing contemporary concern with the nature of subjectivity and in particular subjective autonomy, of the kind that Giorgio Agamben, among many others, has discussed.

When Grandrieux responded to criticism about the dehumanising abjection that the human bodies of his films undergo, his response was as follows: 'I sincerely believe first and foremost that there is no such thing as an inhuman action, however monstrous it may be. Man is attached to his species' (Grandrieux et al. 1999: 39, translation mine). Man is attached to his species, attached to what it is to be human. On the one hand, Grandrieux's comment is a bold statement, acknowledging, like Conrad, Nietzsche, Arendt, Benjamin and Agamben, the ambivalent darkness of the human heart; in effect, this statement acknowledges the contextualisation of Grandrieux's film, both in terms of contemporary French cinema, and in terms of its presentation of objectified, commodified, non-autonomous bodies. This commodification seems particularly pertinent, and persistently ambivalent, where these bodies are those of individuals living in the twilight of human existence – peripatetically, in brothels, or otherwise at the margins of society. On the other hand, it also raises the question of this dual ambivalence, between the human(e) and the inhuman(e), the human and the non-human (the figural), and the human and the animal, particularly in the case of Jean, the wolf-man.[9]

WOLF-MEN AND VIRGINS: INHUMAN ARCHETYPES AND BARE LIFE

Sombre presents the opportunity to think the implications of a different kind of abjected cinematic subjectivity: the evacuation from subjectivity of any kind of autonomy, inclusive rights or self-ownership. This also invokes the political implications of Deleuze's machinic body without organs, the schizophrenic at the heart of capitalism (Deleuze and Guattari 1972). In fact, both Deleuze and Guattari and Agamben share this criticism of the machine of modernity, as Agamben makes clear when he describes the continually ambivalent and dialectical injection and ejection that is invoked by modernity's machine:

Insofar as the production of man through the opposition man/animal, human/inhuman, is at stake here, the machine necessarily functions by means of an exclusion (which is always already a capturing) and an inclusion (which is also always already an exclusion). Indeed, precisely because the human is already presupposed every time, the machine actually produces a kind of state of exception, a zone of indeterminacy in which the outside is nothing but the exclusion of an inside and the inside is in turn only the inclusion of an outside. (Agamben 2004: 37)

Agamben's interest in the ambivalent gestures of inclusion and exclusion and in states of exception arises from his treatment of historical exclusionary practices in ancient civilisations, by contrast to the incomprehensible fluxes of modernity. Much of his writing concerns the Holocaust as emphatically not a transcendent evil but as a paradigm of politicised life, or rather, 'biopoliticised power', where the killing of humans is not only not murder, but also where individuals to be killed are excluded from the realm within which they would be accorded the right to live as human beings (Bernstein 2004: 4). In the first few pages of *Homo Sacer*, he delineates an ancient Greek division between life as pure existence – the life of all, or bare life, *zoe* – and the life of autonomous beings known as human, with all of its constitutive regulations for selfhood, *bios* (Agamben [1995] 1998: 9–11). Agamben views the politicisation of life – that is to say, the production of human autonomous subjectivity with rights and responsibilities within a public arena – as at the heart of modernity, with all the accompanying horror that the incorporation of exclusionary bare life (that is, a life deprived of human autonomy – *bios*) into systems of government might entail. One might, as Agamben does implicitly and explicitly, identify this mode of thought with Hannah Arendt's *polis*, or what according to Foucault, is a process of subjectification whereby man was, for Aristotle, a 'living animal with the additional capacity for political existence' (Foucault 1976: 188, translation mine).

The condition of modernity, then, is where the biological existence of humans at their most basic animal level has become an affair of the state, howsoever formed; life is, in effect, politicised. As such, what is most interesting is where the delineations of humanity and animality are broken down, when humans exist outside, or are deliberately excluded from, the functioning of state, sovereignty and social power. Such exceptions, which to Agamben are constitutive of what then becomes state power, emerge historically as archetypes – the King and the bandit, for example, or the wolf-man (wargus). The figure of the wolf-man in particular draws a fascinating parallel between *Sombre* and Agamben's works, *Homo Sacer* and *The Open*. The persistence of the wolf motif of Jean in *Sombre*, as a puppet, as a mask and as a costume, not only implicates the feared werewolf creature of fables and fairy tales, existing spectrally between the human, the bestial and the outcast, but also implies a more far-reaching engagement with the inhumanity of our age, of living between the human and the animal. The figure of Jean raises the possibility of thinking non-autonomous, exclusionary subjectivity, like Agamben's exclusionary figure of the *homo sacer*, literally without community, but which is constitutive of the possibility of community or society.

This is not a question of morality in a fairy tale, which is what Grandrieux rejects, but an engagement with the ethical questions of subjectivity that emerge from an encounter with Grandrieux's films. In *Sombre* and in *La Vie nouvelle*, the presentation of subjugated, excluded bodies, of the dismemberment of bodies and of their separation from life – whether they refer to the right to a humane and autonomous life, or the actuality of existence – cannot help but call upon ethical issues of subjection and subjugation. David Pellecuer describes the bodies of *La Vie nouvelle* as 'opaque, abyssal, resistant, strange, transformed, weighty [. . .] evaluated, sensed, touched, weighed, shaved, stripped, desired, exchanged, sold' (Pellecuer 2005: 90, translation mine).

Bodies are objects in Grandrieux's films; things are done to them just as they stubbornly refuse to be recognised as human. In *Sombre*, Jean is the figure who manipulates pliant women's bodies as if they were the puppets he carries in his bags; in each of the six murder scenes, he pushes his fingers into the mouths of his victims in an obviously erotically charged act of penetration. This act also represents the locus of life and death; in breaking the skulls of the women through their mouths, Jean's gesture is a ritual, life-annihilating one – a gesture of command but also a gesture of death. Reminded as we are of the significance of gesture rather than linear narrative, in *Sombre* and in Grandrieux's influences from Deleuze's *Francis Bacon: The Logic of Sensation*, it is not surprising that Jean's movements should be so codified.[10] One is reminded equally of Jean's balletic twirling in the hotel room, or his hunched, crouching, inchoate, monstrous body as he wades out into the lagoon after his attempt on Claire's sister's life. Archetypal in gesture and in behaviour, Jean is predatory, incapable of conducting the linguistic complexities of conversation – only grunts, orders and platitudes. As a killer, a traveller, an outcast and a performer, Jean is evidently a figure of exclusion from normative society. His solitude, lack of expression, and predominant absence of emotion all point to a figure without content or interiority: a total exclusion of human subjectivity.

The motif of the wolf is embedded throughout the film in the very performances and gestures of storytelling and puppetry. The wolf puppet and the wolf costume are in Jean's possession but we never see him wearing them – as if Jean shared an embodied but somehow reversible relationship between the symbolic wolf and his body. Strangely enough, just prior to the film's climactic shift, Claire finds the wolf costume in his bags while locked out of her hotel room. Another archetype, the salvational virgin, Claire dons the wolf costume in Jean's room, where he finds her wearing it. Given the intimate symbolism of this fable, this scene is not peripheral; Claire, the source of light (a symbolic name) takes on the discarded, interchangeable skin of the wolf-man, the inhuman, contentless Jean. She illuminates his exclusion, his animality and his attributions of the non-human, while herself not belonging to the exterior world of supermarkets and barbecues in which her sister happily exists.

RETURN TO THE UNREAL

When Grandrieux has been asked in interview to comment upon the setting of his films, he has denied explicit critique either of middle-France's petit-bourgeoisie, or of Eastern Europe's Realpolitik in the case of *La Vie nouvelle* (Grandrieux et al. 1999: 41). None the less, the final scene of *Sombre* does not abandon the viewer to a twilit primal scene in the forest, but is instead a long tracking shot at ninety degrees to a winding road in the Massif Central, slowly moving past spectators who line the road, presumably watching the passage of cyclists during the Tour de France; the camera is held a metre or so above the ground, so that in passing the spectators, their heads are frequently cut off. Consequently, the camera floats past adult bodies that have been effectively decapitated by the framing, while children remain intact; the children's gazes return that of the camera, while the adults frequently do not. Inevitably this motivated camera angle invites reflection upon the watching of the silent spectators and the nature of their watching. The sightline of children also invokes the ecstatically transfixed, screaming children in the second scene of *Sombre*, whose absorption in what they are watching (we assume the puppet theatre of Jean) is so consuming as for their cries to become pre-cognitive, instinctual and subconscious. However, these children are not suspended ecstatically in a darkened theatre; their presence, together with the faceless adults of the final scene, is within a particular contemporary society, one that watches the Tour de France from the roadside, or that overenthusiastically celebrates the return of their older daughters from Paris, as happens for Claire earlier in the film. This final Tour de France scene has been commented upon as a 'return to the exterior world', as Grandrieux suggests in an interview in 1999:

> The final travelling shot of the Tour de France is like the absolute reverse-shot of the entire film. The exterior world exists: we will find it again when we leave the film behind us, and me, I am caught up in this – I do not feel in the least bit distanced from these people for whom I have no contempt whatsoever [. . .] We are these people – they are us. A

little bit abandoned by the side of the road, we watch, it passes us by, we are dazzled by it, and then it has already disappeared. (Grandrieux et al. 1999: 39, translation mine)

In watching the spectators watching (as both the camera and, consequently, we do), the exterior world (of representation and of spectatorship) looks in upon the interior world of the film: the semi-conscious world, as some critics have described it, or the penumbral, archetypal darkness that is excluded from what it is to be human.[11] However, the child-like angle from which the travelling shot is taken suggests that this is not a precise mapping of contemporary petit-bourgeois France on to a hypothetical reverse-shot of the archetypal world of *Sombre*. If Jean is an archetypal, non-human figure, then so too is this reverse-shot a non-human representation, both culturally specific and culturally general. The same exclusionary practices that engulf Jean within the archetype of the wolf-man also constitute the headless people in the tracking shot as distinctly other. *Sombre*'s penumbral world never escapes its own orbit, not even at its end.

Agamben might describe this as the ambivalence of an exclusionary practice of inclusion, whereby the unfolding behaviour of Jean, the murderous figure, 'block of sensations cut off from other men', is placed in relation to a world exterior to him in this last tracking shot. Grandrieux, and we, are complicit with these figures of the exterior; but these figures are only like us in so far as we are complicit in the exclusionary practice of viewing Jean, the werewolf, as the murderous outsider for whom the rules of society have already ejected him from humanity, but which require him to be excluded in order to confirm that same society. Agamben highlights this ambivalent gesture of inclusive exclusion in his chapter on 'The Ban and the Wolf' in *Homo Sacer*:

> [. . .] at issue is not simply *fera bestia* and the natural life, but rather a zone of indistinction between the human and the animal, a werewolf, a man who is transformed into a wolf and a wolf who is transformed into a man – in other words, a bandit, a *homo sacer*. [. . .] the Hobbesian state of nature is the exception and the threshold that constitutes and dwells within it. It is not so much a war of all against all, as, more precisely, a condition in which everyone is bare life and a *homo sacer* for everyone else, and in which everyone is thus wargus [. . .] And this lupinization of man and humanization of the wolf is at every moment possible in the dissolutio civilitatis inaugurated by the state of exception. This threshold alone, which is neither simple natural life nor social life but rather bare life or sacred life, is the always present and always operational presupposition of sovereignty. (Agamben 2007: 116–17, translation mine)

While, in the penultimate scene, Jean merges with the darkened forest, his foetally curled body no longer distinguishable from foreground and background both by the saturation of the image and by the just out-of-focus shot, the final scene returns this sublime pre-social realm of fable and unconscious to the anticlimactic world of what is external to the excluded. Neither confirming nor denying Jean's terrifying alterity, this world cohabits with him, as if the murderous wolf-man in fact confirmed the existence of the actual, autonomous but fundamentally othered human world. *Sombre* draws upon the zone of indetermination across all planes, including the one we might most readily describe as what is real.

Jean invokes the state of exception, which confirms the sovereignty of human autonomy in a social world. For Agamben, the wolf-man exists in the peripheral threshold of human life; just as Jean's hands transform into a wolf puppet and his bag contains a wolf costume, so the murders he commits confirm his liminality as the penumbral, non-human (but all too human) archetype, whose chaos moves with him and engulfs the lives of other, female outcasts – predominantly prostitutes. His exclusion is contagious and he spreads death, disorder and darkness. *Sombre*, in its darkness, presents a world that is both ours and not ours; it is the world of the *homo sacer*, a subjugated and subjugating body. At the same time, this close, unbearably horrifying, pornographic, penumbral world serves to constitute the *bios* of the weirdly othered, human social world – that reverse-shot at the end of the film.

Grandrieux and Agamben here seem to illuminate one another mutually; while Grandrieux exposes the concrete, abstract and figural body's night to the cinematic image, Agamben claims for the ambivalent darkness and horror of the wargus, a body to whom humanity is stripped away but which also strips away humanity from bodies. While this is not a morality of the kind Hainge or Grandrieux imagine, it is an exposure of the darkness of humanity, or indeed the inhumanity within and without humanity. Pertinently, Agamben notes the opacity of thinking this inhumanity in terms very similar to those of Grandrieux:

> Until we become aware of the political nature of bare life and its modern avatars (biological life, sexuality, etc.), we will not succeed in clarifying the opacity at their centre. Conversely, once modern politics enters into an intimate symbiosis with bare life, it loses the intelligibility that still seems to us to characterize the juridico-political foundation of classical politics. (Agamben 1998: 120, translation mine)[12]

If Grandrieux's films move close to presenting via a corporeal image the opacity of bare life, or 'the body's night', then far from being a form of pure aesthetic intimacy or cinematic experimentation, they are no less than an engagement with the ethics of being, through principles of the aesthetic. If this is the case, a caveat should none the less be added. Agamben has been criticised heavily for his transformation of bare life into the pure witnessing of bare life in the figure of the Muselmann in his *Remnants of Auschwitz: The Witness and the Archive*, as a gesture that becomes an aesthetic act inducing a pornography of horror, not an ethics of witnessing (Bernstein 2004). This ambivalent ethical position is one shared by *Sombre*, and suggests that a deep ethical and aesthetic engagement with the film cannot easily dismiss the anger of audiences that watch it. J. M. Bernstein's critique of Agamben, which rests on Adorno's refutation of discursive engagement with inhumanity and in particular with Auschwitz in his *Negative Dialectics*, is fascinating, and its relation to *Sombre* and the film's sensory and archetypal engagements with inhumanity is the subject of another study. None the less, the shadows of being in *Sombre* succeed in traversing both cinematic reception and cinematic production, via the irruptive affects of the archetype. In *Sombre*, at least, the ethical materiality of the archetype presents and illuminates, but certainly does not articulate, the darkness of the human body's night.

NOTES

1. We should be reminded that Nagisa Ôshima's ground-breaking film of 1976 displaying real sex and simulated genital violence, *In the Realm of the Senses*, was banned under anti-obscenity laws including those of the US, UK, Germany and Japan, and was only passed uncut by the British Board of Film Classification in 1991, and re-released worldwide in 2001. Attitudes towards *In the Realm of the Senses* exemplify some of the fundamental shifts that had taken place by this time in terms of legal attitudes to so-called 'obscene' audio-visual material across the world. Since the film could not have been released in Japan under the strict censorship laws (and still cannot be screened in Japan without optical masking of explicit scenes), the negatives of the film were originally developed in a French laboratory and the film was produced by Argos Films, Chris Marker's French production company. See BBFC (2009a) and Alexander (2003).
2. Perhaps unsurprisingly, while *Un Lac* retained many of the formal experimental features of Grandrieux's previous two feature films, its much-reduced sexual and violent material drew a far warmer response from the critics. *Le Monde* described it as 'une histoire de sensations' (Douin 2009).
3. Martine Beugnet describes *Sombre* as part of a collective cinema of evil or of terror in contemporary French cinema: 'Unusually categorized as art or auteur cinema, these works construct heterogeneous forms, mixing elements from "sub-genres" such as the gothic, gore, horror and pornography, with references to high art and literary and artistic underground trends' (Beugnet 2005: 175).
4. Some examples of this phenomenon of non-linear narrative and non-narrative-driven dialogue: *À ma sœur!* (Breillat, France, 2001); *Flandres* (Dumont, France, 2006); *Irréversible* (Noé, France, 2002); *5 × 2* (Ozon, France, 2004); *Batalla en el cielo / Battle in Heaven* (Reygadas, France, 2005).
5. Michael Witt, co-curator of the Tate Modern series, 'Paradise Now! Essential French

Avant-garde Cinema, 1890–2008', which ran from 14 March to 18 May 2008, mentioned to me the very heated accusations of misogyny and dehumanisation aimed at Grandrieux, who was present at the screening of excerpts of *Un Lac*, his video installation *L'Arrière-saison* (2007) and his 2002 film *La Vie nouvelle*. Similar anger was expressed by audiences at a screening of *La Vie nouvelle* at the Cambridge Film Festival in September 2008, at which I assisted in the interpreting of a Q&A in a direct video link to Grandrieux in Paris.

6. The internal quotation is from Fabien Gaffez's account of *La Vie nouvelle* (Gaffez, cited in Hainge 2007: 34).
7. Beugnet treats the 'archetypal dimension' of such films as *Sombre* as an analogous act of becoming other. Drawing upon Deleuze's *Cinéma I – L'image-mouvement*, she describes these archetypal filmmaking practices/generic codes as a flux between the contemporary world and an originary world of the Deleuzian any-space-whatever:

    The archetypal dimension thus sends us back to the crux of the matter: the attempt to create a cinematic experience that connects us, even fleetingly, with those pre-objective sensations and affects that operate before desires and drives are inscribed (defined, encoded, fixed) in the linguistic or discursive planes of organisation. (2007a: 128)

    However, this does not make any distinction between an archetypal dimension and the presence of an archetypal figure; if the archetypal dimension is pre-objective, then the archetype is also a deep configuration that speaks to the narrative strata of human subjectivity. As sensational as the archetype may be, it also enters the realm of the defined, encoded, inscribed desires of human subjectification via its own transmission: namely, in the act of storytelling.

8. When I interviewed Grandrieux, he was about to travel to the Congo for his next project, a study of Conrad. Given Grandrieux's attraction to the body's night, it seems pertinent to note his next cinematic excursion into the *Heart of Darkness*.
9. Beugnet also picks up on Jean's wolf-man-like presence as inflecting the 'nightmarish tale' that unfolds in the film (2007a: 115).
10. In my interview with him in June 2008, Grandrieux also explained that he felt the Deleuze text that engaged most deeply with the cinema was not in fact *L'Image-temps* or *L'Image-mouvement*, but Deleuze's *Francis Bacon: Logique de la sensation*, which discusses gesture rather than the figural as a key mode of engagement with Bacon's work.
11. See Beugnet (2005). Grandrieux also comments on his spectatorial directions: 'I'd like the spectator to be somewhere between sleep and waking, in a state of semi-consciousness' (Grandrieux et al. 1999: 40, translation mine).
12. See also Grandrieux (2000: 92) and Brenez (2003).

CHAPTER 7

Eastern Extreme: The Presentation of Eastern Europe as a Site of Monstrosity in *La Vie nouvelle* and *Import/Export*

Michael Goddard

Despite the breakdown of the Cold War division of Europe into separate Western and Eastern political zones, there is still a discernible economic boundary between these two spheres and this is reflected in the ways they are presented cinematically. Whereas Western Europe is presented unproblematically as a synecdoche for Europe as a whole, as its civilised centre, Eastern Europe is presented condescendingly as the 'new Europe' as if it had no history prior to 1989 and above all in terms of abjection and monstrosity. This chapter will focus on this presentation of Eastern Europe as a site of the extreme and of monstrosity in two recent (Western) European art movies: namely, Philippe Grandrieux's *La Vie nouvelle* (2002) and Ulrich Seidl's more recent *Import/Export* (2007). On the surface, these films can seem quite similar to the recent spate of horror movies such as *Hostel* (Roth, US, 2005) or *Severance* (Smith, UK, 2006), in which Eastern Europe is represented as the primitive other of Anglo-American civilised normality. Certainly, the clichéd tropes of Eastern European primitivism such as prostitution, mafia-like violence, semi-poverty and alienating socialist architecture are present in both these generic and art movie examples. However, a closer examination of *La Vie nouvelle* and *Import/Export* reveals other dimensions in which Eastern Europe functions not only as the primitive other to the civilised West but as a radical destabilisation of these relations. Moreover, this is done not by avoiding clichés about Eastern European monstrosity but by pushing them to a higher level of intensity. In this respect there is a continuity between these two films and other examples of the French new extremist cinema dealt with in Martine Beugnet's book, *Cinema and Sensation: French Film and the Art of Transgression*, even if in *La Vie nouvelle* and *Import/Export,* the irruption of transgressive alterity and visceral sensation takes place in the more geopolitically specified sites of Eastern Europe and Austria.

This chapter will argue that while both films could be accused of conforming to a clichéd, primitivist view of Eastern Europe, their resort to violence, monstrosity and extreme sensations is essential to the political questions the films raise about the still-divided constitution of contemporary Europe. Before addressing these films directly, however, I will look at the reduction of Eastern Europe to the status of primitive, monstrous other, as developed in the work of Marina Gržinić and other critics.

EASTERN EUROPE AND/AS MONSTROSITY

Several different theorists have already noted that, historically, European identity has been defined by the drawing of an eastern border that would delineate the civilised and non-civilised parts of the continent, most recently reaffirmed in the Cold War division of Europe into Eastern and Western zones. However, this is only a recent example of a series of drawings and redrawings of the map of Europe, constantly redistributing what is included or excluded, civilised or primitive, normative or monstrous. Dina Iordanova, for example, points out that the end of the Cold War 'did not mean an automatic deletion of the entrenched ideas of European fault lines; either new associations were to be found to mark the differences or older division lines from before the Cold War were to be re-established' (Iordanova 2003: 13). As Iordanova indicates (13–15), the polemical critical attempts to claim an East-Central or simply Central European identity for the part of countries like the Czech Republic or Poland can be seen as so many attempts at remapping these European fault-lines against associations with either Soviet Russia or the Balkans and in favour of an integration or reintegration with the 'heart of Europe'. Another key factor in Eastern and Western European relations after 1989 are phenomena of mobility and migration which are perceived as 'new', even though, as Mazierska and Rascaroli point out, in some cases these forms of mobility have historical antecedents going back more than a century (Mazierska and Rascaroli 2006: 139–40). Nevertheless, the fall of the Berlin Wall definitely operated as an accelerating factor in European East–West mobility, which, as Mazierska and Rascaroli show, has been expressed in a range of European films, to which *La Vie nouvelle* and *Import/Export* could certainly be added. As Mazierska and Rascaroli acknowledge and as these films demonstrate, while this movement is mostly from the East to the West, it is also accompanied by the reverse movement to the East, to the site of monstrosity itself. This is not to mention the potential of Eastern Europe as a giant film set, complete with a well-trained but relatively inexpensive labour pool of both crew and performers, a potential tapped into not only by Seidl and Grandrieux but also by David Lynch and other more commercial filmmakers who select Eastern Europe as an ideal site for making cheap genre films.

Behind this cultural, political and economic exclusion and exploitation of the East are several mythical ideas about Eastern Europe. According to Gržinić, one of these is the romantic mythology taken up by Marxist–Leninism that would locate Eastern Europe, due to its technological backwardness, in terms of 'the myth of a grand brotherly community and total sexual freedom' and its flipside of 'an exclusively totalitarian project and a realisation of an Eastern despotism in which poverty, misery, mucus and blood decant incessantly' (Gržinić 2008: 71). It is this latter dystopian vision of Eastern Europe that, according to Gržinić, is dominant today, and certainly elements of this myth are clearly evident in both the films I will be discussing. While Gržinić points to these myths in the dissolution of the brotherly project of Yugoslavia into a monstrous bloodbath characterised by ethnic cleansing and mass graves, the same could also be said of the image of contemporary Russia as a return to imperialist politics embodied by leaders like Putin and accompanied by a sinister mafia. For Gržinić, the Western response to this monstrosity is to exclude it, even when, as in former Yugoslavia, monstrous events are taking place in the heart of Europe: 'this same Europe can renounce this heartland, for it has renamed it the "Balkans"' (72). These processes of exclusion/inclusion are clearly evident in the response to Eastern European migrations through the construction of the European Union in terms of 'Fortress Europe'; even while certain Eastern ethnic groups are allowed in, this is only on the condition that they accept the most menial and degrading forms of labour and a gross economic inequality that is itself a form of monstrosity, a point that is emphasised in Seidl's *Import/Export*. For Gržinić the response to this from an Eastern position must involve a rejection of this mythology in favour of a re-appropriation of history against both its effacement and renaming by the socialist machine and its evacuation through its neocolonial reduction to the status of primitive other by the West: 'For the East there is one constant concern: History and its re-appropriation' (72). Elsewhere, however, Gržinić advocates a very different strategy of adopting the place of exclusion and abjection projected on to the East by the West, by becoming the very surplus Europe that the West tries to banish from its borders, what Gržinić refers to as the Eastern European 'piece of shit' (48). For the purposes of this chapter, I am not dealing with the question of an Eastern European position but two Western European versions or visions of the East that are clearly related to this abject vision of Eastern Europe as, in Gržinić's terms, 'an excremental remainder' (51). I would like to propose the value of this second strategy in which the abjection of the East is not avoided, denied or taken for granted but instead emphasised and exaggerated as paradoxically a way of exploding the very myths to which both films I will be speaking about may appear at first glance to subscribe.

LA VIE NOUVELLE: BIG TROUBLE SOMEWHERE IN EASTERN EUROPE

Grandrieux's *La Vie nouvelle* – The New Life – is highly suggestive of the geopolitics of 'new Europe', as is evident both from its title and its setting in an 'any-Eastern European space-whatever' that is, in fact, Bulgaria. This last expression is adopted from Gilles Deleuze's account of Italian neorealism and its use of the bombed-out cities of Europe as a new kind of delocalised cinematic space analogous to Marc Augé's concept of the 'non-place' (1995). It is worth pausing over Deleuze's description of these traumatised non-places: 'the post-war period has greatly increased the . . . places we no longer know how to describe. These were "any spaces whatever," deserted but inhabited, disused warehouses, waste ground, cities in the course of demolition or reconstruction' (Deleuze 1989: xi). Post-Cold War Eastern Europe provides many similar examples of destroyed and anonymous non-places in which degraded and collapsing socialist architecture provides a perfect spatial expression for a damaged and anonymous sociality exploited in both the movies under consideration.

However, the 'new life' implied by the title is not limited to this other zone of the East but implies a future development of life in Europe and perhaps the world in general, situating Eastern Europe in the avant-garde of new modes of biopolitical existence characterised by violence, decaying and alienating urban environments, mafia-style capitalism and especially the reduction of the body to an animal-like commodity. This points to another resonance of the title – namely, to Sade's 'new Justine' – and certainly, an early scene in which young women are rounded up like cattle at an auction is a highly Sadean vision, resonant of Pasolini's *Salò* (1975), while at the same time an exaggeration of one of the most common clichés about Eastern Europe. Finally, as the book devoted to the film, *La Vie nouvelle/Nouvelle Vision*, edited by Nicole Brenez, emphasises through its organisation into different circles of hell, the film is a precise reference to Dante. Indeed, the film takes its name from Dante's first text and can be read as a contemporary version of the descent into hell, in which the metaphorical journey described by Dante takes place in the all-too-real destroyed cultural environment of the 'new Europe'.

And yet this really says nothing about what the film is like, since this monstrous space is presented in the film through a series of affectively intense images in which narrative and language have been subtracted, leaving a cinema and a space of pure sensation, as has been commented on in several critical responses to the film. If the film has a relation to any 'actually existing' Eastern Europe, it is one that reaches the West in terms of rumour and vague knowledge from the media. As Bellour points out in one of the texts devoted to the film, it is 'a physical, psychic world about which one knows nothing, which arrives as in a fog' (Bellour in Brenez 2005: 16, translation mine). For this reason the film operates according to a 'subtractive' form in which all the usual transformations of images into a sense-making series of narrative steps is substituted by a chaotic flux of images and sensations; nevertheless, a type of proto-narrative is still perceptible through these images but is one that partakes precisely of the unformed in the Bataillean sense of the term.

This sensory, unformed experience of the film is explored in Martine Beugnet's book, *Cinema and Sensation*. Beugnet points out that, instead of a regime of conventional representation, the film operates at the synaesthetic intersection of the visual and the haptic, a zone that she relates to the work of Merleau-Ponty on the 'limit between the body and the world' (Beugnet 2007a: 108). This zone creates an ambiguity between the self and the world so that, in Beugnet's terms:

> What is at stake, then, which film, as the medium of sensation, 'thinks' through so vividly, is the evocation of the complementary poles that define the relation of the subject to the world, caught as it is between the daunting sense of the void on the one hand, and the sense of a diminution or temporary loss of subjectivity on the other. (ibid.)

Plenitude and loss, the inanimate and the living, are therefore subject to a destabilising gaze that evokes the indescribable and unutterable through synaesthetic means. *La Vie nouvelle* is certainly not the only film to do this but it is a privileged example in Beugnet's book for the radicality of its attempt to use cinematic means to remain entirely on the side of the unformed and the evocative, as opposed to the clear and distinct vision of mainstream cinema: 'the unfathomable gaze of the inanimate, of the landscapes, objects and buildings that bear witness to that which, in Deleuze's words, "we no longer know how to react to"' (1989: 109).

For example, in the beginning of the film we are confronted with a series of nocturnal faces, which, in their manner of presentation and in conjunction with the soundtrack, give the impression of being the survivors of some traumatic collective event that suggests everything from the purges of totalitarian power to ethnic cleansing without this cause ever being revealed. Instead, all our attention is focused on these unnamed faces that plunge us into a world of bodies and sensations, before things are named or identified. This scene, in fact, sets the tone of the entire film in which events are on the borders of the perceptible and only subject to a minimal articulation through language. This also draws attention to the space of the film, which is precisely the any-space-whatever of a mythic Eastern Europe as imagined from the West; as Hélène Fleckinger puts it, it is 'a world in ruins, as if after a disaster . . .

An Eastern country, it matters little which one' (Fleckinger in Brenez 2005: 104, translation mine). While both the film and critical responses to it such as the one cited above could be seen as a further erasure of Eastern European history, on another level the film uses this destroyed space as a site for the projection of desires surrounding a commerce in human bodies that is all the more political for being devoid of any precise geographical referent. In a sense, what several critics have identified as the primitive, pre-human or pre-historical in the film could rather be seen as a level of abstraction that is in communication with the 'real abstraction' of transnational capital, which similarly transgresses national boundaries and stable identities. In *La Vie nouvelle* bodies are a kind of 'living currency', to use the expression of Pierre Klossowski, which circulate entirely according to exchange value, a situation that is only a hyperbolic form of capitalism in general (Klossowski [1970] 1994). For this reason, I would argue that the film should not be seen as a return to a primitive pre-human past but rather as the dystopian evocation of a posthuman future in which the real subsumption of capital has progressed to the extent that there is no distinction between the human body and the commodity form.

This reading of the film is one way of making sense of the figure of Melania, the prostitute who is the object of Seymour's desire or love and appears in the film as a figure of absolute submission. First shown in a masochistic submission to a ritualistic and eroticised cutting of her hair, symbolising that she is now the property of another, Melania performs throughout the film in the role of an object. Her submission to the role of the commodity is dramatised in her performance of the song 'Smell my scent', which is redolent of a Lynchian atmosphere pushed to a greater degree of intensity and deterritorialisation; unlike in the world of *Twin Peaks* or *Blue Velvet* there is no small town or suburban 'apple pie' light relief to alleviate the performance of submission, violence and the exchangeability of human flesh presented in the film. This scene seems to be posing the question of what becomes of human life when it is entirely reduced to the level of an exchangeable object and Melania's performance can be seen as one answer to this, combining as it does an absolute submission with a disturbing eroticism. The final descent into hell via a barely graspable scene of mutual vampirism and cannibalism, filmed by an infra-red camera in which bodies are sensed via the heat they give off rather than having any clear visibility, is perhaps the ultimate answer the film gives to this question of the 'new life' into which Eastern Europe and the rest of the world are entering.

Melania's performance of absolute submission can be related to Gržinić's ascription of a feminine position to Eastern Europe precisely in relation to the kind of submissive abjection that she performs in the film; the question is whether to read the film as merely an 'arty' reinforcement of this cliché, or whether in its exaggeration and hyperbole it is capable of suggesting a type of immanent critique of the hyper-capitalist reduction of subjectivity to the commodity form that none of the figures in *La Vie nouvelle* is capable of escaping. This is to confront the reception of the film in terms of not sensation but sensationalism, as pointed out by Nicole Brenez:

> the critical reception of *La Vie nouvelle* . . . included contempt, sarcasm, insults and even defamatory comments . . . Even for those who had been passionate about Grandrieux's first feature, *Sombre*, *La Vie nouvelle* represented an aesthetic shock . . . only two journals defended the film. (Brenez 2005: 11)

As Beugnet, who also quotes this passage, indicates, it is precisely the film's proximity to raw visceral sensation that makes it vulnerable to charges of sensationalism, to being perceived as merely designed to shock. In this respect, the film is close to some of the other examples of the new French extremism treated by Beugnet. However, rather than a simple gesture of transgression, what this film, along with the other examples of the new extremist cinema, is attempting is to maximise cinematic intensity by 'destabilising normal patterns of perception and distance . . . [and] tread[ing] close to formal chaos and bodily abjection' (Beugnet 2007a: 31). What needs to be added in the case of *La Vie nouvelle* is a geopolitical and biopolitical dimension in which the film becomes the expression, not of European political reality as such, but rather of its political unconscious: the cruel desires that animate it through economies, not only of money and objects, but also of human bodies and modes of subjectivity that are generated by the unequal logics of economic exchange that characterise and constitute contemporary Europe. These issues are focused on even more directly in Ulrich Seidl's *Import/Export*, albeit via radically different cinematic strategies.

IMPORT/EXPORT

Import/Export also engages directly with these questions of the exchange of bodies between the East and the West but in the more literal sense of having two parallel trajectories that never meet, in which the main protagonists are 'exported' from one zone to the other. Olga's life, from the beginning, is like a compendium of conventional images of Eastern Europe; shown trudging through snow from her socialist apartment block to her work as a nurse, she is paid only 40 per cent of her wages. Next she tries her hand at internet porn but is hampered by her lack of knowledge of foreign languages, as she is unable to understand the erotic commands barked at her by the Western European clients. Leaving her child behind, she goes to Austria, where she works at a number of menial jobs, eventually becoming a hospital cleaner, an ironic and frustrating position since, despite her training as a nurse, she is unable to work as one and provokes resentment when she attempts to make contact with the elderly patients. Meanwhile, we first see Pauli going through a brutal and absurd training as a security guard, a job he holds only briefly as he is fired after being beaten up and humiliated in a car park. Seeming to owe money all over town, he takes the opportunity to go to 'the East' with his stepfather Michael, to sell outdated fruit and amusement machines. It soon becomes apparent that his stepfather prefers to combine business with pleasure, his trip culminating in an encounter with a prostitute, after which Pauli decides to depart from his company.

As with Grandrieux's film, however, the plot gives no indication of the experience of watching the film, which evolves as a series of vignettes on which Seidl tends to linger beyond the needs of the narrative or the comfort levels of the audience. Examples of these scenes that border on the intolerable include the opening one of a screaming baby in the Ukraine, who seems to be attended to in a cold if not cruel manner, and the numerous scenes of elderly patients in Vienna, who are real patients suffering from dementia. Many reviewers have pointed to what they perceive as gratuitous cruelty in these scenes and have raised ethical questions about Seidl's filmmaking that will be returned to shortly. In many ways, it is often quite everyday scenes that are the most disturbing, such as when Pauli brings his new dog, who he is training in an aggressive manner, to his girlfriend's apartment; the latter is terrified of dogs and begs him to leave, while Pauli taunts her for 'over-reacting'. This scene seems to go on interminably to the point that it is hardly surprising when it leads to a disintegration of their relationship, sealed by the dog's violent attack on the girlfriend's teddy bear. Another key scene is when Olga is first employed in Austria as a maid and she is being instructed on the correct way to care for the taxidermy heads of various hunting trophies. As with several other scenes of 'training' in the film, this scene directly presents a diagram of unequal power relations, which is only reinforced by Olga's subsequent shoddy treatment at the hands of this bourgeois Austrian family.

The question of work and training is fundamental to the film and is clearly connected to service professions that could broadly be understood in terms of a biopolitical paradigm; Olga goes from being a nurse and a pornographic performer to a maid and a cleaner, all of which are low-paid service positions, typical for female and migrant labour. This seems to correspond quite closely to Hardt and Negri's account of biopolitical production and their distinction of biopolitics from biopower; paradoxically it is via the experience of precarious forms of biopolitical labour that a challenge to contemporary biopower can best be posed (Hardt and Negri 2000: 22–7). Pauli similarly works as a security guard, which has become a paradigmatic job for the former male industrial working class, before getting involved in the low end of business, where he is primarily of use for his ability to lift the heavy, anachronistic merchandise his stepfather is selling to the East. For almost all these kinds of work, Seidl shows training sessions that range from the condescending and humiliating (the care of taxidermy and industrial cleaning) to the brutal (Pauli's security guard training) and to the black humour of Olga's foray into internet sex and its rather darker parallel of Michael's training of the Ukrainian prostitute to behave like a dog: a scene that explicitly recalls both Pauli's training of his new dog and his own training as a security guard.

Pauli, Olga and the many other anonymous workers are reduced by these disciplinary processes not to a form of bare life but to the potentials of their bodies – their physical labour power, whose value is directly dependent on their capacity to perform as disciplined bodies. Nevertheless, there is something unruly about both Pauli and Olga that seems to escape this discipline and to be alive to other corporeal potentials, despite their inscription in the regimes of post-industrial labour that service the new Europe. For example, while Pauli seems to accept the macho world of security and physical training, he rejects the hedonistic lifestyle of his stepfather, even if he can barely articulate the reasons for this rejection. Similarly, while Olga is willing to accept the menial positions offered to her in her working life in Vienna, she resists their constraints by making a real connection with one of the hospital patients who she sneaks in food for and dances with in a hospital basement; she also fights back when one of the nurses attacks her in a fit of xenophobic resentment. These gestures of resistance may seem small in relation to the otherwise bleak environments they take place in but nevertheless they are key to the whole film and can defend it from the charge of gratuitous miserabilism or of being a Michael Haneke-like provocation of bourgeois guilt. While Seidl does hold up a critical mirror to Western European and specifically Austrian society, presenting it as in many ways a more cruel and cynical environment than its neighbours to the East, this is done not to provoke guilt but to discern possibilities for biopolitical resistance, to be located not in the consciences of the middle classes but in the biopolitical experiences of the protagonists as participants in these proletarianised service industries of the new Europe. The juxtaposition of these two trajectories, as well as the two spaces of the East and the West, is not to judge one according to the values of the other – and Seidl clearly is more critical of Austria than he is of the East – but to point to the painful knowledge produced by the mobility between these zones which, whatever the difficulties it encounters, nevertheless develops moments of resistance and even joy.

It is in this context that the notorious scene in which Michael is 'training' the Ukrainian prostitute should be understood; most of the reviewers of the film, even those sympathetic to it, singled out this scene as gratuitous and pornographic, and also as evidence of a poor sense of film ethics. This latter charge was due to the fact that this performer – like many of the Eastern Europeans, not to mention the elderly people who appear in the film – was no doubt 'really' a prostitute and therefore was obviously being exploited. However, closer attention to this scene reveals something more complex at work. Apart from the fact that this scene is pivotal to Pauli's decision to abandon Michael to his hedonistic and admittedly repulsive excesses (clearly predicated on unequal power and economic relations between the East and the West), there seems to be an ambiguous dynamic between Michael and the prostitute; the more he attempts to humiliate her, the more he comes across as completely ludicrous. As in many of the scenes of the film, problems of language and translation are paramount and have a tendency to undermine power relations, as without communication, diagrams of power are susceptible to falling apart. The power of Seidl's film derives at least in part from its quasi-documentary procedures. Indeed, several of the main characters and many of the incidental ones are not played by professional actors but by subjects performing either their own 'roles' or ones that are very similar; in the press kit for the film the actor playing Pauli (his real name) is described as 'loving fighting and dogs' and having 'no fixed address', while Ekaterina Rak, who plays Olga, really was a nurse, the profession she has at the start of the film. This proximity to documentary should not be mistaken for any naïve attempt to 'represent reality' or claims to authenticity, so much as an articulation of cinematic production in proximity to the forms of work presented in the film. Performing in the film is therefore just one more form of biopolitical production engaged in by the performers, in many cases not that far removed from the various modes of performance, such as internet porn, required for economic survival in the 'new Europe'. However, what the film enables is a more reflexive mode of performance capable of crystallising the political unconscious of the unequal economic and power relations constituting contemporary Europe, not only for the audience but also for the producers of the performances in the movie itself.

In conclusion, while both these films engage with the primitivist clichés associated with Eastern Europe that one can find repeated both in the mass media and in exploitation films such as *Hostel*, they both in their own way render these clichéd perceptions unstable by implicating the West in the emergent modes of life of the 'new Europe'. Furthermore, both films do suggest possible transfigurations of this situation, whether through their own aesthetic procedures or through the gestures of resistance in *Import/Export* or the affirmation of desire in *La Vie nouvelle*, both of which destabilise the dominant Western mappings of new Europe. Despite the differences in the aesthetic strategies of the two films, they both constitute ethical engagements with post-Cold War Europe, reminding the Western European viewer of the biopolitical labour, humiliation and violence on which 'fortress Europe' is founded, while also presenting destabilising perceptions of this situation amounting to a radical critique of the European political unconscious operating on the level of cinematic affect and sensation.

CHAPTER 8

Naked Women, Slaughtered Animals: Ulrich Seidl and the Limits of the Real

Catherine Wheatley

Within critical discussions of the new extremism, the figure of Austrian director Ulrich Seidl is all too often conspicuous by its absence. And yet his work demonstrates many of the tenets which underpin the amorphous term, characterised as it is by a rigorous aesthetic and provocative narrative content that spans subjects such as bestiality, pornography and violent misanthropy. Indeed, his first theatrical release, *Dog Days*, premiered at Venice in 2001 to precisely the type of critical uproar that Tim Palmer sees as both beneficial and foundational to the careers of many of the new extreme directors (Palmer 2006a: 23), prompting immediate comparison with the likes of Virginie Despentes, Gaspar Noé and Bruno Dumont. Having built a reputation as one of the most important Austrian documentarians of recent years (if not *the* most important), with a body of works characterised by a rigorously controlled aesthetic and a span of incendiary subject matter, ranging from pornography (*Models*, 1997) and violent misogyny (*Der Busenfreund/The Bosom Buddy*, 1994; *Die Letze Männer/The Last Real Men*, 1994) to the spectre of bestiality (*Tierische Liebe/Animal Love*, 1995), Seidl was, in his own words, 'forced into fiction' for *Hundestage/Dog Days* (2001) and his subsequent film, *Import/Export* (2007). This was not, as might perhaps be supposed, in order to leverage funding or raise his international profile, but rather so that he might be able to portray shocking events – such as rape, assault and death – that, he states, 'in a non-fiction film wouldn't be possible' (Wheatley 2008: 49).

Given the prominence accorded to the real within discussions of the new extreme by critics and theorists alike, the implication of Seidl's statement – that there are certain tropes that are acceptable within the context of fiction but not within the documentary – is one which, to my mind, merits some attention. Of course, the inclusion of documentary elements is common to many of the films that are subsumed under the moniker of the new extremism, which draws heavily on neorealist principles. This chapter will therefore use

Seidl's films as a launching pad for an exploration of the status of the 'real' in relation to the new extremism, raising questions about the contribution that the incorporation of documentary elements might make to these films' 'shock value'. However, it will also examine whether the deployment of the real – or rather the self-imposed limits that these filmmakers place on it – might not in fact point to a paradoxical conservatism within this body of works both reified and vilified for their insistence on exploding societal and cinematic norms.

In what follows, therefore, I shall be using Seidl's works as a lens through which to examine the manner in which the real is both mobilised and contained by the films of the new extreme. For if what defines this body of works, as Martine Beugnet suggests, is 'transgression' and the testing of 'boundaries of the representable [. . .] to the limit' (2004a: 295), I hope to discover something about where exactly these boundaries and limits might lie. And it seems to me that Seidl's films occupy a privileged position within the discourses of the new extreme, provoking responses that go beyond the now-familiar unease that we have come to associate with extreme cinema. It will be my contention that he achieves this effect not by testing the limits of the representable, but by testing the limits of the real.

EROS AND THANATOS

The division of Seidl's work into the categories of documentary and fiction is, to a large extent, an artificial and deeply reductive one. In interviews and public appearances Seidl himself has rejected such a binarism, stating that all his films 'have documentary and fictional elements' (Wheatley 2008: 46). It is a statement that close attention to his works bears out. Both the œuvre as a whole and the individual films traverse a range of realities, from the clearly staged (the rape of a young disabled woman in *Dog Days*) to the incidentally observed (a small child wailing helplessly in the opening scenes of *Mit Verlust ist zu Rechnen/Losses to Be Expected*, 1992), with the vast majority occupying a space between these two extremes. Thus a 'documentary' such as *Models* features professional mannequins placed in a series of contrived encounters (a one-night stand, a battle of sexual wills with an aggressive photographer, an explicit drugs and drink binge), while the 'fictional' *Import/Export* (2007) devotes a substantial proportion of its running time to capturing the daily existences of residents in a genuine geriatric ward, its cast of largely non-professional actors seemingly playing variants on themselves (Trinity Distributors, 2008).

Seidl's deployment of the 'real' within the fictional context of *Import/Export* and *Dog Days* both converges with and, as I hope to demonstrate, transcends its operation within works by a great many of the other directors subsumed under the banner of the new extreme. Even taking this very brief description of his working methods as a starting point, we might think, for example, of Lars von Trier's incorporation of unwitting members of the public into *Idioterne/The Idiots* (Denmark, 1998), Bruno Dumont's insistence on the use of non-professional actors and 'found' locations in *L'Humanité* (France, 1999) and *La Vie de Jésus/The Life of Jesus* (France, 1997), or Catherine Breillat's inclusion in *Romance* (France, 1999) and *Anatomie de l'enfer/Anatomy of Hell* (France, 2004) of scenes of non-simulated sex. In each of these cases, as in Seidl's films, reality is mobilised in the service of authenticity, in order to heighten what Beugnet calls the 'affective and aesthetic force of shock' that is the effect of viewing these films (2007a: 38). So while von Trier's Dogme 95 edicts aim to *épater les bourgeois* through what John Orr terms its 'traducing realism' (Orr 2004: 313), in Dumont's films intense bursts of 'convulsive violence' (Quandt 2004) collide with the film's 'hyperreality' (Beugnet 2007a: 174), which takes the form of the profoundly banal. Breillat's appropriation of elements of pornography, meanwhile, seeks to outrage through its sheer incongruity (Downing 2004: 266).

Yet if the real is thus incorporated into these fictional narratives, it is also bound by them. That is, as in Seidl's films, we see real people, real places, real sex, and yet there is no place here for real assault, death or rape. Instead, where violence occurs, it is either consigned to the off-screen space (as in the films of Michael Haneke and Dumont) or swathed in shadow (Philippe Grandrieux, Claire Denis); dealt with perfunctorily and matter-of-factly (Breillat) or else stylised in the extreme (Gaspar Noé, Marina De Van). It is perhaps no coincidence that the two genres most frequently referenced within this body of work are pornography and gore – the one dependent on bare-faced reality, the other on its total absence. In the face of their inability to show 'real' death, these directors turn to its opposite: the exaggerated and obvious artifice of, as Jean-Luc Godard would have it, 'Not blood. Red' (Godard 1972: 217).

It seems some boundaries cannot be transgressed. This in itself is not a bad thing, of course. The implications of what would be involved were these directors to show us real violence are, in many ways, terrifying. But the complicity of film and spectator with respect to this unspoken, unbroken taboo offers, I believe, a set of limits within which we can safely engage with the onscreen spectacle: as in all functional sado-masochistic relationships, the rules of the game are clear to both parties. Viewing these films, which skirt around the borders between the real and the fictional, spectators can move back and forth between absorption within their cinematic universe and rational awareness of their pre-agreed boundaries. This dualistic position is most clearly illustrated in the instance of rape scenes, in which sex and violence collide. Let us take, for example, the infamous scene in Coralie Trinh Thi and Virginie Despentes's *Baise-moi/Fuck Me* (France, 2000), which involves a real penetration, shot in close-up (although censored in the UK). Here, we know that the penetration is indeed real; yet we also know the 'rape' is not, since the sexual act that we are watching is taking place with the full consent of the actors involved. To this end, our rational, intellectual faculties serve as a counterbalance to the 'haptic' experience of film which Beugnet sees as characteristic of viewings of many of these works (Beugnet 2007a: 1), and which is described by Laura U. Marks as a process of 'gradually discovering what is in the image rather than coming to the image already knowing what is' (Marks 2000: 178). Confronted with the image of violence, we can wrap ourselves in that age-old safety blanket, 'It's only a movie.'

THE DYING ANIMAL

The human face of Eros may be revealed to us in all its splendour and abjection by the films of the new extreme, then, but the human face of Thanatos remains safely consigned to the sidelines. There is, however, one exception to the rule permitting real sex but not real violence, a trope repeated throughout the films of the new extreme: scenes in which audiences are party to the real-life slaughter of animals. The dead or dying animal (always of the domestic or farmyard variety) is perhaps most prolific in the films of Michael Haneke (live fish flap helplessly as their tank is upturned, a pig has its throat slit, a dog is bludgeoned to death – off screen, a chicken is beheaded and horses are shot). It is most relentless in Gaspar Noé's *Carne* (France, 1991) and *Seul contre tous/I Stand Alone* (France, 1998). And it is Lars von Trier's onscreen slaughter of a donkey in *Manderlay* (Denmark, 2005) that may constitute the most infamous example of this practice; as a result of the extremely negative responses to the scene (many of which were based upon its appearance in the film's trailer), the director eventually cut the scene from the finished work (Longworth 2005). But it reverberates throughout the films discussed in this collection. Indeed, as testament to the reliability of this trope we might take Richard Falcon's comment on the scene in *Dog Days* in which security systems salesman Hruby, the nearest thing the film has to a bridging character, advises a prospective client that his dog, far from being a deterrent, will itself need protecting. Falcon sagely counsels that, 'In the context of extreme arthouse cinema, we know he's right' (2002: 53).

The image of the dying animal is far from unique to the films of the new extreme. A history of its deployment within the cinema would perhaps start with Buñuel's *Un Chien andalou* (France, 1929)[1] and the indelible vision of a knife slicing through a calf's eye, and extend through the cart-wheeling rabbits of Renoir's *Règle du jeu* (France, 1939) to Franju's slaughterhouse in *Le Sang des bêtes* (France, 1949) to the blood, not red, of another rabbit – one whose throat is graphically slit in Godard's *Weekend* (France, 1967). The new extreme, however, imbues the trope with a new set of meanings, first amongst which is a metaphorical significance. Employed as a substitute for the human deaths that lie beyond Beugnet's proposed boundaries of the acceptable, animal slaughter offers an insight into what 'real' death might look like. Derek Bousé has astutely drawn the parallel between the kill scene in wildlife films as its chief guarantor of authenticity and the function of the 'cum-shot' in XXX-rated films, as described by Linda Williams (Bousé 2000: 43; Williams 2008: 45).[2] Here, within a body of works concerned with 'the body as flesh' (Beugnet 2007a: 2), the blow that strikes down the living animal is the violent equivalent of the penetration shot, offering 'proof' of an act which shocks by its very reality. However contrived the context, there is no dividing line between the simulated and the real.

The consequences for the animal body in the depiction of violence are much more extreme, however, than that for the human body in the depiction of sexuality. And the fact that we are watching animals, not humans, dying, may in fact intensify emotional responses to this taboo-breaking. For as Jonathan Burt explains in his brief but thorough overview of the use of animals in film:

> Animal imagery in film has a peculiar status in that, despite a general awareness of the contrivances of the medium, audiences often respond differently to animals or animal-related practices than they do to other forms of imagery. It appears that certain kinds of animal imagery, magnified and intensified precisely by the artifice of film, are responded to more emotionally and are therefore less mediated by the kind of judgements that might normally apply to other kinds of imagery. (Burt 2002: 10)[3]

This peculiar status is accorded to animals because, argues Burt, 'the animal is caught in an uncertain space between the natural and the contrived' (Burt 2002: 10). That is, animals, on film, can 'act' – in that they can follow instructions and perform gestures (one need only think here of Lassie, or to choose a more pertinent example perhaps, Robert Bresson's Balthazar) – and they can be 'faked', all the more so in the light of recent technological innovations; but they cannot 'feign'. Or, more precisely, they cannot feign suffering. So when, in the opening scenes of Haneke's *Benny's Video* (Austria, 1992), we are confronted with the image and soundtrack of a pig being stunned and slaughtered, we are left in no doubt as to the painful realities of its protracted agony; likewise, the snorts and squeals of the sacrificial ass in von Trier's *Manderlay*. Confronted with a 'real' human death on screen, we would most likely dismiss it as cinematic trickery. The image of the dying animal is not so easily disavowed. It invokes that which Baudrillard calls 'the brutal irruption of their death *en directo*, in real time, on-screen [. . .] the absolute, no appeal event'

(Baudrillard 2001); and by these means, it erases the requirement 'to analyse the impression of reality by differentiating between perception and representation' (Baudry 2004: 220), because the reality is simply indisputable.

THERIOMORPHOSIS

What seems to incite the most outrage amongst those spectators who complain of the cruelty of Haneke and von Trier's films on internet message boards is the animal's innocence, its inability to participate willingly or knowingly in the violence to which it is subjected. In this case, the invocation of taboo imagery raises ethical questions relating to issues of exploitation, at stake within which are questions of knowledge, consent, self-awareness and responsibility. These are the same terms which underpin the act of spectatorship itself, but they are also, crucially, the terms which inform much of the debate surrounding Seidl's deployment of the real within his filmic works. This is not because his films feature a particularly excessive number of dying animals (although they have their fair share). Rather, when applied to Seidl's films, the question of exploitation relates to his use of human subjects.

Peter Bradshaw's thoughtful review in *The Guardian* newspaper perhaps most succinctly crystallises the ambivalence towards Seidl's treatment of his human subjects within *Import/Export*, for example:

> Very often, it's an all-but-unwatchable ordeal [. . .] there are the startling sequences in the Austrian hospital ward in which Seidl films old people in advanced stages of dementia, moaning and gibbering, and uses what are surely genuine non-professionals. In some ways, this is radically confrontational: why have pretending and play-acting, when you can get the real thing? Seidl appears to be saying – here, this is how life ends, and these are the people on whom we place the necessary burden of care and compassion; now take responsibility for consuming this misery as onscreen entertainment. Yet what informed consent can these people have given to be in the film? I have no idea, and I am not sure whether I can endorse these sequences, excoriatingly potent though they are. (Bradshaw 2008)

The critic's response to the film thus negotiates the filmic and the real in much the manner that imagery of the dying animal prompts us to do. Watching the images in question, it is not enough simply to accept these images as filmic representations; we are forced by their apparent authenticity to scrutinise the image, to determine what is safely bound up within the confines of the fictional world and what spills out, frighteningly, into real life.

The troubling sense that what we are seeing in the scene described is somehow wrong and unethical, that someone is being exploited, depends greatly on Seidl's choice of subjects; as Bradshaw underlines, the elderly and mentally unstable residents of the geriatric home in which Seidl filmed appear, for the most part, to be unaware that they are appearing in a film, or unable to indicate that this is the case. But elsewhere, too, Seidl chooses to place on screen social groups whose ability to give consent is similarly uncertain; the very elderly and the very young are recurring figures within his films, as are characters whose linguistic abilities may prevent a clear understanding of what is happening to them. In another scene in *Import/Export* we see Paul and his bellicose stepfather pick up and abuse a Ukrainian prostitute, who is seemingly baffled by their instructions to wheel her legs as if she was riding a bicycle and intone after them, in a language completely alien to her, 'I am a cunt.' The scene, striking for its naturalness, becomes all the more so when one learns from the film's press notes (and subsequently, the majority of the film's press coverage) that the 'actress' in question was indeed a Ukrainian prostitute who spoke no German. Despite Seidl's contention that 'it was arranged in advance what was possible' (Wheatley 2008: 49), it nonetheless remains the case that in both film and reality the prostitute was paid to humiliate herself for the entertainment of others: and more specifically, for the enjoyment of Western spectators. Without wishing to enter into feminist debates regarding prostitution and power, it is fair to say that this *mise-en-abyme* has a vertiginous effect, one which is somewhat troubling, to put it mildly.

As one of his many demands of the prostitute, Michael, Paul's stepfather, insists the young woman crawl on all fours and bark like a dog, as he holds her hair like a leash. It is, to my mind at least, a strikingly literal vision of the way in which Seidl's camera, to all intents and purposes, theriomorphosises his subjects. Indeed, Justin Vicari aptly characterises Seidl's œuvre as a whole when he writes of *Dog Days* that 'Seidl's subject is the limits of the human – the human becoming all-body, becoming animal' (Vicari 2006: 40). Indeed, we might say that Seidl's films serve as illustrations of the collapse of humanity that Giorgio Agamben describes in the following statement from his 2004 *The Open: Man and Animal*:

> When the difference [between man and animal] vanishes and the two terms collapse upon each other – as seems to be happening today – the difference between being and the nothing, licit and illicit, divine and demonic also fades away, and in its place appears something for which we seem to lack even a name. Perhaps concentration camps are also an experiment of this sort, an extreme and monstrous attempt to decide between the human and inhuman, which has ended up dragging the very possibility of the distinction to its ruin. (22)[4]

What is the difference between human and animal? For Agamben, after Heidegger, what distinguishes the two might be man's awareness of his captivity contra the animal's unawareness of it. Yet stripped by nationality of language and, in some cases, by virtue of advancing age and diminished reason, it is not unreasonable to suppose that the men and women subjected to the gaze of Seidl's lens might be stripped, too, of the awareness of the ways in which they are captured and captivated before the camera.

As hellish and hopeless as such a vision of humanity might seem, it is worth turning briefly to Jacques Derrida's investigation of what he calls the 'question of the animal', in order to ask how it might offer a more productive method of spectatorial engagement (Derrida 2008). Here, Derrida emphasises that the fundamental ethical bond we have with non-human animals resides in our shared finitude, our vulnerability and mortality as 'fellow creatures' (11). Following on from Bentham, Derrida contends that the fundamental ethical question with animals is not 'can they talk?' or 'can they reason?', but 'can they suffer?' (27). The question, Derrida explains, is disturbed by a certain passivity. It bears witness, manifesting already, as question, the response that testifies to sufferance, a passion, 'a not-being-able'. 'What of the vulnerability felt on the basis of this inability?' he asks (28). 'To what extent does it concern us?' (28). It concerns us very directly, he argues, because 'mortality resides there, as the most radical means of thinking the finitude that we share with animals, the mortality that belongs to the very finitude of life, to the experience of compassion . . . the anguish of this vulnerability' (396).

Derrida might be speaking directly to the non-human humans who populate Seidl's films. Consigned to the status of the animal, all that is left for them is to suffer before us. Yet this suffering can, just as Derrida describes, engender a human connection with the Other, as we are confronted with their vulnerability and, in consequence, with our own (397). This being the case, the climate of uncertainty in which Seidl cloaks his films, in which any act may go beyond its fictional boundaries and become part of our own world, may serve to increase the proximity between this suffering and us. The methods by which he achieves this rapprochement are deeply uneasy and perhaps not, ultimately, ones that we, like Peter Bradshaw, can countenance; after all, as I suggested earlier in this chapter, the implications of putting real violence on screen – and the suffering that Seidl's films depict does indeed bear the traces of real violence – are deeply frightening. None the less, they are, at their best, effective.

Unfortunately, it is beyond the limits of this chapter to consider in any greater depth the ethical implications of what might well be seen as a brutal denial of his subjects' human essence, although it is a matter that undoubtedly deserves deeper consideration, especially with regard to the educated, middle-class Seidl's proclivity for taking his subject matter from what Eva

Hohenberger tactfully refers to as 'society's disadvantaged' (Danquart et al. 1996: 35).[5] But whether or not the ends justify the means, it is none the less Seidl's accomplishment, through his willingness to test the limits of the real, to bring us into contact with realities of human suffering in a manner unprecedented in the other films of the new extreme. The coincidence of this suffering with the spectre of exploitation which hovers beyond the edges of the frame, edges to which our attention is constantly drawn, makes for a deeply unsettling experience – one which pushes even those spectators who have entered the cinema in search of such transgressive materials, we knowing devotees of the new extreme, to question the boundaries of acceptability. Let us leave the last word to Bradshaw, writing once more of *Import/Export*: 'There is one thing that is beyond doubt: this extraordinary film makes everything else around look comfy and pedestrian' (2008).

NOTES

1. As Jonathan Romney states, 'In cinema, it was Surrealism that inaugurated the school of extremism' (Romney 2004).
2. Interestingly, both Bousé and Williams take the photographic work of Eadweard Muybridge – in one case his nature films, in the other his sequences of naked women in motion – as a principle object of analysis. These are the naked women and slaughtered animals who have inspired this chapter's title.
3. The commonplace that people are more sensitised to, or disturbed by, film violence concerning animals than they are to that involving humans is difficult to assess or quantify, particularly in the absence of detailed studies of the impact of animal imagery on audiences. However, when such sentiments are expressed by people protesting against instances of screen violence, as in the case of *Manderlay*, it does suggest that the suspension of belief that is normally in play with regard to humans on screen does not work in the same way for animals.
4. It is a conclusion echoed by Cora Diamond in her essay 'The Difficulty of Reality and the Difficulty of Philosophy', in which she compares the mechanised killing of animals in its scale and violence to the Holocaust, while for his part Cary Wolfe states that: 'The sacrifice of the animal [. . .] makes possible a symbolic economy in which we can engage in a 'non-criminal' putting to death (as Derrida phrases it) not only of animals, but of other humans as well, by marking them as animal' (Wolfe 1998: 39).
5. It is worth noting in this respect that, in keeping with the philosophical tendency to see the non-human animal as somehow more 'natural' than man, Seidl describes his subjects, 'those on the edges of society', as 'in some ways truer'. 'People who are more educated', he states, 'aren't true to themselves – they're performing, presenting an image' (Wheatley 2008: 48).

PART III

Watching the Extreme: Cultural Reception

CHAPTER 9

Watching Rape, Enjoying Watching Rape . . .: How Does a Study of Audience Cha(lle)nge Mainstream Film Studies Approaches?[1]

Martin Barker

Look closely at the two quotations below, which both relate to Catherine Breillat's *À ma sœur!* (2003). Although quite different in their conclusions, they share a problematic characteristic. The first is an extract from a summary of the reasons for the decision at the British Board of Film Classification (BBFC) to cut the final scene of the film:

> There was some concern that the older sister is repeatedly sexualised throughout the film, that this presentation could appeal to haebophiles, and that the scene of her seduction . . . could be used by a potential abuser as a script for seducing underage girls. However the presentation of the girls was thought to be well contextualised within the narrative. The character of seducer Fernando was said to be sketchily drawn, allowing for little ego identification by a male viewer. In any case, the seduction scene was thought more likely to act as a warning to young girls. More problematic for many was the final rape of the younger sister. Considerations included: breast nudity could give an erotic tinge to the rape, as could the focus on the girl's passive, submissive expression. The younger sister seems glad that it has happened. This could be thought to endorse the 'rape myth' about child rape, ie. that they 'like it really'. On the other hand the nudity is brief and the focus is held fairly resolutely on the younger sister's face during the rape. The scene is also the culmination of the whole film.[2]

The quotation summarises the BBFC's debates and shows the kinds of reasoning they used. Note the term 'haebophiles', a category putatively depicting men who are by nature sexually attracted to just-pre-adolescent girls. Note the deployment of the concept 'ego-identification', borrowed from a particularly American style of cognitive psychology. Note too the use of the concept of the 'rape myth', originating in the work of Martha Burt. The BBFC's arguments and judgement are made possible by a collation of circulating theories, each with a particular – and highly arguable – provenance. Crucial is that all these are essentially *predictions* of possible audience responses.

Consider now this extract from a substantial review of *À ma sœur!*, which appeared first in the British film magazine *Sight & Sound*. It is by leading French film academic Ginette Vincendeau:

> *À Ma Sœur!* is no feminist tract and we should know better than to expect a politically correct analysis from a director who enjoys cultivating an iconoclastic image. In *À Ma Sœur!* Anaïs' earlier expressed preference for first time sex without love is horrifically fulfilled in the film's bloody climax in which Elena and her mother are brutally murdered, with Anaïs watching unblinkingly from the back seat. She gets out of the car and is raped by the man in the woods, though she later denies this to the policeman who finds her. Of course such acts of violence are committed by men against women on an almost daily basis, but the constant reiteration in Breillat's cinema of such events, together with her ubiquitous dysfunctional families and the absence of any pleasure – sexual or otherwise – for her female protagonists threaten to make her films simply grim, repetitive and punitive. It has been argued that female frustration is the subject of Breillat's films, but the films themselves can provoke frustration in the spectator. (2001)

Vincendeau is concerned to evaluate from a feminist point of view – is Breillat's film 'good for women'? Her conclusion, while cautious, is that it is not. The final sentence, the one which brings her to her concluding judgement, introduces a 'figure' much found – indeed, much depended upon – in film studies: 'the spectator'. 'She' will be frustrated by the film. Its grimness offers little of benefit or hope to any woman because it becomes a form of punishment. That last point, of course, ties Vincendeau's argument to wider claims within film studies about the emergence of a 'cinema of cruelty'. But again, the conclusion hangs on that prediction of an 'audience response'.

These two quotations operate in quite different sectors, and were produced for very different purposes. But they share this important characteristic. Both operate with what I have come to call 'figures of the audience': that is, predictive claims built out of theorisations – sometimes purely speculative, sometimes supported by a scatter of (often laboratory-based) research – of the ways in which films might affect audiences. Such 'figuring' is a very widespread feature of both general film culture and of academia.[3] It is particularly disappointing and disturbing that it is so prevalent within academia, since surely our role should be not simply to do the same as other social actors but in less penetrable language. It ought at least to include weighing the claims of others, and producing good grounded evidence which measures the validity of social arguments and policies. That, sadly, seems rarely to be the case in our field at present.

In 2005 an opportunity arose for me and a group of colleagues to work with the BBFC,[4] on a research project into the ways in which real audiences (not, that is, audiences artificially assembled for purposes of a laboratory-like 'test') make sense of and respond to watching sexual violence on screen. How this opportunity came about was semi-accidental. But it was too good to miss. The BBFC nominated five films which had given them pause when they were submitted for classification, because of their inclusion of scenes of sexual violence: *À ma sœur!*, *Baise-moi* (Despentes and Trinh Thi, France, 2000), *House on the Edge of the Park* (Deodato, Italy, 1980), *Ichi the Killer* (Miike, Japan, 2001) and *Irréversible* (Noé, France, 2001). Our working agreement with them settled that they would not interfere with our processes and methods of research while we would not seek to speak directly on policy matters.

In addressing the issue of screened sexual violence, we were very aware just how fraught this area is. While in many ways the topic of sex on screen has become relatively uncontentious – at least for adult viewing – and while the issue of violence has at least become more nuanced (with much greater awareness of the importance of context, motivation and narrative positioning, for instance), the mixing of sex and violence on screen remains a virtual no-go area. It is not simply that people do not like it; it is seen to hold a host of dangers. I would identify five aspects to these:

1. There is a belief that to show, for instance, a rape on screen is – unless very strict protocols are followed – almost to enact the rape for real. The line between the represented and the real is seen to be particularly fragile in this case.
2. There is a working assumption that if any woman is shown to be violated on screen, in effect *every* woman is threatened. A raped woman is a universal entity.
3. Crucially, the protocols for presentation are focused more than anything on *taking sides*. The first question to be asked of any representation of sexual violence is: whose side is it on – the woman's or the man's?
4. Vitally connected with this, a key measure is that under no circumstances should a representation of sexual violence produce sexual arousal. To do so, would be to be directly promoting the real occurrence of sexual violence.
5. Finally, and more topically, an underlying theorisation in all this is that notion derived from Martha Burt, that our culture produces and installs in

many men myths about women (Burt 1980) – that while they may say 'no', they are secretly turned on by the idea of rape.

I can do no more here than point towards these, and say that I find it very striking that I cannot find in the literature around this any significant questioning or critical examination of these ideas. They are part of a current 'common sense', which is sufficiently taken for granted as to need little argument.

Their currency is unarguable. As Tanya Horeck summarises it: 'The representation of rape continues to be one of the most highly charged issues in contemporary cinema' (2004: 115). The same idea is present in public debates, as evidenced in this discussion thread:

> Rape is a very sensitive subject matter to film, and I agree if there is to be rape scenes they should have a point for being included in the plot and shouldn't be filmed to arouse the viewer in any way, although there will be certain individuals who will be.[5]

In attempting to design and carry out audience research in this area, of course, these assumptions generate constraints on what we might be able to do. Audiences would be well aware just how sensitive this topic is, and how their responses might be judged. Indeed, the BBFC's view before we began was that we were extremely unlikely to be able to learn anything about one question which certainly fascinated me: how might audiences – both male and female – talk about their own physical arousal responses on watching scenes of sexual violence? What might this be able to tell us about the place and role of arousal in meaning-making?

The full report of our research is available as a download from the website of the BBFC, and for that reason I say only a few things here about its design and conduct. Over a six-month period a team of us undertook a three-phase project:

1. We gathered and analysed evidence about the ways the five films were discussed on 243 websites across the five films. In particular, we were interested in the kinds of debates each film aroused and what was involved in being a *positive* discussant of the film.[6]
2. We designed and mounted a complex online questionnaire, which we publicised as widely as we could, asking people to tell us their thoughts on any of the five films. The website design allowed us to associate together the responses of people who had seen more than one of the five, so that we could explore how judgements compared and related.[7] The questionnaire recruited 859 individuals who gave us 1,257 responses to the five films.
3. Our questionnaire included at its end a request for people to say if they would be willing to talk further to us. Selecting people who had particularly

positive responses (since the BBFC accepted our argument that those who rejected a film were in important senses less engaged with it; therefore a focus on positivity allowed us to get closest to possible influence), we organised four focus groups per film at many different locations around the UK (from Scotland to the south coast). Forty-four women and sixty men took part in these.[8]

Behind our whole approach was the way of thinking about audiences that can broadly be characterised as the cultural studies tradition. This tradition is frequently misunderstood so I very briefly lay out its key premises here – aware, as I do so, that not all those who research under the broad cultural studies umbrella would agree with every proposition I put down. Our approach begins from the conviction that nobody ever encounters a film or any other media experience devoid of their location in history, culture and society. We come to every experience thoroughly imbued with the time, place and circumstances in which we live. The idea of an abstracted 'spectator', 'viewer' or 'reader' can only therefore be an analytic construct. *All real* audiences come with prior knowledges, hopes, fears and expectations. They belong to communities (real, imagined and hoped-for), and have a sense of who they are and what they want from the encounter. Any research method that seeks to bypass these can take us nowhere helpful, and any method that seeks to derive some 'necessary response' from textual characteristics achieves even less. The term 'audience', in consequence, always has to be pluralised. And the methods of research we use must be capable of capturing differences that arise from varying cultural, social and historical circumstances and goals.

To these complex demands must be added the problem that the media, and indeed all cultural forms, come with discursive baggage attached to them – this is part of the very way in which they come steeped with history. As Pierre Bourdieu brilliantly outlined, and as many following him have also shown (deepening Bourdieu's account even as they have criticised particular aspects of it), societies create and operate through taste structures that enact judgements of both the various forms and of their audiences. As we research a topic like screened sexual violence, therefore, we encounter those discourses in the field of production, and in the very terms in which it is supposed to be debated, researched and managed. Those 'figures of the audience' are not just arguable claims; they are part of the cultural fabric within which the films appear, circulate and are responded to.

To all this must be added one feature that arises from my own (and others') research: that media and cultural encounters have different degrees of salience for different viewers. The encounters that resonate the most with us, which we engage with richly – and maybe repeatedly, and which in some way connect with our sense of who we are and what we want to do and be: these work differently from those which are more routine or quotidian, or which leave us critical or bored. While it is by no means a single or simple dimension between engagement and detachment, the differences are vital. And, for instance, they are one of the key problems with laboratory-based research that depends upon the arbitrary gathering of disconnected audiences, without any check on their prior interests in what they will be seeing. And, crucially, research has shown that there are systematic differences between how engaged and disengaged audiences attend to the media, what they notice, how they interpret, and what they take away from the experience. Put at its baldest, the experiences which critics impute to the 'figures of the viewer' do not match those which engaged viewers say that they experience.[9] From this premise, then, our research into our five films sought to identify the distinctive ways in which (what we came to call) 'embracing' and 'rejecting' audiences perceived, understood and judged them. That involved also exploring what they knew in advance – what sorts of reputation and prior debates tilled the ground of responses before viewing. In the case of À ma sœur!, this proved quite complicated.

We found, first, that a number of distinctive themes ran through debates about À ma sœur!, and that these played into the interpretations people made and the judgements they arrived at about it. To UK viewers, the name 'Catherine Breillat' already carried with it a set of connotations, of 'Frenchness' and of 'feminism'. Discussions of À ma sœur! were inevitably touched by these wider considerations. But these were not fixed quantities. 'Frenchness' could mean the tradition of difficult, art-house cinema, with overtones for some people of pretentiousness. But for others it signified seriousness, and more than anything a refuge from Hollywood formula films. A second dimension was the wider debate about film and under-age sex – of course, a hot topic because of its links with issues of paedophilia, but linking in to other debates over, for instance, Nabokov's *Lolita* and the two film versions thereof. Of course, the complexity here was that it was a woman directing the film – so accusations (and there were plenty) turned less on the issue of *showing* under-age girls engaging in sex and more on the question of whether the young actresses were being exploited and endangered. Thirdly, and inevitably, many online debates dipped into the murky waters of 'pornography' – a term which 'benefits' greatly from being very slippery but morally charged.

One other dimension came powerfully into view. While many viewers found early parts of the film challenging (especially the two 'bedroom scenes' in which Elena is seduced), more than anything debates turned on the ending: what exactly had happened, what did it mean, how did it 'close' the film and what light did it throw back on earlier parts, and what did it show about Anaïs? What also emerged very clearly was yet another confirmation of my earlier general point, that Critics are poor predictors of what a film will mean to those who Embrace it.[10] In this case, Critics really struggled to make sense of it, often unable to see how the ending related to, was motivated by, what had gone before. Typical comments included:

'Too contrived and did not flow with the rest of the film.'

'The ending felt like it had wandered into the film from a completely different film and I struggle to see what the point of it was except to shock the viewer.'

'A silly way out of the issues it raised.'

'I'm sure the director was trying to make some point but I felt cheated and manipulated by the ending – it came from nowhere at the end of what was up till then a fairly gentle film.'

The first is primarily a report on failure – this just did not make sense. In the second comment we can see added a glimmer of a concept of 'the viewer' – but hardly articulated. The third is interesting in taking for granted that it is clear what the 'issues' were, and indeed that they can be known independently of the ending. The last, the most personal, is a cry of anguish, based on a sense that the film had misled him – that even if there was a point, it was too hurtful to shatter an established ('gentle') way of watching.

In other ways Critics of À ma sœur turned the 'Frenchness' of the film against itself. One internet reviewer damned the film in a revealing way:

This piece of junk is the usual French sh-t. Two sisters, one fifteen, nice looking and the other thirteen and fat are vacationing with their family. The older girl gets involved with a young Italian man, and they end up making love (shown very explicitly) in the same bedroom as the younger sister. When the affair is revealed, the mother hauls them away. On the trip back to Paris, the mother and the older girl are killed, and the younger daughter is raped. What is this all about? What is the point?

This retelling of the narrative decouples all the events – they are a meaningless sequence, which is the 'usual French sh-t'. The closing questions are strictly rhetorical – this retelling by its very nature makes meaning impossible.[11]

Embracers began entirely elsewhere. Their reactions can pretty uniformly be characterised as beginning from 'knowing something's coming' – yet still, importantly, being shocked at what does happen. Many different reasons were given. Some were 'local' to the point in the film: a sense of slowly rising tensions . . . accentuated by the mother's rage, her tiredness, the horrible drive . . . tiny incidents like the face of the lorry-driver that looms at them as he drives past them . . . even a knowledge that the film is going to end soon. To these are added some other claims; that the very 'everyday-ness' of the film could not possibly continue, not least (and here the connections with those wider discourses leak in) because 'it's French.' French films do the unexpected – that is their *raison d'être*. In light of this, *À ma sœur*'s Embracers focused in on the ending and gave it close, studied attention.[12] And everything turned on *accompanying* Anaïs, and watching what happens to her, what it means for her and what it tells us about her. Individuals would do it differently (and, of course, would then often share their thoughts) but among the things they thought about, and mobilised in their interpretations, were the following: before the attack, Anaïs says something to her attacker: 'You're not going to hurt me' – but is it a question or almost an order? While Anaïs is being raped, she looks – steadily, apparently calmly – at her attacker. She keeps her eyes open throughout as if she is communicating with him in some way. She seems to put her arms around him. When the rape is over, she moves 'silkily' when he releases her. When next morning she is led out of the woods, she does not speak for herself – her words are 'ventriloquised' by the policeman. But when she says 'You don't have to believe me,' she turns and looks at 'us'. Building on their detailed attention to these tiny elements, Embracers began to wonder what Anaïs is 'thinking' (something which, of course, cannot be known directly, has to depend on audience 'work') and what she is becoming, now that she is alone. Many of them evince the view that in this final scene we see her become older, more mature – perhaps even now the most 'adult' person in the film (well captured in the questionnaire response which concluded that 'This film showed the wisdom of the ugly duckling'). And in contrast to those critics who attacked Breillat's (mis)use of her two young actresses, their coupling becomes something to celebrate: 'She's the narrator's persona, in a way, cos she's the one that's got more intelligence than anyone else in the film.' Embracers found nothing to concern them in a character like Anaïs becoming the embodiment of a director's vision.

All this led many to think back over the rest of the film, to find in some cases a logic of shocking repetitions from earlier events. Wasn't the wolf-man's rape simply the overt expression of the predatory male attitude embodied in Fernando's seduction of Elena? Isn't the 'male ownership' of women expressed in the assertions of control over Elena recapitulated in the casual police takeover of Anaïs's speech? On such an approach, it would be simply meaningless to say that the ending overturned established themes – the themes could only become fully apparent in and through the shock of the ending. Many of these, of course, were hinted at or briefly indicated in web debates. In our interviews people were encouraged and given time to spell out their thinking at length. And the *processes* of meaning-making become much more overt through this. Take as an example this lengthy response from a woman:

I found it in some ways realistic, because you hear very often cases of rape and it's like consensual rape. And you can find that a lot especially in many countries where there's always been a bit oppression like in the religion for people, it's not the first case I've heard of someone that actually got raped that actually said, oh, no, it wasn't the case, you know. And the Italian guy was very tidy, he was very Italian, and I've also met many girls of my age, as long as someone's got a nice car and takes them out for dinner, back home where I come from they will accept that. You know, they wouldn't care if the person is not a nice person, that they don't keep their own dignity. So I found it in many ways really an excellent movie. And in the end, yes, it's typical French movies, they're always tragic in the end. And I was watching it on the computer so you could still see there was only seven minutes left or something, and I thought, OK, they're going back home and see what happens, and then the end, I mean like it was, oh!, you know, and I felt a bit shocked by it, but at the same time I thought, well, this is one of the most unpredictable films I've ever seen, you know, I like films that are unpredictable in many ways.

This woman moves back and forth from the film to her own experience, using components of the latter to make sense of what she admits was 'shocking' – although, watching the time on the film, she had known and expected that something of this kind would occur (because of its 'Frenchness').

Of course, many people were equivocal, and it is interesting to see that ambivalence had its own characteristics. In one web debate we monitored, where people were typically debating the ending, one contributor picked up on a detail that others had missed and built an account on it. Early in the film, Anaïs had told Elena that she wanted her first sexual experience to be with someone she did not like – to get it over with. Then, just before the attack, Elena and Anaïs discuss what has happened, and Elena – declaring her hatred for her mother – wishes herself and the mother dead. Just before, Elena had left the car to go for a pee. Might this not provide a base for understanding the ending – that Elena *set it up* for herself and the mother to be killed, and her 'parting gift' to Anaïs was the loss of her virginity? That set a debate rolling:

> Goodness! I never made that connection, however when the killer breaks the front-shield, I assumed that the noise would have woken Elena up. It looked to me like for a split second, before he struck her, they were looking at each other in silence. I was wondering why she didn't scream, or struggle, or even look surprised. I figured she was in shock. However, if what you are saying is true, then that would explain why she wasn't surprised when he came, cos she had in fact asked him to. It would also explain why he didn't kill Anaïs. Also, half way through the rape Anaïs

stops struggling. Maybe because she thought it was futile and gave up, or maybe she realised that her sister set the whole thing up?[13]

Now it can make a *kind* of sense to someone previously befuddled by it – but at the price of taking the focus away from Anaïs and back on to Elena. It can make sense now, but it is not a sense to be embraced, only to be acknowledged as a way out of confusion.

Interpretations have consequences. They take audiences to different places. And films thereby become the embodiments of different *kinds* of meaning. But they are not all of the same kind. What is most striking to me is that Embracers of the film are the ones least likely to generate and work their accounts of the film through 'figures of the audience'. Their own engagements are rich and complex, and weave together their personal experiences with a way of understanding characters, their experiences and motives. Critics, on the other hand, tend to impute more to others what they themselves, of course, would never do . . . *In extremis*, these imputed responses become the basis for demands for controls, cuts and censorship. Characters, too, are less 'real' to them, because they cannot build an account of their motivation, as one critic put it: 'The film seemed very schematic: a sermon rather than a work of art. I have seen several films by the same director and this was typical. A rather French – overly philosophically determined – take on sex. The participants were ciphers rather than real characters.'

I want to stress that I am not *agreeing with* or *celebrating* Embracers' interpretations. I am arguing that we need as film scholars to *learn how to learn from them*. Much can be learnt about the character and social location of a film from the ways in which people, sometimes with damaging self-honesty, admit things about themselves in the act of appreciating a film. Here are two closing quotations which seem to me to do just this – here, two respondents, the first a young woman, the second an older man, reflect on which part of *À ma sœur!* made them most uncomfortable (a key question we asked in our questionnaire):

Anaïs watching her sister have sex for the first time. Although Anaïs' own rape was uncomfortable to watch in the uncut version, I did not find it half as uncomfortable as seeing her sister have consensual sex. It possibly reminded me of my own experiences and how naïve this young girl was.

The prolonged seduction of the girl in the first part of the film with her sister in the room. I hated this greasy opportunist for trying so forcefully to manipulate her, but as a bloke I think at the back of my mind was the realisation that I've tried the same tactics as him in the past, so I guess there was some self-loathing and guilt there too.

In the spaces of self-reflection that each accomplishes, we can see why, in the case of *À ma sœur!* we felt able to tell the BBFC that we could see a distinct pattern in audience responses. It was *younger women* and *older men* who were most likely to fall into the Embracer position – the women because it dramatised their sense of their own move from naïvety to maturation, the men because it pushed them to reflect on their own guilt at the temptations of sexual manipulation.

Audience research is *hard*, in many ways. Not doing it, however, and substituting untested 'figures' to be stand-ins for us is becoming inexcusable.

NOTES

1. This essay is an elaborated version of the presentation I made at 'The New Extremism: Contemporary European Cinema' conference at Anglia Ruskin University on 24–25 April 2010.
2. This quotation is taken from a BBFC digest of their reasons for cutting *À ma sœur!*, provided to researchers at Aberystwyth University in 2006.
3. There is a scatter of important work on the role and provenance of these 'figures', variously naming them among others as 'myths' or 'conjectures'. See, for instance, Klaus Schoenbach (2001) and Edward Schiappa (2008). See also Richard Maxwell (2000).
4. The opportunity arose almost by chance, out of a combination of two things. The BBFC had expressed interest in finding out what could be learnt from our international project on the reception of *The Lord of the Rings* about the responses of young viewers – since some concerns had been expressed that, even though the story was evidently fantasy, the film might none the less be rather frightening for them. While delivering them with a summary of what our evidence revealed on this, their attention was drawn to work I had recently done on audience responses to *Straw Dogs*, and in particular the ways my findings challenged certain assumptions built into work they had previously commissioned (published under the title 'Where Do You Draw The Line?'). Out of these discussions arose the notion that we might design and submit a proposal for this research.
5. This quotation, and all others of this kind, are taken from our project materials, gathered May to December 2006.
6. This aspect of the research is situated within the recently emergent tradition of reception studies, which concerns itself with the ways in which it is possible to locate, within naturally arising materials, traces of the working criteria, modes of participation and judgement of different audiences. These, it has been argued, constitute framing *discourses*, through the lens of which groups of viewers make sense and build interpretations of films. This approach has its roots, more than anywhere, in the work of Janet Staiger, but has since spread and somewhat loosened its association with the wider theoretical framework that Staiger has proposed.
7. The questionnaire owed a great deal to the conceptions and design used in the *Lord of the Rings* project, in the way it combined quantitative and qualitative questions.
8. We discussed with the BBFC the notion of organising single-sex groups and originally planned to use these. As we began to talk to possible participants, we found to our surprise that, overwhelmingly, women and men said that they would prefer these discussions to be

mixed, as they wanted to hear how the 'other sex' thought about the issues. Only one woman strongly said that she only wanted to take part in a single-sex group.
9. See, for instance, Martin Barker, Jane Arthurs and Ramaswami Harindranath (2001).
10. The distinction I am using here, between Critics and Embracers, was used in our research for the BBFC. Its logic is that people who reject a film, or hold it at a distance, are for that very reason less engaged with it, and therefore less likely to carry any residual influences (other than memories of dislike and discomfort) away from it. But it is a distinction with wide ramifications, since it also turns out that Embracers of a film tend to see and experience different kinds of things as going on within it. It bears the important implication that those hostile to a film are unreliable sources for determining its significant contents. This is actually an idea with a considerable history in cultural studies-influenced work on audiences on many kinds of cultural materials. It was at work in, for instance, Ien Ang's discovery that those who loved the soap opera *Dallas* had different languages for describing it from those who scorned or dismissed it (see her *Watching Dallas*). It was also at work in Janice Radway's *Reading the Romance*, as she very cleverly draws out from her readers' responses the conditions for a successful story. And it is, of course, at work within the very wide range of work on fans, as particular kinds of audiences who work in quite distinctive ways on their chosen materials.
11. A great deal can be learned through attending to the manner in which reviewers recount a film's narrative. This is a largely ignored way in which the analysis of reviews can contribute to our understanding of audience responses.
12. The concentrated level of attention can be gleaned from one response recorded within a focus group. One man was struggling to articulate his feelings about the ending, and recalling what happened in great detail. Of course, he said, it was important that we could see so much because it was all so brightly lit . . . wasn't it? And from the responses of people around him, he realised that he had *constructed* it as brightly lit in the course of watching so attentively.
13. This quotation is among those discussed in Melanie Selfe's (2008) essay on our project, 'Inflected Accounts and Irreversible Journeys'.

CHAPTER 10

Censorship, Reception and the Films of Gaspar Noé: The Emergence of the New Extremism in Britain

Daniel Hickin

The late 1990s saw the British Board of Film Classification (BBFC) enter a period of transition that would transform the policies and ideology of British film censorship. The changes seen at the BBFC were numerous and wide-ranging, and contributed to the Board adopting an increasingly liberalised approach to film censorship, with a greater emphasis on accountability and classification. The era coincided with the emergence of a number of films now being discussed as part of the new extremism within contemporary European cinema; featuring scenes of graphic violence and explicit unsimulated sexual activity, films such as *The Idiots* (von Trier, Denmark, 1998), *Seul contre tous* (Noé, France, 1998), *Romance* (Breillat, France, 1999), *Baise-moi* (Despentes and Trinh Thi, France, 2000), *À ma sœur!* (Breillat, France, 2001) and *Irréversible* (Noé, France, 2002) are characterised by their calculated attempts to question the limits of cinematic representation and challenge the boundaries of film censorship. No filmmaker exemplifies this approach better than Argentinean-born French director Gaspar Noé, whose confrontational style has proved controversial. His debut, *Seul contre tous*, was optically censored by the BBFC in 1999, while his second feature, *Irréversible*, became a *cause célèbre* within the British media after being approved uncut in 2002. While the censorship and classification of both films illustrated the increasingly liberal approach of the BBFC, its newfound openness was reflected by the willingness to rationalise its decisions through a series of press releases, interviews and reports. In providing an analysis of the censorship discourses surrounding *Seul contre tous* and *Irréversible*, this chapter builds upon the work of scholars such as Annette Kuhn (1988) and Martin Barker et al. (2001) by exploring how the ideology of British film censorship has changed since 1998. In doing so, I argue that the BBFC has distanced itself from the concept of 'censorship' towards a policy based on 'classification' and the principle that adults should be free to choose their own viewing (provided it does not contravene British law). In light of this shift, it is necessary to reconsider the critical approaches to British film censorship, particularly with regard to how the changes implemented by the BBFC corresponded with the emergence of the new extremism.

The first in a series of changes at the BBFC in the late 1990s saw the departure of BBFC President Lord Harewood[1] and the appointment of Andreas Whittam Smith[2] as his replacement in January 1998. Within months, Whittam Smith made a commitment to openness and accountability that included the issuing of press releases regarding any potentially contentious decisions and initiating the first in a series of nationwide public consultations which sought the views of the public as part of a major review of film and video classification policy. This led directly to the first official set of published BBFC guidelines in 1998, since revised in 2000, 2005 and 2009 (BBFC 2009b). The move towards greater transparency gained further momentum with the launch of the BBFC's website, also in 1998, through which a variety of materials have been made publicly available.[3] In terms of liberalisation, the period saw the implementation of the Human Rights Act 1998, which for the first time in its history required the BBFC to consider freedom of expression when making its decisions. A further change in personnel saw the retirement of long-serving BBFC Director James Ferman,[4] who was replaced by Robin Duval[5] in January 1999. Thus within the space of a year, a combination of personnel changes, technological developments and the implementation of new initiatives, policies and laws helped to instigate a notable shift within the perception and ideology of British film censorship.

As my analysis of *Seul contre tous* and *Irréversible* will demonstrate, the wider cultural impact of the revisions seen at the BBFC during this period was to challenge the concept of 'censorship' radically for adult audiences in Britain. Thus a fresh theoretical approach to the subject can foreground the positive role of classification, rather than the negative act of censorship. In discussing the cultural meaning of the term, Annette Kuhn argues:

> Censorship is understood first and foremost as an act of prohibition, excision, or 'cutting-out' – a practice through which certain subjects are forbidden expression in representations. Debates on censorship, both pro- and anti-, invariably see it as a prohibitive process, assuming that a censored text, by distorting 'reality' or in some other sense falling short of it, is in some sense partial in its representation. (Kuhn 1988: 2)

The acts of 'prohibition' and 'excision' have thus been central to our concept of censorship, and part of what Janet Staiger has described as the 'repression of forbidden knowledges' (Staiger 2000: 77). The prohibitive aspect of the classification process excludes certain age groups from viewing unsuitable material, and the question of what is permissible within each certificate (Uc, U, PG, 12, 12A, 15, 18, R18) is defined within the Board's policy guidelines and supported by existing British law (BBFC 2009b).[6] Prior to 1998, cuts to scenes of sex and violence were common, with 16.6 per cent of '18' certificate theatrical releases cut between 1986 and 1997 (BBFC 2010). This compares to only 1.6 per cent between 1998 and 2009, which accounts for just eleven films, all of which were cut between 1998 and 2003, with none between 2004 and 2009 (BBFC 2010). The dramatic decrease can be traced to the changes previously described, which helped to establish freedom of choice for adult viewers, most notably through the implementation and interpretation of the Human Rights Act 1998 by the new leadership team of Whittam Smith and Duval. Since 1998, the primary policy concern relating to excision at the '18' category had been the depiction of sexual violence, specifically those scenes that, according to the BBFC, appear to endorse or eroticise such acts. With the considerable fall in the number of '18' certificate films being cut, the ideology of British film censorship has increasingly moved towards a policy based primarily on classification. The negative aspects of 'censorship', the acts of excision or 'cutting out', as Kuhn states, have thus been significantly reduced in the years since 1998.

CENSORSHIP AND *SEUL CONTRE TOUS*

Within the first half of 1999, the BBFC approved the release of *The Idiots*, *Seul contre tous* and *Romance*.[7] Notable for their provocative representations of disability, incest and sexuality, each film featured arguably the most transgressive characteristic associated with the new extremism: namely, the depiction of unsimulated scenes of sexual activity, including scenes of erect penises, oral and vaginal penetration, cunnilingus and male ejaculation.[8] Images that were previously considered 'hard-core' pornography were now featuring within a European cinema destined for nationwide distribution and exhibition. In terms of their censorship, the BBFC placed significance on their context within each film as a whole. For example, in the press release for *Romance*, the film is judged 'a serious work' (BBFC 1999c) and its explicit sex scenes were not considered pornographic but instead contextually justified. Such readings proved problematic for sections of the British press, and the role of media controversy can be seen as central to the wider cultural understanding of where the boundaries of film censorship lie, as certain films are identified as being potentially transgressive.

The collective significance of *The Idiots*, *Seul contre tous* and *Romance* was highlighted in January 1999 by Richard Falcon (1999), who, by combining his analysis of the films, recognised that a new form of provocative cinema was emerging from within European cinema. Other notable films from this period include *Funny Games* (Haneke, Austria, 1997), *Sitcom* (Ozon, France, 1998), *Pola X* (Carax, France, 1998) and *L'Humanité* (Dumont, France, 1999). Collectively, they can be identified as part of the first wave of the new extremism. Discussion of the 'New French Extremity', as examined in 2004 by James Quandt in response to films from Gaspar Noé, Catherine Breillat and Bruno Dumont amongst others, has therefore been incorporated into a broader European context – one previously alluded to by Richard Falcon in 1999. Thus the emergence of the new extremism at this time coincided with a transitional period for British film censorship, and the BBFC's move towards liberalisation is reflected in how all the aforementioned films were approved uncut for theatrical exhibition, with the sole exception of *Seul contre tous*.

Set within the industrial suburbs of France in 1980, Gaspar Noé's *Seul contre tous* follows the misadventures of the Butcher, first introduced in the short film *Carne* (1991). Separated from his beloved daughter, the Butcher finds himself prowling the city streets, his increasing sense of alienation detailed in the character's omnipresent voiceover. In one of the film's key scenes, the Butcher visits a porno theatre and muses upon the nature of love, sex and death while viewing a sex film. Shots of him watching from his seat are intercut with two passages from his point of view, lasting approximately twenty-nine seconds and twenty-one seconds respectively, which focus on the close-up scenes of 'hard-core' sexual intercourse presented on the cinema screen before him. Despite the film's provocative representations of bigotry and incest, these two shots became a feature of the film's pre-publicity as part of a discourse on British censorship.

Following the film's world premiere at the Festival de Cannes in May 1998, *Seul contre tous* received its UK premiere in August at the Edinburgh International Film Festival. In *The Guardian*, Dan Glaister's interview with Noé from 19 August 1998 identified the porno theatre scene as potentially problematic for the BBFC. Anticipating the scene's removal, Noé stated: 'if you cut the scene it wouldn't really change the movie' (Glaister 1998), later suggesting that the idea of the film being banned appealed to him. Thus the challenging nature of the film was highlighted several months prior to the film's classification and release, serving to create a level of hype and expectancy that aided the proliferation of censorship discourses on the depiction of unsimulated sexual activity within European *auteur* cinema. Amelia Gentleman's article in *The Guardian* from 22 February 1999 discussed the examples of *Seul contre tous* and *The Idiots* with newly appointed BBFC President Andreas Whittam Smith. Although unable to comment on the fate of Noé's debut prior to the Board's decision, he reflected on what he considered to be the public's changing attitude towards sex on screen:

The board is not inflexible – the amount of explicit sex we see in cinemas has gradually increased. I believe that in this country public tolerance of violence and particularly sexual violence is declining, while tolerance of sexual explicitness is increasing. We have no way of stopping cultural trends. (Gentleman 1999)

Thus, according to Whittam Smith, the possible uncut approval of explicit sex scenes would merely be a response to the changing cultural climate. This view is supported by the research undertaken by Martin Barker et al., who noted that while scenes of sexual violence remain a concern for British audiences, separate scenes of graphic violence and consensual sex have become increasingly acceptable (Barker et al. 2007: I). Nevertheless, the comments from Whittam Smith could be seen as an attempt to downplay the BBFC's role in such a potentially divisive decision: one likely to be supported by the liberal readership of *The Guardian* and those opposed to censorship. The greater test for the film's potentially transgressive impact would be in the response of the popular tabloid press, who purport to represent the views of the public but who failed to enter into the pre-release debates surrounding the film. In addition to Whittam Smith's own interview, the issuing of a press release provided the Board with an opportunity to address any concerns about the film, while becoming part of the same censorship discourses upon which it sought to comment.

The notion of a BBFC press release, whose remarks are attributed to the Board rather than any named individual(s), raises certain issues regarding a film's reception. Although there were seventeen (subjective and opinionated) examiners in 1999 when *Seul contre tous* was classified (BBFC 1999c), the BBFC is one body of opinion with various figureheads, such as Whittam Smith, who act as the Board's public face. Examiners do, however, share the same viewing space when assessing a given film. Janet Staiger has referred to how 'interpretations depend in part upon the subjectivity of the various readers, but also significantly upon the context of the experience of encountering the text' (Staiger 2000: 77). Although the body is made up of differing opinions, the viewing context at the BBFC is one of a collective, collaborative experience with the shared purpose of evaluating the text for public consumption. The 'press release' thus provides a direct dialogue between the BBFC and the media concerning its collective, agreed interpretation of a film.

The press release for *Seul contre tous* was issued on 15 March 1999, and detailed the Board's decision to classify the film for theatrical exhibition with an '18' certificate and minor optical changes. It began by emphasising the French identity of the film (which I later explore in relation to *Irréversible*), before addressing the censorship of the porno theatre scene. Despite Whittam Smith's suggestion of a more tolerant attitude towards screen sex, the BBFC made a change to the scene through the process of 'optical softening', which created a blurred effect over the offending shots. Yet with the soundtrack left intact, British viewers were left to imagine the onscreen images denied them by the BBFC. In discussing the scene, the Board appeared sympathetic towards it, and provided an insightful reading into its relevance in understanding the main protagonist:

> The loveless images on the screen reflect his bleak views about sex and human relationships. The Board recognized that the images performed a function within the context and structure of the film as a whole. They were nevertheless of a particularly extreme nature which exceeded the boundaries of acceptability for BBFC classification in any medium. (BBFC 1999b)

The 'extreme' and prolonged nature of the images meant they were unacceptable under the current BBFC guidelines, despite the Board having understood their importance within the context of the narrative. Thus it appears contradictory to provide a rational justification for the significance of the scene, only to require the removal of certain images which helped create its meaning. The inconsistency between the BBFC's reading of a text and the interpretation of its own guidelines was further highlighted within the Board's 1999 annual report, which noted that while the scenes in *Seul contre tous* could not be justified by their context, those in *The Idiots* and *Romance* were (BBFC 1999c: 4). Both the press release for *Seul contre tous* and the annual report for 1999 refer to *The Idiots* as a precedent, having been approved a month before on 15 February 1999. For the BBFC, the crucial difference between the films was the prolonged close-up shots in *Seul contre tous*, compared to the brief shots of penetrative intercourse seen in *The Idiots*.

The reviews that accompanied the British release of *Seul contre tous* on 19 March 1999 provided an opportunity for critics to react to its censorship. A frequent detractor of the BBFC, *Evening Standard* critic Alexander Walker had previously criticised the decisions to pass such films as *The Devils* (1971), *Crash* (1996) and *Lolita* (1997). His review of *Seul contre tous* failed to produce such a reaction, conceding that it was 'powerfully toxic stuff' (Walker 1999) before concurring with the BBFC's decision to pass the film with one minor alteration. James Christopher of *The Times* was similarly engaged, claiming he had 'rarely seen a more savage piece of celluloid' (Christopher 1999). Such views were echoed by Jonathan Romney in *The Guardian* (Romney 1999) and Philip French in *The Observer*, with the latter conceding: 'you won't easily forget *Seul contre tous*, and you won't rush to see it a second time' (French 1999). The reviews reveal that there was little to distinguish between those of the supposedly conservative and liberal media, the consensus being that the film was a powerful experience, yet difficult to enjoy. The strongest opposition to the film was provided by Christopher Tookey of the *Daily Mail*, who has become synonymous with censorship debates, having previously united with Walker in his calls to ban *Crash* (Barker et al. 2001). Unlike Walker's, Tookey's review of *Seul contre tous* provided a damning critique, calling it 'repetitive, tawdry and tedious beyond belief' (Tookey 1999). Nevertheless, his criticisms were not aimed at the BBFC for approving the film's release; instead, he attacked the director for his 'pathetic attempts to get noticed', while any potential viewer would have to be a 'sad, pretentious git' in order to appreciate it (ibid.). The role of the director was also discussed by Tony Rayns in *Sight & Sound*, who, despite appreciating the film's visual energy and invention, nevertheless criticised Noé's self-conscious desire to shock his audience, noting that: 'sadly there's a typically punk hollowness at the core of Noé's rhetoric' (Rayns 1999). The desire for provocation was self-evident from Noé, who at the time of the film's release described his pleasure at shocking his audience, stating: 'I'm happy some people walk out during my film' (Noé 1999), before condemning the Board's censorship of the porno theatre scene in one of the few post-censorship articles to do so. While both Walker (1999) and Tookey (1999) applauded the alteration, critics such as French (1999) focused on how the scene invited comparisons to *Taxi Driver*. Despite the provocative themes and imagery present within the film, the censorship of the porno theatre scene appeared to eliminate its most transgressive element. Consequently, *Seul contre tous* lacked the desired qualities required to incite the conservative press into calling for the film to be further cut or even banned.

CLASSIFICATION AND *IRRÉVERSIBLE*

Following the first wave of the new extremism in the late 1990s, an identifiable second wave appeared between 2000 and 2002, most significantly *À ma sœur!*, *Baise-moi* and *Irréversible*.[9] Other notable films of the period include *Intimacy* (Chéreau, France/UK, 2001), *La Pianiste/The Piano Teacher* (Haneke, Austria/France, 2001), *Trouble Every Day* (Denis, France, 2001), *Le Pornographe/The Pornographer* (Bonello, France/Canada, 2001) and *Hundstage/Dog Days* (Seidl, Austria, 2001), all of which have been incorporated into the notion of contemporary European extreme cinema. Prior to the BBFC's classification of *Irréversible*, both *Baise-moi* and *The Pornographer* had received cuts to scenes of unsimulated sexual activity. In *Baise-moi*, a ten-second cut was required to a 'hard-core' rape scene in accordance with the BBFC's guidelines on sexual violence, leaving intact the numerous scenes of explicit consensual sex. Meanwhile, in *The Pornographer*, a graphic close-up shot in which a man ejaculates on to a woman's face was cut by twelve seconds.[10] While the depiction of graphic unsimulated sexual activity was still a concern for the Board, no such images were present in Gaspar Noé's second feature, *Irréversible*. In the film, a simple rape and revenge narrative is told in reverse, with the early part of the film dominated by a graphic murder scene involving a man being repeatedly hit in the head with a fire extinguisher. As the film progresses, the narrative details the events leading to the murder, including a nine-minute rape scene shot in a single take. As with *Seul contre tous*, the discourses surrounding *Irréversible* would focus on specific scenes considered potentially transgressive, which would provide a challenge for the revised policies of the BBFC.

As with Noé's debut four years earlier, *Irréversible* received its world premiere at the Festival de Cannes in May 2002 before screening at the Edinburgh International Film Festival in August 2002. Early British press reports described the film as 'the new French shocker' (Norman 2002) and its Cannes screening proved highly controversial, having 'divided critics' with 'quite a few walking out' (Romney 2002). The film was further perceived as being 'designed to provoke this year's moral panic' (James 2002: 16), thus providing a cynical early reading of Noé's intent and the censorship difficulties it could face. At Edinburgh, these concerns were placed within a specifically British context, whereby the issue of a British general release gave rise to a series of discourses surrounding the representation of sexual violence and the likelihood of the film being passed uncut by the BBFC. Within the context of contemporary European cinema, Angelique Chrisafis in *The Guardian* from 17 August 2002 believed the film would be passed by the Board, but would be added to a group of films, including *Baise-moi* and *The Pornographer*, 'where Britain has broken from the rest of Europe and requested cuts' (Chrisafis 2002: 9). The belief that cuts would be made reflects the notion that the film overstepped the boundaries of acceptability in relation to its scenes of sexual violence, while contributing to the censorship discourses and hype surrounding the film. As part of these discourses, Andreas Whittam Smith discussed *Irréversible* prior to the Board issuing its decision on the film, just as he had previously with *Seul contre tous*. After leaving his role as BBFC President in July 2002, Whittam Smith wrote an open letter to his successor Sir Quentin Thomas[11] in *The Independent*. The recent controversial decision to approve *Baise-moi* with only a ten-second cut had been one of Whittam Smith's last acts as President, and he offered Thomas the following note of caution regarding the media's role within censorship discourses:

> Sometimes, though, press coverage prevents one from keeping one's mind free from preconceptions. I see that one film critic has already warned you that the explicit nature of Gaspar Noé's rape revenge movie, *Irréversible*, [. . .] will make even *Baise-moi* look tame. [. . .] It is much

more difficult to make a balanced decision if a film arrives with a notorious reputation that has already generated a long debate in the press before its British opening. (Whittam Smith 2002)

Although insightful, such comments equally contribute to the reactionary media coverage Whittam Smith was himself attempting to downplay. While the violence in *Irréversible* is brutal and prolonged, the film did not contain the mixture of violence and 'hard-core' sex present in *Baise-moi*. *Irréversible* would thus be an example of how the media attempted to set the agenda on how the film should be perceived by the Board. One article that was a direct attempt to influence Thomas came from Alexander Walker. As part of his profile on the new BBFC President, he informed Thomas that '*Irréversible* is coming up soon: nine-minute rape sequence in an underpass' (Walker 2002a: 29). Walker's focus on reducing the film to one scene sets out to distinguish *Irréversible* as problematic, and define it purely as a 'rape film'. This provocative warning would also have created a highly negative perception of the film for the *Evening Standard* readership, adding further pressure to the impending BBFC decision on the film.

The Board's press release for *Irréversible* was issued on 21 October 2002 and sought to address the negative media discourses surrounding the film. It began by noting the film's French identity, thus clearly identifying it within the context of French cinema, as done previously with *Seul contre tous*. By highlighting this point, the BBFC were alluding to certain preconceptions and stereotypes, linking French cinema with intellectualism and explicit sexuality, which Mark Betz has traced back to the marketing of European cinema in the 1950s and 1960s (Betz 2003). As with *Romance* and *Baise-moi* previously, *Seul contre tous* and *Irréversible* were discussed in terms of their 'serious intent' and 'artistic merit'. Such comments fuel the belief that the BBFC takes a more lenient approach in its censorship of foreign-language and art cinema compared to English-language and genre films, based on the problematic assumption that those who watch the former tend to be educated and middle-class, while the latter appeals more to a younger, less sophisticated audience. Criticism of this approach was evident in July 2001 when Mark Kermode (2001) highlighted the BBFC's decision to pass films such as *Romance* and *Baise-moi*, yet continue to oppose the uncut release of the American rape-revenge exploitation film *Last House on the Left* (1972).[12] Although *Baise-moi* and *Irréversible* could also be viewed within the rape-revenge sub-genre of exploitation cinema, their national identity allowed them to be viewed within the context of French and European art cinema, thus providing a sense of cultural and artistic respectability that excused their explicitness and legitimised their release. Having cited *Irréversible*'s national identity, the press release went on to acknowledge that the depiction of sexual violence was a major concern as a matter of BBFC policy, but that a clinical forensic psychiatrist had been consulted on the film:

> She agreed with the Board that the scene is a harrowing and vivid portrayal of the brutality of rape. However, it contains no explicit sexual images and is not designed to titillate. The Board was satisfied, therefore, that no issue of harm arose in the context of a cinema release for adult viewing only. (BBFC 2002a)

The notable inclusion of 'she' strongly emphasised that a female psychologist considered the scene acceptable, thereby deflecting any potential criticism that could arise from providing a male response to the scene. More importantly, it was the view of a professional, whose opinion the media and the public should acknowledge and respect. The press release further explained how the film was viewed firmly within an 'adult viewing only' context, and accepted that it included shocking and unpleasant scenes, 'but these are not reasons for censoring them for adults' (BBFC 2002a). Reflecting on the film within the pages of its annual report for 2002, the BBFC reiterated many of the points concerning *Irréversible* first made within its press release. However, one notable difference lay in the further comments on the media pre-publicity surrounding the film, which the report suggested had been based on assumptions made by those who had not seen the film (BBFC 2002b). Having addressed the media's concerns within the press release, the Board appeared to use its annual report to criticise the media openly for their inaccurate and sensationalist approach to discussing the film. Having concentrated on responding to the critical concerns in the original press release, the statement itself became the target of the very critics whose concerns it aimed to reassure.

The BBFC's announcement that *Irréversible* would be released without cuts confirmed the fears of the conservative media, and was seen by David Taylor of the *Evening Standard* as part of the 'increasing liberalisation' (Taylor 2002) of a Board that had only recently approved *Intimacy* and *Baise-moi*. Kate Sherry produced a similar response in the *Daily Mail*, claiming the BBFC had failed 'to restrain levels of gratuitous sex and violence' (Sherry 2002). The debates within the conservative media thus became dominated by an anti-liberalisation, anti-BBFC agenda, further exemplified in articles by Tookey (2002) and Walker (2002b). As with the reports of Taylor and Sherry, Tookey's article on *Irréversible* was primarily an attack on the BBFC for wanting 'only to advise the public about how offensive a film may be, not protect them by demanding cuts or refusing a certificate' (Tookey 2002). By providing advice rather than making cuts, the Board had abandoned what Janet Staiger has described as one of the key aspects of censorship: namely, the process of 'inflicting the moral view of one group onto another' (Staiger 2000:

77). The failure to impose its own moral view thus provides further evidence of the BBFC's shift from censorship to classification. The issue of morality was echoed by Alexander Walker, whose review of *Irréversible* from 30 January 2003 focused on attacking the film's supporters and those who were complicit in its release through their failure to speak out against it. His 'contempt' goes beyond the film, and 'extends to those mealy-mouthed commentators who fear to endorse it, but are politically incapable of damning it' (Walker 2003). Thus an ineffectual media are blamed for the film's release and reflect the growing influence of liberalism and political correctness in British society. Walker's failure to re-engage critically with the film in his review was shared by Tookey, who simply republished a condensed version of his previous *Irréversible* article criticising the BBFC (Tookey 2003). The conservative media's discussion of *Irréversible* thus centred on its classification and the lack of censorship by the BBFC, ostensibly at the expense of any critical evaluation of its artistic merits (or lack thereof).

For those who wished to engage with *Irréversible*, such as Peter Bradshaw in *The Guardian*, the film was representative of Noé's 'rage against modern life, against progress, against hypocrisy, against political correctness, against everything and nothing' (Bradshaw 2003). Yet the nihilistic *Irréversible* was deemed 'empty' and 'shallow' in comparison to the 'radical commentary on the dark heart of France' provided by *Seul contre tous* (ibid.). Such comments draw attention to the original response to Noé's debut, which received cautious praise from both sides of the political divide, in distinct contrast to the reception of *Irréversible*. Despite the differences in their censorship and critical response, the films shared a degree of pre-publicity dominated by discourses surrounding sex, violence and censorship, in the process reducing the discussion of each film to individual shots. This issue has been highlighted by Martine Beugnet (2007a), who has noted how the term 'extreme cinema' can be too limiting and simplistic, often failing to acknowledge a film's other merits and achievements. The term also feeds into the publicity and expectancy surrounding certain films and their censorship. Noé's capacity for self-promotion contributed to the hype surrounding *Seul contre tous*, and Richard Falcon states how 'Noé claims to have wanted his film banned at least somewhere to prove its confrontational power' (Falcon 1999: 13). Although not rejected by the Board, the film was censored, and therefore overstepped the boundaries of acceptability at a time when the process and policies of British film censorship were being revised. With its most controversial shots obscured, the film failed to have the transgressive impact suggested within the pre-publicity. With *Irréversible*, Noé tested the limits of the Board's newly revised guidelines and its policy towards the representation of sexual violence. The subsequent media controversy surrounding its uncut release suggests that its scenes of sexual violence were socially transgressive and deemed unacceptable by those opposed to the Board's shift away from censorship towards classification. Its release thus created a new precedent in the onscreen depiction of rape in British cinema and provided evidence of the BBFC's move towards providing freedom of expression for filmmakers and freedom of choice for adult viewers. The release of *Seul contre tous* and *Irréversible* heralded the emergence of a new form of provocative European cinema that coincided with the beginning of an increasingly open, accountable and liberalised form of British film censorship. This shift, alongside the BBFC's engagement with censorship debates through a variety of consultations and publications, helped to aid the proliferation of discourses surrounding the subject. As part of those discourses, this chapter reflects the need to consider further the relationship between film censorship and the cultural impact of the new extremism.

NOTES

1. BBFC President George Harewood, aka Lord Harewood, aka George Lascelles, 7th Earl of Harewood (June 1985–December 1997): a music enthusiast and former Director of the Royal Opera House, and former Chairman and Musical Director of the English Opera House.
2. BBFC President Andreas Whittam Smith (January 1998–July 2002): an Anglican and former journalist, and founding editor of *The Independent* in 1986.
3. The website http://www.bbfc.co.uk contains such information as a comprehensive database of all classified films, news and press releases, consumer advice, policy documents, guidelines and legislation, annual reports and statistics, information for customers, and various reports and studies.
4. BBFC Director James Ferman (June 1975–January 1999): an American-born freelance filmmaker, known predominately for producing documentaries.
5. BBFC Director Robin Duval (January 1999–September 2004): a former Deputy Director of Programmes at the Independent Television Commission, TV regulator and writer/producer/Head of Production at the Central Office of Information (COI).
6. As noted in the BBFC Guidelines 2009, the laws include: the Human Rights Act 1998, the Cinematograph Films (Animals) Act 1937, the Obscene Publications Act 1959, the Protection of Children Act 1978 and the Video Recordings Act 1984/2010.
7. *The Idiots* approved 15 February 1999, British theatrical release 14 May 1999; *Seul contre tous* approved 15 March 1999, British theatrical release 19 March 1999; *Romance* approved 19 July 1999, British theatrical release 8 October 1999.
8. Examples of contemporary European cinema depicting unsimulated sexual activity include: *La Vie de Jésus* (Dumont, France, 1997), *Assassin(s)* (Kassovitz, France, 1997), *Sitcom* (Ozon, France, 1998), *Pola X* (Carax, France, 1998), *The Idiots* (von Trier, Denmark, 1998), *Seul contre tous* (Noé, France, 1998), *Romance* (Breillat, France, 1999), *Baise-moi* (Despentes and Trinh Thi, France, 2000), *The Pornographer* (Bonello, France, 2001), *Intimacy* (Chéreau, France/UK, 2001), *The Piano Teacher* (Haneke, Austria/France, 2001), *Dog Days* (Seidl, Austria, 2001), *Lucía y el sexo* (Medem, Spain, 2001), *The Principles of Lust* (Woolcock, UK, 2003), *Anatomie de l'enfer* (Breillat, France, 2004), *9 Songs* (Winterbottom, UK, 2004), *Destricted* (Noé, Abramovic, Clark, Brambilla, Barney,

Taylor Wood, Prince, 2006, UK/USA), *Taxidermia* (Pálfi, Hungary, 2006), *Ex Drummer* (Mortier, Belgium, 2007), *Import/Export* (Seidl, Austria, 2007), *Puffball* (Roeg, UK, 2007) and *Antichrist* (von Trier, Denmark, 2009).

9. *À ma sœur!* approved 7 November 2001, British theatrical release 7 December 2001; *Baise-moi* approved 26 February 2001, British theatrical release 3 May 2002; *Irréversible* approved 21 October 2002, British theatrical release 31 January 2003.

10. Although the cut scene in *The Pornographer* could not be contextually justified in accordance with '18' certificate classification guidelines, the film was approved uncut on DVD/video with an 'R18' certificate, reserved for pornographic sex works sold only through licensed premises.

11. BBFC President Sir Quentin Thomas (August 2002–present): a former Head of the Broadcasting Department at the Home Office and Northern Ireland Office civil servant.

12. *Last House on the Left* endured a turbulent history with the Board, which includes being rejected for theatrical release in 1974 and 2000, and rejected on video in 2001 before being released in a heavily cut version in 2002. It was finally approved uncut on 17 March 2008.

CHAPTER 11

'Sex and Violence from a Pair of Furies': The Scandal of *Baise-moi*

Leila Wimmer

X-rated in its home country and censored throughout the world, *Baise-moi*, Virginie Despentes's notorious first feature, is a highly controversial example of the new extremism in French cinema. Co-written and co-directed with porn actress Coralie Trinh Thi and starring Karen Bach (Nadine) and Rafaëlla Anderson (Manu), the film's combination of low-brow, hard-core pornography within a violent neo-*noir* female revenge narrative provoked such a scandal on its release in Paris on 28 June 2000 that its commercial life was brutally interrupted. Known for taking 'the representation of sex into a new domain for French women's cinema' (Tarr and Rollet 2001: 284), *Baise-moi* had originally been granted a '16+' certificate accompanied with a warning by the Ministry of Culture. But three days after the film opened, under pressure from far-right pro-family values groups, the State Council reclassified the film as '18+' on the grounds that it 'constituted a message which is both pornographic and an incitement to violence' (Camy and Montagne 2002: 219). Since the '18+' rating was abolished in 1990, *Baise-moi* had to be given an X certificate to be forbidden to minors. As a result the film would receive no state or financial aid, would be heavily taxed and could only be shown in licensed outlets, which have mostly disappeared since the advent of video, cable television and the internet. Despentes, Trinh Thi and producer Philippe Godeau refused to accept the decision and the film was removed from distribution. What came to be called *'l'affaire Baise-moi'* generated a huge polemic and cinematic circles promptly mobilised in support of the film. Fellow filmmaker Catherine Breillat, similarly noted for her graphic portrayals of sexuality, initiated a petition demanding a reform of the law. This was subsequently signed by several film personalities, including directors Romain Goupil, Tony Marshall, Jeanne Labrune, Claire Denis and Jean-Luc Godard; a demonstration was also organised in Paris on 5 July that same year. The French Minister for Culture eventually re-introduced an '18+' certificate and the film was re-released legally in mainstream cinemas on 29 August 2001 (Camy and Montagne 2002; MacKenzie 2002).

In a sense, the X-rating of Despentes and Trinh Thi's film was rather surprising if we consider that several contemporary European sex-based art films feature non-simulated sex acts as well as graphic violence. A self-reflexive rape and revenge narrative that draws from low-brow sexploitation pictures and horror films such as *I Spit on your Grave* (Zarchi, US, 1978) and *The Exorcist* (Friedkin, US, 1973), *Baise-moi* has been described as 'an extreme example of the blurring of boundaries between pornography and art cinema' (MacKenzie 2002: 316). While the film almost certainly corresponds to the notion of a typical French art film to foreign audiences, *Baise-moi* appears to have been more problematic for French censors and critics. The outrage caused by *Baise-moi* in both the mainstream and cinephile press seems to suggest that the film had a powerful symbolic charge. In this chapter, I will argue that the film's power to shock and outrage audiences and censors had less to do with its use of pornographic codes and conventions than it may at first appear. Indeed, as Angela Carter has suggested, when pornography serves 'to reinforce the prevailing system of values and ideas in a given society, it is tolerated; and when it does not, it is banned' (Carter 1979: 18). The disappearance of *Baise-moi* from French screens caused a media storm, albeit one, as I will show, accompanied by much moral and critical disdain for the film itself.

The aim of this chapter is to examine the scandal surrounding *Baise-moi* upon its release in France. I want to consider its problematic critical reception in the context of contemporary expectations and debates about appropriate French citizenship, interrogating the nexus of gender, ethnicity and class that informed its aesthetic dismissal. As Carrie Tarr and Brigitte Rollet point out, 'the film is driven by a notion of sexual difference as unavoidable and grotesque, where the only answer to women's victimisation by men is to make men the victims' (Tarr and Rollet 2001: 284). It is my contention that the controversy around *Baise-moi* makes visible some of the key anxieties and fears of the contemporary cultural moment, reflecting upon French culture in ways that are telling and troubling. I want to argue that the scandal of *Baise-moi* was predicated on the film's exposure of difference. I will conclude that for French critics *Baise-moi* challenged and troubled the French Republican rhetoric of universalism that is based on a disavowal of difference in order to maintain white, middle-class, heterosexual and Catholic masculinity at the centre. Foremost, the *banlieue* where the film begins connotes racial and social exclusion, a space within the French context that is often the object of moral panic and occupies a structural position in debates about national identity and citizenship. To understand the scandal of *Baise-moi*, the film needs to be located within the culturally specific French context from which it emerged and it is to this that we now turn.

Baise-moi is based on Virginie Despentes's best-selling first novel, a cult neo-*noir* crime fiction that made a considerable impact on its publication in 1993. Part of the new generation of women writers that emerged in the 1990s, Despentes's writings have been identified as belonging to a literary tendency known as 'trash', a trend associated with marginalised youth, worthlessness and exclusion, a space outside mainstream society (Jordan 2004: 115–19). Her work is also linked to the *noir* tradition of French crime fiction, 'expanding in new directions the left-wing political engagement of the 1970s and 1980s *neo-polar*, a vigorously anti-bourgeois form intent on critiquing the economic and social structures that determine power relations' (Jordan 2004: 126). *Noir* fiction is arguably an essentially virile and misogynistic genre where violence against women features as an important element. In recent years, it has been appropriated by French women writers who explore its significance, subverting its gender politics and offering representations of powerful independent female characters. In the case of Despentes, the appropriation of *noir* is marked by 'role reversals that serve to highlight the deeply entrenched understanding of the female body as a victim's body on which crime fiction has traditionally depended' (Jordan 2004: 129).

In terms of its explicit sex scenes, the work of Despentes also fits within the French cultural context, where a growing number of women are appropriating pornography and producing texts 'which push at generic as well as cultural boundaries and which seek to wrest pornography from men' (Jordan 2004: 54). Described by Christian Authier as 'hard female narratives' in which 'women have taken over sex' (Authier 2002: 13), what characterises these contemporary works is 'a form of protesting neo-feminism' (ibid.: 9), whose 'fascination for fluctuating identities and mutating bodies' is representative of a 'new queer culture' (ibid.: 141–2).[1] Shot in six weeks on low-budget digital video, *Baise-moi* is the story of Manu and Nadine, two marginal lower-class young women from the brutal environment of the Parisian *banlieue* who both work in the sex industry. They meet after Manu is brutally raped and kills her brother while Nadine has killed her roommate in a fight and her best friend has been shot. Together, the hard-boiled twosome embark on a journey of casual sex and revenge murders in a fantasy of eradicating masculine agency and representatives of the bourgeoisie that ends tragically. Breaking the taboo of women as perpetrators of violence, *Baise-moi* is circumscribed at the outset by its rhetorical strategy of spectatorial address. Bleak and brutal in terms of its gender politics, the film, as Judith Franco has suggested, 'problematizes male spectatorship in its foregrounding of the "open" yet empowered female body (represented realistically rather than monstrous, as it often is in action films), and its emphasis on female bonding' (Franco 2004: 7). Indeed, in *Baise-moi*, '[r]esisting the homophobic link between lesbianism and criminality as well as voyeurism', Despentes and Trinh Thi 'refuse to give male spectators what they want to see' (ibid.: 4). Instead, throughout the film, male spectators are confronted by 'the spectacle of other men humiliated through ridicule and death' (ibid.: 9).

In a film where graphic scenes of sex and violence are performed by two hard-core *beur* (second-generation children of North African immigrants) actresses, sexuality imbricates not only with gender, but also with national identity, an issue that is central to contemporary French society. What has largely remained undiscussed in relation to *Baise-moi* is how the film explores the socio-political and economic system of heterosexual patriarchy and the particular position of women in relation to the national body. In addition to its formal politics, Despentes and Trinh Thi's film can be read as a series of 'social vignettes where class-consciousness is exacerbated' (Spoiden 2002: 74, 75). Furthermore, as Phil Powrie has observed, the film foregrounds 'exclusion both at the level of race (both women are *beurs*) and gender (both are women)' (Powrie 2007: 76), exploring the structures of power in which men dominate women and how this dominance is shaped by class and other social forces at work in the economically devastated, socially fractured and multi-ethnic cityscape of post-industrial France.

Baise-moi thus constructs a specific imagining of national identity as the inter-ethnic female bonds that develop between Manu and Nadine emphasises the hybrid nature of Frenchness. Racism is alluded to when Manu asks her friend Karla if she is French enough to get unemployment benefits and is evoked obliquely in a particular episode when in a sex club Manu protests at being fondled and the lecherous patron replies: 'We are not in a mosque here!' Significantly, of the two, it is Manu, the one most clearly marked racially, who is brutally raped. But despite these sequences the major issues are gender and class, rather than cultural difference. Manu and Nadine's symbiotic friendship is cemented largely because of their difference as marginal young women who are outside the French bourgeois mainstream. In contrast with the original novel (where they come to the 'ethical' agreement of not killing *beurs*), in the film, ethnic difference is to a certain extent minimised in order to foreground female solidarity and the knotting together of issues of class and gender under the oppressive system of late capitalist patriarchy.

Baise-moi must be seen as taking place in a contemporary French context 'marked by challenges to sex and gender roles that have produced what is often described as 'a "crisis of masculinity" and an increase in the level of violence against women (which is the highest in Europe)' (Tarr and Rollet 2001: 20). Since the 1990s French women have made new inroads in terms of their representation in the social and political spheres. Yet, as Tarr and Rollet have suggested, they 'accept a level of sexism and misogyny in the media and in academic and political life which would be unacceptable in Britain and America'. Moreover, 'there is still a high premium on traditional "feminine" elegance and seductiveness' (ibid.: 21).

The historical notion of a universal French identity based on assimilation has recently been threatened by the increasing demands of minority groups, such as women, immigrants, and gays and lesbians. French universalism has been on the defensive under the impetus of the debates around the movement for women's parity in politics, the controversies surrounding same-sex relationships and the inception of the PACS (*Pacte Civil de Solidarité*). Furthermore, there has been a revival of militant feminism at the same time as lesbian and gay issues found new prominence – from the *Chiennes de garde* to *Act-Up*. French politics in the 1990s 'was full of debates about universalism', a concept according to feminist historian Michelle Perrot, which is 'in fact a big leaf that only covers over the masculinity that has served to exclude women from the government of the polity' (Perrot in Wallach Scott 2004: 41). Thus, 'Whatever the issue, citizenship for North African immigrants, greater access to political office for women, or domestic partnership for homosexual couples [. . .] its proponents and critics framed their arguments as critiques of, appeals to, or defences of a universalism thought to be distinctively French' (Wallach Scott 2004: 32–3). Debates around Islamic headscarves, seen as a challenge to the principles of the secular Republic established in 1905 and which insists upon the separation of Church and State, erupted in 1989, 1994 and 2003, and were extended in 2010 around the wearing of the burqa in public spaces. Such debates have been presented in terms of the identification of the French nation with a universal model of individual integration. As Diana Holmes has suggested:

> In a France which defines itself as 'one and indivisible', equality is achieved through integration and the erasure of difference, and otherness is ignored or equated with inferiority. Women's otherness has been celebrated, but the rhetoric of adoration is merely euphemised contempt. French citizens from other cultures can achieve acceptance, but to be fully part of the nation, they must renounce alternative models of identity. (Holmes 1996: 278)

The way that gender and nation are imagined in *Baise-moi* is thus central to these debates and provides a useful perspective through which to explore the hostility of the critical establishment towards the film. Essential to the understanding of this aversion are the modernist dynamics of French film culture. In reading French reviews and critical commentary on *Baise-moi*, one finds an almost exclusive focus on form, centring largely on its pornographic properties, on the characters' violence, their hatred and their pleasure in killing. The criteria that underline such judgements are, of course, socially produced and, as such, necessarily bound up with issues of taste within French film criticism. The male critical establishment (only a handful of critics are women) is inscribed within France's Republican tradition where issues of difference are obscured by the rhetoric of universalism. Since the advent of the French New Wave, the main paradigm of film criticism has been the concept of the *auteur* and the notion of universal aesthetic and moral values. French film culture is dominated by a modernist conception of cinema as an art with a discourse advocating formalist autonomy against a feminised mass other and an art that rejects contextual issues or the reading of films from a gender or cultural studies perspectives. A good part of this hostility stems from an implicit refusal of 'any manifestation of differences in the field of artistic creation [...] It is as if women, *beurs* or gays are indirectly discouraged from making films dealing with issues that are particular to them' (Rollet 2005: 175). The claim to universalism, then, often masks hidden exclusions and hierarchies and 'the flagrant contradictions of a universalism that is in fact synonymous with the masculine, white, heterosexual, Catholic' (ibid.: 176).

THE SCANDAL OF *BAISE-MOI*

Catherine Breillat's *Romance* (1990) and Despentes and Trinh Thi's *Baise-moi* have both generated scandals and acted as catalysts for debates around the advance of pornography in mainstream film, though the first was not greeted with an opprobrium similar to that which confronted *Baise-moi* on its release in its home country. Tanya Krzywinska has suggested that European art films distinguish themselves from low-brow hard core through their framing of sex in terms of established art values: 'the cinematic representation of real sex, it seems, is sanctioned only on the conditions that certain signifiers of "art" are present.' *Baise-moi*, on the other hand, 'has far fewer conventional signifiers of art than the current trend' (Krzywinska 2006: 226).

Though, as noted earlier, the X certificate triggered a widespread polemic about freedom of expression and the policing of public morality, the disgust and the outrage played out in French reviews suggest that it was its graphic depictions of violence and sexual acts performed by women that were the source of *Baise-moi*'s scandal. Thus, although all Parisian newspapers ran pieces on the affair, defending the film against what was perceived as outright state censorship and arguing for the freedom of expression, critical responses to the film itself were overwhelmingly hostile. Decried as pseudo-pornography, an important strand of the reviews consisted of violent rhetorical dismissals of the film on artistic grounds: 'if one agrees that only masterpieces deserve our insurrection to be protected, then *Baise-moi* did not merit this battle,' declared a critic in the prestigious daily *Le Monde*. *Baise-moi* is 'formless, chaotic, uncontrolled, a primal film of flashes, no doubt inspired by a certain hopeless drive, but signalling a total incapacity to frame, to align two shots, to project anything besides a declaration of intent', argued another (Douin 2000). For the satirical political weekly, *Charlie-Hebdo*, the film was 'not even vile, just worthless, a trash version of *Thelma and Louise*' (Boujut 2000). *Baise-moi*, the critic continued, 'is a film made of hatred and revenge. This is why it is pornographic. Yet don't rely on me to approve the State Council's decision to give it an X-rating' (ibid.). The cinephile establishment represented by the monthly *Positif* and *Cahiers du cinéma* concurred on the grounds that this was a film of 'gratuitous violence [. . .] essentially primitive' (Vincendeau 2000), displaying the 'worst populist impulses' which 'added nothing' (Joyard 2000).

The link between sex and violence in all these arguments is also about the violence of women during times of change and transition. What is at stake in the debates around *Baise-moi* is the notion of women responding to violence, which was perceived as extremely disturbing to reviewers. The discomfort posed by this portrayal is expressed in reviews where the film is described as 'disgusting' (Assouline 2000), 'a butcher film' (De Bruyn 2000), 'disgusting and fascist' (Joffrin 2000), 'reheated junk with hot sauce' (Gorin 2000). The key issues explored by the film are thus largely sidelined in favour of a discussion of the increasing advance of non-simulated sexual acts in mainstream cinema and of the aesthetic features of the film. In what they referred to as 'shock tactics', several reviews derided *Baise-moi*'s graphic concoction of sex and violence as meaningless sensationalism and a cynical marketing ploy. For the daily centre-right, *Le Figaro*, this was an 'embarrassing feminist letting off steam by two old adolescent girls battered by life' (Gianorio 2000), while the Catholic *La Croix* suggested that *Baise-moi* was 'not art' but merely 'a commercial operation of the worst kind, oversold in a transgressive packaging doubled with the most barbaric vision of life' (Ph. R. 2000). Similarly, the daily *Les Échos* claimed that the film was 'repetitive, ugly, [. . .] touting a disgusting violence more shocking than the touting crudeness of the sex scenes [. . .] an appallingly empty and boring provocation [. . .] of no interest whatsoever' (Copperman 2000), while for the weekly *L'Express*, *Baise-moi* was 'neither a film nor cinema' (J. P. D. 2000). Though a few comments on *Baise-moi* posit some aesthetic innovation – 'a Copernican revolution in cinema since the sexual scenes are on an equal footing with others' (Rauger 2000) – they decline to engage with the concerns explored by the film. A few dissenting voices were offered by female critics for whom the film constituted 'a passionate piece of work, sincere and feminist' (Attali 2000), but overall, the critical consensus was that from a formal point of view Despentes and Trinh Thi's film 'does not represent cinematic art and is thus beyond aesthetic judgement' (Dufreigne 2000); it offered 'nothing new, no real experimentation [. . .] Humiliation, sadism, stupidity are the driving force behind *Baise-moi*' (Mérigeau 2000).

These formalist reactions speak of a refusal, or even a denial, of the representation of the power relations that underpin the film. This refusal to engage with the underlying gender relations is especially surprising given comments made by Rafaëlla Anderson and Karen Bach during interviews for this film that 'pornography is similar to rape,' and with Virginie Despentes explaining that 'We did not invent rape [. . .] I've been raped and one of my actresses has been raped' (Garcin 2000). Indeed, the most significant aspect of *Baise-moi* – namely, its engagement with gender politics – went largely unspoken or was condescendingly brushed off. This speaks of the enduring structural lack of engagement with issues of representation, at a time when women's roles were being rethought, with the issue of women's political representation in the public sphere and the link between postcolonial questions ('the colonial breach') and social fragmentation ('the social breach') much discussed in the popular media and in the French cultural and intellectual landscape. In his analysis of the scandal of *Baise-moi*, Noël Burch has commented on the hypocrisy of newspapers and has seen their attacking of the film from a formal, stylistic perspective as a strategic pretext. According to Burch, the film was not banned 'because there is an association between sex and violence a little more "raw" than in other films, but because this sexual violence is perpetuated by women against men and it stirs up unspeakable fantasies and fears' (Burch 2007: 160). To Burch, the film exposes 'the reality of carefully hidden female anger against the male establishment; the crime that caused its banning is the crime of *lèse-phallus* [outrage against the phallus], thus a new language was needed: the protection of childhood, the letter of the law' (ibid.).

THE RETURN OF THE REPRESSED

While I largely agree with Noël Burch that the formal dismissal of *Baise-moi* covers over anxieties and fears triggered by the disturbing portrayal of female characters responding to violence with violence, this contempt for the formal politics of the film also worked to mask and neutralise several other issues that are flagged there. On the surface, it seems that the unpalatable display of female violence and graphic sex alone in *Baise-moi* presented critics with a problem. But the controversy it engendered and the discomfort which is played out in some reviews also hint at wider struggles over the meaning of citizenship and national identity that have characterised French culture since the late 1980s, reflecting growing concerns with the politics of identity, the 'integration' of immigrants, feminism and homosexual rights.

In its July 2000 issue, the prestigious political and cultural weekly *Le Nouvel Observateur*, published a dossier entitled 'Pornography, Violence: The Freedom to Say No', discussing the worrying cinematic 'panegyric of violence', particularly in current Hollywood cinema. In a telling diatribe comparing *Baise-moi* with 'the most uncouth American action films', commentator

Laurent Joffrin addressed the identity politics that he identified as lurking behind the film. Having opened his review by declaring that '*Baise-moi* is a disgusting film,' Joffrin then accused *Baise-moi* of being 'openly racist' by showing that 'it's fine to savagely kill people as long as they don't belong to minority groups' (Joffrin 2000). This article is noteworthy in terms of its outrage at the fact that violence in the film is solely meted out against the white majority. (Symptomatically, Joffrin is misguided since Manu kills her own brother, who is also of North African descent.) Despentes's thought, continued the article, stands for 'the apology of force allied with communitarianism [. . .] What do we call this exalted combination of violence and identity, the cult of force and community?', he asks, rhetorically. 'Fascism,' Joffrin concludes. 'Virginie Despentes has made a fascist film' (ibid.).

The negative connotations of the word communitarianism can be seen as a metonymical signifier of larger social and cultural issues. The above review exposes that which is tellingly absent from most reviews of *Baise-moi* and in doing so highlights the ideological stakes governing critical discourse when difference is affirmed. According to Joffrin, *Baise-moi* posed a threat to the cultural establishment because of its representation of difference, arguably through the character of Manu, linking these fears to postcolonial anxieties and identity politics. Indeed, according to Étienne Balibar, 'the post-colony haunts the French situation – in many respects it is its repressed' (Balibar 2007: 55). What the critical outrage around the film reveals, then, is culturally specific concerns around the politics of identity and difference, such as the fear of separatism between the sexes, the cultivation of cultural difference by immigrant populations, and the rise of gay and lesbian activism against discrimination, a central source of concern during the 1990s. Moreover, the description of *Baise-moi* as akin to 'the most uncouth American film' also links the film to 'the counter-model of the United States', a rhetorical model which in the period under consideration 'was constantly evoked, especially in debates regarding minority issues – ethnicity as well as gender and sexuality' (Fassin 2003: 27).

Under pressure in the 1990s in light of demands by particular groups for state recognition, the notion of French universalism was remobilised and reinforced. Significantly, the United States provided a counter-model to the French ideal of assimilation and integration. The American cultural practice of recognising the existence of particular identities was, and still is, perceived as an anti-French Republican model, doing away with the Jacobin notion of equality that posits that differences of race, religion, gender and sexuality are subsumed under the abstract model of the citizen, emphasising the prevalence of citizenship and universalism over interest groups and specific identities. Catherine Raissinger has suggested that recent political debates have imagined 'the virile body of the nation as being assailed by a series of threats from foreign forces that, if not controlled, can weaken and ultimately destroy it. Current dominant representations of the national body, therefore, depend on the othering of a number of human bodies, most prominently, post-colonials, women and homosexuals' (Raissinger 2002: 77).

CONCLUSION: POST-PORN, POST-FEMINIST, POSTCOLONIAL

Tanya Horeck has offered a perceptive examination of how 'the raped woman is not only a sexual other. She is often marked out as other by virtue of ethnic and class positioning' (Horeck 2004: 115). According to Horeck, 'the representation of sexual violence as well as commentaries on it, bring to light cultural unease concerning gender, race and ethnicity' (ibid.). *Baise-moi*'s formal and political engagement with such issues of gender, race and identity was neutralised in favour of a less threatening debate about the visibility of violence and pornography within mainstream cinema. As Despentes suggested in an interview, the film aroused fear and hatred because:

> our two lead actresses have both African roots, one is half-Moroccan, the other half-Algerian and in France, don't harbour any illusions, it is visceral this problem. A lot of people don't want to see two North African women who have been raped taking up arms and shooting European men. That's a bit too close to historical reality. (Despentes in Sharkey 2002)

The privileging of form over questions of representation, particularly when it comes to gender, is typical of French cinephilia's entrenched masculinist perspective where questions of content can easily become evacuated, removing films from their social and cultural context and fostering a fixation on form at times exerting a politically and socially conservative influence (Wimmer 2009). The evacuation of meaning in film culture is also not surprising given a French context where socio-cultural difference is often occulted in order to cultivate an abstract universal ideal. Critical materials engaging with the film and the main questions it has provoked debated its graphic representation of sex and violence and discussed the film itself in formal rather than textual terms, occulting the important way in which issues of sexuality and gender intertwine as well as the link between economic marginalisation and sexual violence which is portrayed in the film. The texts I have just examined thus put the emphasis on graphic sex and the excessive display of physical violence from women, but choose to ignore or separate other socio-cultural issues. Minimising the socio-economic context of the film and avoiding the question of violence against women, critics have mostly stressed the issue of pornography, occulting in the process how the condition of violence in the film and its setting of the *cité* (suburb) can be seen as a metonym for other differences (ethnic, class, sexual and religious).

Decried in the press as exploitative pseudo-pornography and the object of much controversy, *Baise-moi* has been appropriated as a cult film. Flaunting its trash aesthetics, it took a step away from mainstream 'good' taste. Moya Luckett has suggested that 'femininity emerges as arguably *the* structuring force in cult films, and in the process, recasts cinematic intervention into sexual difference' (Luckett 2003: 142, emphasis in original). The controversy around *Baise-moi* also demonstrates the continuing influence of 'art' and 'trash' distinctions and the discourses of taste that circulate and regulate women's engagement with explicitly sexual images. Indeed, that Despentes and Trinh Thi elicited such a response confirms that feminist filmmaking is still perceived as a threat to aesthetic values and to the cultural distinction they seem to warrant. This demonstrates the continuing influence of 'high' and 'low' distinctions and how struggles over taste remain inflected by class, gender, sexuality and cultural difference. What the dynamics of its reception also indicate is the masculinist value system that constructs criteria for good cinema and inclusion into the canon.

The scandal of *Baise-moi*, then, was that it exposed the underlying logic of the abstract republican ideal of universalism, exploring some of the structural inequalities that are foundational to the French republic. The reception of the film revealed unresolved anxieties and concerns about ethnicity, citizenship, gender and sexuality that are played out in contemporary French society. The film was disturbing because it brought to the surface what should best remain hidden: namely, the social salience of class, ethnic and gender difference in the context of new challenges to national identity by minority groups. Marie-Hélène Bourcier has perceptively diagnosed these hostile critical reactions and commented that the film represented 'a threat to Frenchness and dominant French masculinity: white and heterosexual' (Bourcier 2005: 187–206). Bourcier suggests that the film was troubling and hence the subject of fierce controversy and debate 'because of its association with post-integration, post-colonial French culture' (ibid.). Moreover, Bourcier has attributed hostile reactions to the film in terms of its challenging pornography's traditional heterosexist and masculinist content, which she connects with queer strategies of re-appropriation: 'We can thus read the banning of the film as a rejection of the identity politics that threaten republican universalism and hegemonic white heterosexual masculinity' (ibid.). 'By filming like men,' pursues Bourcier, 'the girls of *Baise-moi* have effected a change in traditional gender roles. They deconstruct and re-signify modern pornographic discourse. *Baise-moi* is thus post-feminist, post-pornographic' (ibid.). Despentes and Trinh Thi's film is deliberately rooted in a specific portrayal of French life and it is this very specificity that led to the dismissal of the film. Located at the intersection of feminist, postcolonial and queer concerns, *Baise-moi* appears to have heralded the violent return of that which is repressed in dominant constructions of French national identity.

NOTE

1. All translations from the French are mine.

CHAPTER 12

'Close Your Eyes and Tell Me What You See': Sex and Politics in Lukas Moodysson's Films

Mariah Larsson

In the autumn of 2004, Swedish poet and director Lukas Moodysson released his fifth feature film, *Ett hål i mitt hjärta/A Hole in My Heart*. Most Swedish film reviewers praised the film and its maker, but the film was only seen by around 25,600 spectators in the cinemas. Moreover, some of these 25,600 spectators actually left the theatre during the screening.[1] Regardless of the fact that there is often a rift between critical and audience responses to films, these statistics are still noteworthy, especially considering the large audiences that Moodysson's earlier films had attracted. His second comedy *Tillsammans/ Together* was actually the number one box-office hit in Sweden in 2000, and his third film, *Lilja 4-ever/Lilya 4-ever*, made number three on its release in 2002 despite its sordid and tragic subject matter.[2]

Most probably, the low attendance numbers had to do with the fact that *A Hole in My Heart* was very different from Moodysson's earlier films. Its topic – the shooting of a porn film – was sensationalist indeed, but the film also had no clear linear narrative and contained some deeply disturbing images, amongst them close-ups of plastic surgery on the labia and open-heart surgery. In this regard, the film aligns itself with a comparatively new tradition of extremity within European art cinema and American independent cinema. Like Lars von Trier's *The Idiots* (Denmark, 1998) or Catherine Breillat's *Romance* (France, 1999), *A Hole in My Heart* does not shy away from showing graphic and explicit representations of genitals, sex or violence. Although Moodysson's films have always, in some sense, concerned themselves with human relations in a capitalist, patriarchal and heteronormative ideological system, and although most of them have also dealt with sexuality in different ways – for instance, lesbian love in small-town Sweden in his debut *Fucking Åmål/ Show Me Love* (1998), the sex slave trade in *Lilya 4-ever*, transgenderism in *Container* (2006) and sex tourism in *Mammoth* (2009) – the explicitness of *A Hole in My Heart* and its provocation of the spectator is an unprecedented turn for Moodysson. In this chapter, I will argue that this turn toward a so-called 'new extremism' in *A Hole in My Heart* is motivated by a political principle, which can be understood in relation to the debates about pornography in Sweden. This context is important, since the Swedish debates about pornography have, in a sense, moralised the issue to the extent that only certain standpoints have been viewed as legitimate. Compared with the American pornography debates in the 1980s – the so-called 'sex wars' – an equivalent 'war' in Sweden never really took off since the anti-porn position quickly came to be taken for granted. Moodysson has, from his first film, placed himself on the anti-porn side in political discussion. Despite Moodysson's reputation as a progressive or even radical filmmaker, his films tend to emphasise a platonic, if not puritan, view of sexuality and human relations. As this chapter will demonstrate, there is a political conservatism at the heart of Moodysson's work that is at odds with the more subversive aspects of his filmmaking, including its recourse to disturbingly explicit imagery in *A Hole in My Heart*.

LUKAS MOODYSSON AND THE CONSTRUCTION OF A NATIONAL *AUTEUR*

To date, Moodysson has directed seven feature-length films. One of them, *Terrorister – en film om dom dömda / Terrorists – The Kids They Sentenced* (2003), is a documentary, co-directed with Stefan Jarl, while another, *Container*, is more a piece of video art than a film and was, accordingly, shown in museums as well as released in cinemas.[3] His feature film debut, *Show Me Love*, was an unpretentious comedy, filmed with handheld cameras and featuring young, untrained actors, and had an enormously favourable reception. Almost overnight, Moodysson was seen as a saviour of Swedish cinema, and his next film, *Together*, also a comedy, was the most successful Swedish film of that year. Although the reception of *Show Me Love* was accused of embracing heteronormativity – emphasising the experiences of growing up in small-town Sweden rather than the lesbian experience (Rosenberg 2002: 103–15) – Moodysson had already gained a reputation as a political radical, one which, on the release of *Lilya 4-ever*, was further amplified to the point of figuring Moodysson as a gender political hero.

Although *Lilya 4-ever* was, again, not a very graphic film (perhaps because of the youth of the actors), it seems that Moodysson's political views at this point became a more explicit and transparent part of his authorial persona. In a newspaper article about the film at the time of its release, Moodysson stated: 'It is a film about the society in which we live where everything can be sold and bought, even body parts, like big breasts' (cited in Mårtensson 2002). Nevertheless, the use made of the film by the Swedish government sat uneasily with Moodysson: 'I don't make films to influence the people in power,' he said in an interview in *Dagens Nyheter*, Sweden's largest daily newspaper, in 2003. 'Laws are nice, but the world won't change just because a social democratic politician proposes a new law. That is like a band-aid instead of real medicine' (cited in Wennö 2003).[4]

This quotation from *Dagens Nyheter* discloses, to a degree, Moodysson's ideological positioning and its importance for the construction of his authorial image. The message here is one of radical political intent. We cannot change the world by changing laws; we need to propose a new system. Curing the symptoms is not enough; we need to cure the cause of society's disease. Although *Lilya 4-ever* was not as successful with Swedish audiences as Moodysson's comedies had been, it received much positive attention from Swedish politicians, who financed screenings of the film abroad as well as in Sweden. The intention of these screenings was to inform audiences about trafficking for sexual purposes and to deter people from the practice of buying sex (Hedling 2004). Students in high school, young men doing their military service, and politicians and policy-makers within the European Union as well as the Russian *duma* were shown screenings of the film (Gentele 2003).

The power of the film's message was strongly conveyed by the widely known fact that it was based on a true story. Although the tactic of claiming a film is 'based on a true story' is always a useful marketing device, this time it was especially so since the fate of Dangoule Rasalaite, a young victim of sex trafficking, had been covered extensively in Swedish newspapers.[5] Furthermore, the film was to a large extent shot with handheld cameras, on location in Paldiski, Estonia, with Russian actors and mostly Russian dialogue. These devices further enhanced the claim to authenticity made by the film, an authenticity which reinforced the sense that 'this kind of thing happens for real,' which is a common reaction to the film, judging by user comments and user reviews – for instance, on www.lovefilm.se (a Swedish internet DVD-rental site), but also in an international context, such as the Internet Movie Database (www.imdb.com).

Lilya 4-ever has been widely discussed both within Sweden and abroad. Swedish scholars Olof Hedling and Sven Hansell have, as I have pointed out elsewhere, made similar analyses of the film but drawn different conclusions from it.[6] Where Hedling regards the film as reproducing a national, hegemonic perspective, gender theory scholar Hansell contends that Moodysson is a subversive gender political hero (Hedling 2004; Hansell 2004). Both, however, point to the film's argument that global capitalism is one of the more pressing reasons for Lilya's fate. Furthermore, film scholar and Slavonist Lars Kristensen has compared this film with the Russian film *Interdevochka* (Todorovski, 1989), which has a similar story. Kristensen contends that the Swedish film, although featuring Russian actors and Russian language, portrays concerns that 'largely address the Nordic context' – a contention which is in line with Hedling's argument about a national hegemony (2007). In short, Moodysson's films prior to the release of *A Hole in my Heart*, and the construction of his authorial persona, reflect an ambivalence in Sweden about questions of sex, gender and politics.

NEW EXTREMISM IN SWEDEN

A Hole in My Heart had gained notoriety before it was even released, as the tabloid papers reported that there would be 'warning labels on Moodysson's new film', adding that 'the role was too much for Flinck [the male lead],' who was left nauseated by the film's disgusting climax.[7] No doubt the topic – the shooting of a porn film – stimulated curiosity and was spoken about in highly sensationalist terms. Where the tragic story of *Lilya 4-ever* has a linear narrative and works to evoke pathos in viewers, *A Hole in My Heart* has a scant narrative framework and is more of an intellectual, essayistic attempt to evoke feelings of disgust and uneasiness.

Although Sweden has a reputation for its liberal attitudes toward sex, sexually explicit, extreme cinema has not necessarily had a favourable reception with cinema-goers or critics, suggesting that there is much more ambivalence in Sweden around the question of sexual representation than is immediately apparent. In a study of Swedish film criticism in the first few years of the millennium, Swedish film scholar Charlotte Wiberg points to the conflicting views presented in reviewers' opinions about films that deal with pornography (2006: 267–302, 295). Comparing the reception of Catherine Breillat's *Romance* with that of *A Hole in My Heart*, Wiberg claims that reviewers found Breillat's use of her female lead exploitative whereas Moodysson's similar handling of his female lead was not criticised (ibid.: 295). The negative responses to both *Romance* and *Baise-moi* (Virginie Despentes and Coralie Trinh Thi, France, 2000) need to be seen in the context of the close relationship they establish with the genre of pornography. As Wiberg points out, reviewers saw these films as being 'contaminated by' their closeness to pornography (ibid.). In *Romance*, this is related to the use of well-known porn actor Rocco Siffredi and in *Baise-moi* to the directors'/writers'/female leads' connections to the porn industry (ibid.: 299–300). As a result of this compromising closeness to pornography, these films were unfavourably received by the Swedish critical establishment. Given this outright rejection of French new extremist films, the critical endorsement of Moodysson's film – which details the shooting of a porn film in graphic detail, and replicates many of the visual strategies of other new extreme cinema – seems somewhat puzzling. It is worth noting that while Swedish critics rejected the French films as being complicit with the pornographic industry, *A Hole in My Heart* did not receive the same treatment, and its message was taken to be unambiguously critical. These responses to *A Hole in My Heart* are bound up with Moodysson's authorial persona; critics were able to read, and in many senses take for granted, the film's critical message because of Moodysson's reputation as a politically subversive filmmaker, despite the film's ambiguous play with tropes and images of pornography. Furthermore, as Wiberg argues, Moodysson can be regarded as belonging to a distinctly male tradition of cinematic subversion (which includes *auteurs* as diverse as Pier Paolo Pasolini, David Cronenberg, Lars von Trier and Vilgot Sjöman, the latter of *I am curious* fame), whereby a 'male priesthood in the arena of film [is] consecrated' (ibid.: 295).

According to stories that sprung up around the shooting of *A Hole in My Heart*, the actors stayed in the cramped and sordid one-bedroom apartment which is the site of the film for the whole shoot, bringing reality TV shows such as *Big Brother* to mind.[8] There are four characters in the film: the producer/director of the porn film, Rickard (Thorsten Flinck); the two performers, Tess (Sanna Bråding) and Geko (Goran Marjanovic); and Rickard's teenage son, Eric (Björn Almroth), who has nothing to do with the porn shoot and stays in his room for most of the film. The interaction between the characters is intertwined with different kinds of images and scenes which show, among other things, plastic surgery of the labia, open-heart surgery, Barbie and Action Man playing kinky games, and a woman's genitals and anus (eventually disclosed as artificial) being penetrated by different types of dildos. These graphic images run alongside the appearance of less confrontational, more traditionally beautiful images, such as when the character Geko runs in a field. These images and scenes are juxtaposed with the interactions in the apartment, forming intellectual montages clearly meant to disturb us and make us think simultaneously. At key moments in the film, Moodysson uses the added effect of a soundtrack to counter the visuals; such moments appear to have an overt 'message' to reveal, as when the plastic surgery of the labia is accompanied by the characteristic moans and cries of a woman in a porn film. The message of the film, therefore, is not wholly reducible to its narrative framing. Rather, the narrative would appear to offer a pretext for its ideological statements, conveyed through audiovisual analogies and intellectual montages. These statements have to do with the relations between power, sexuality and violence in the dominant capitalist and patriarchal ideological system; they are about alienation in a Marxist sense of the word, the commercialisation of the everyday and the commodification of human beings. This may be why Moodysson chose to make a film about the shooting of a porn movie, because this context offers a privileged relation to such critical positions – at least if your political perspective as regards pornography is first and foremost the degradation of women, as a 'handbook' in how to oppress women.

There are interesting links here between Moodysson's film and the Swedish anti-porn movement (such as Riksorganisationen för kvinnojourer och tjejjourer i Sverige, ROKS, which is still active; and Folkaktionen mot pornografi, which was active between 1985 and 1999). Such movements have historically been influenced by the anti-porn side of the so-called 'American sex wars', as well as by the early feminist anti-porn movement in Sweden of the early 1970s, exemplified, for instance, by the socialist-feminist group Grupp 8.[9] For certain (and for many years predominant) kinds of Swedish feminism, the relation of patriarchy to capitalism is self-evident, the one dependent on the other in order to reinforce the status quo. Moodysson's film would appear to reinforce such associations through its treatment of commercialised sex as both a form of empty commodification (as exemplified by the references to plastic surgery) and degradation on a par with other systemic forms of violence, such as torture and, by extension, war. The teenage son, Eric, who plays the role of truth-teller in the film, points out at one point that torture, violence and war are all practised by men. In one scene, Geko and Rickard attack Tess – who is expecting to shoot a regular porn scene – with masks over their faces and baseball bats. The scene illustrates the film's argument that porn and violence only exist on a sliding scale, that they are not separate from one another. There has been and still is a widespread notion that pornography not only constitutes violence against women in itself, but also that it allows for sub-genres such as snuff films (films allegedly showing real murders) and films showing torture to flourish as part of this same patriarchal logic of violent aggression.[10] Later in the film, Geko and Rickard shoot at a picture of a nude model where the head has been replaced by a target. However, they do not aim at the target but at the model's nipples and vagina. Again, the scene might be seen as an illustration of the closeness between objectification, pornographic sex (the nude model) and phallocentric violence.

THE DESTRUCTION OF VISUAL PLEASURE

A Hole in My Heart would appear, then, to be not only an anti-porn film that takes issue with the degradation of women in the name of masculine pleasure, but also a film that aims for what Mulvey describes as the 'destruction of pleasure as a radical weapon'. In the introduction to her seminal article 'Visual Pleasure and Narrative Cinema', she states: 'It is said that analyzing pleasure, or beauty, destroys it. That is the intention of this essay' (2009: 15–16). One could claim that *A Hole in My Heart* ventures something similar: by analysing the (still male-dominated and constructed) terms of pleasure and beauty as they are exemplified by pornography, Moodysson's film attempts to thwart them. Like other films associated with the new extremism, *A Hole in My Heart* seems very consciously determined to destroy any experience of visual pleasure – or pleasure of any other kind – for the spectator. Although Mulvey's article, written in 1975 about classical Hollywood cinema, may seem somewhat out of place in this discussion of recent extreme filmmaking traditions, it nevertheless remains a key reference point in a Swedish context, having been translated not only once, but twice, into Swedish in 1995 (when Moodysson studied directing at the Dramatic Institute) and in 2001.[11] Through *A Hole in My Heart*'s visual style, through its non-linear, fragmented narrative and through its highly disturbing events (such as the 'snuff' sequence) and its explicit imagery (such as the surgical inserts), the film arguably seeks the destruction of (visual) pleasure. There is a consistency to this strategy, which has to do with both the reification of humans and a capitalism that is still dependent on patriarchy to uphold its hegemony. Furthermore, from the ideological perspective of the film, contemporary Swedish society is regarded as placing too much emphasis on the surface and the superficial, thereby creating a desire for what we can look at but never really reach. However, such a message invariably jars against the film's own visual strategies, which revel in precisely this kind of superficial and exploitative imagery. In this respect, the film's opening line, 'Close your eyes and tell me what you see,' is telling; it is only by closing your eyes you will be able to see the truth, because the gaze evokes desire and desire is corrupted by the patriarchal, capitalist system. At the end of the film, Eric puts band-aids over his eyes; in the film's logic this gesture is easily interpreted as a way to avert the corruption of the gaze, an attempt to grasp at an inner truth rather than look at the superficial surface (Larsson 2006). The obvious paradox here is that such an injunction would also apply to the film's own recourse to explicit images. Hence, such a quest for enlightenment is something that the film both advertises and thwarts.

At the beginning of the film, we see the characters in very brief shots, sitting in the cramped and untidy apartment. All of them – Tess, Geko and Rickard – are naked, except for the son, Eric, who is dressed in the black clothes he will wear throughout the film. Again, the film uses a subverted logic – a clichéd take on this opening would be that they are naked and therefore 'natural' and 'true' – but in the film, nakedness is associated with vulnerability and superficiality, whereas the son – the only character who is always fully dressed – is the one who speaks the truth. Nudity is clearly not the path to liberation or enlightenment. Moreover, although Tess is shown through much of the film dressed in pornographic clothing – sequined underwear, high heels, hair extensions – she is always shot in a way which does not enhance her sexiness but rather makes her look as if she is masquerading as a porn star. This is true for the male actors as well, who are never shot in a flattering way but are always made to look unattractive so as to emphasise the caricatured nature of their performance. Moodysson thus carefully avoids the objectification of his characters, inflecting their roles with a critical vision that makes links between pornography, the superficial logic of commodification, and a systemic and pervasive patriarchal violence.

After the 'snuff' sequence, Tess leaves the apartment but returns later with a shopping trolley full of snacks and junk food. In these sequences, food displaces sex as the main focus of the film, and is used as an extended metaphor for sex. Geko, Rickard and Tess indulge an orgy of junk food consumption which is every bit as disgusting as the earlier scenes detailing the shooting of the porn film, if not more so. For instance, Geko urinates in a wine glass which Tess drinks from, they squirt ketchup on each other, and Geko pushes food and then squirts washing-up liquid into Tess's mouth. Rickard films it all with his camera. The orgy culminates in a sequence that clearly evokes a pornographic cum shot: Tess is instructed to lie on the couch and to open her mouth as wide as possible. Meanwhile, Geko sticks his fingers down his throat in a gesture that, in the terms of this analogy, resembles masturbation. When he is about to vomit/come, he turns towards Tess's face and vomits into her mouth and face while Rickard is filming. A more obvious (and more disgusting) statement against pornography could not be made. By replacing sperm with vomit, the film defamiliarises what pornography has normalised – the degradation of women.

Hence, this finale accomplishes a critique similar to those sequences in which pornographic sounds accompany the images of plastic surgery of the labia (Larsson 2006: 255). These images, genital close-ups reminiscent of those in pornographic films (which in Swedish anti-porn rhetoric are often termed 'gynecological images'), also function to destroy visual pleasure, together with the images of open-heart surgery. When I saw the film at the cinema on its premiere, these were the scenes when people left the audience. As images of surgery, they function to abject the human body, both by showing body parts which are usually hidden from view, and by showing the human body passive, immobile, as if dead, and in connection with strange and defamiliarising objects, such as the scalpel. Additionally, these images pathologise the female genitalia. But why should it be acceptable and non-exploitative to show female genitalia in close-up with the intent to shock and disgust but not with the intent to arouse?

One way of answering this question could be to argue that Moodysson's films are moral and ethical statements on the Western, capitalist, consumerist world in which we live. If the gaze corrupts us, the only possible strategy would be to close our eyes. If close-ups of female genitalia objectify and harm women, then it is perhaps a worthwhile destruction of pleasure to show abject close-ups of surgery of the labia, accompanied by the moans and cries of a porn film soundtrack. One could say, too, that by evoking these questions,

Moodysson opens up an ethical discussion about Western society and ideology. However, as Michele Aaron contends in *Spectatorship: The Power of Looking On*, there is a difference between how 'some films nurture reflection, recognition and responsibility, and some prevent it' (2007: 109). Discussing the Dogme 95 manifesto and the films made in connection with it, Aaron claims: 'Spectatorship, then, is neither to be cosied by the blanket of fantasy, nor animated, temporarily, by the shock of the real, but insistently elbowed by ethical implication' (2007: 107). Although it seems to me that Aaron tends to idealise the Dogme film makers such as Lars von Trier, she emphasises a spectatorial position which is not necessarily promoted by the strategies of a film such as *A Hole in My Heart*. Instead, *A Hole in My Heart* risks either preaching to the converted or simply alienating audiences who fail to see past the film's visual provocations. Attempting to shock the spectator into a political realisation, *A Hole in My Heart* could well be regarded as a propagandistic film if not for its essayistic construction, which undermines its potential for widespread popularity, but also calls into question some of its presumed political messages.

Sex, in Moodysson's work, is part of the corruption of society. In *A Hole in My Heart*, the metaphor of food for sex in the second part of the film is, in this sense, crude but apt: junk food equals pornographic sex. What, then, are we to make of Moodysson's recourse to explicit imagery in *A Hole in My Heart*, and the film's persistent use of pornographic tropes and conventions which seem to be complicit with just such a corrupt society? This explicitness needs to be seen in light of Moodysson's presumed unambiguous political standpoint, which in its turn finds its justification in the national context of the debates around pornography in Sweden. Since the evil of pornography has been well established in Swedish ideological discourse, providing a moral benefit for those who are against pornography, there has been little effort to problematise or complicate these debates, which remain highly polarised: either one is 'for' or 'against' pornography. Moodysson's films tap into, while subtly reconfiguring, the terms of this polarity.

The release of *A Hole in My Heart* coincided with a backlash that was developing during these years against a particular type of feminism in social-democratic Sweden, the crux of which concerned the question of pornography. In 2000, for instance, a documentary about the porn industry entitled *Shocking Truth*, directed by Alexa Wolf, was released, and it caused an outcry. Strongly critical of pornography, it was shown to the Swedish parliament in an influential screening. As a result, alterations were made to Swedish film censorship laws. (The period a censor could work was changed from a maximum of twelve years to a maximum of six years.) However, the strong anti-porn tendency witnessed during this period would shift, and by 2005, a highly controversial documentary in two parts, *Könskriget*, about one of the organisations financing Alexa Wolf's film (ROKS), was aired on Swedish television. The documentary provided a cutting critique of hegemonic feminism in Sweden, undermining many of the arguments made by ROKS about the relation between pornography and violence against women. Although the bias of the documentary was fiercely debated by leading feminists, its impact was still remarkable. And in 2008, the Swedish Film Institute funded a collection of short films, consisting of twelve feminist porn films, *Dirty Diaries* (Engberg, 2009). Although these films were feminist, the juxtaposition of the words 'feminist' and 'porn' had been unconceivable only a few years earlier and was actually debated in newspapers and on blogs after the release of the collection.

In order to endorse feminist values, the debates in Sweden around pornography created a climate in which, to be 'politically correct', one had to eschew any kind of engagement with 'pornographic' imagery of the kind Moodysson's work appears to revel in and exaggerate. Although Moodysson has never backed away from showing gruesome images – such as, for instance, the tricks filmed with a subjective camera from Lilya's point-of-view in *Lilya 4-ever* and the drab milieus of Paldiski in *Lilya 4-ever* and of Chernobyl in *Container*, or the children scouring for something sellable or edible in the rubbish dump somewhere in the Philippines in *Mammoth* – it is in *A Hole in My Heart* where he most aggressively attacks the visual pleasure of the viewer by using abject images, juxtaposed with sound in a manner clearly intended to evoke strong emotions and make the audience draw intellectual conclusions. The explicitness of the film's engagement with sexual display, combined with the seeming transparency of Moodysson's 'messages', is likely to render his films problematic in a changing hegemonic context, and perhaps especially so in the very small cultural environment of Sweden.

Through the construction of his authorial persona, his films have been aligned with a strong political pathos that can be located within the political left and the social movements of the past ten years or so, yet these politics are contradicted by the platonic strains of his work. Indeed, for all of his political posturing, there is also a more conservative strain running through Moodysson's films, which tend to romanticise certain kinds of relationships and call into question his status as a subversive filmmaker. Consider, for instance, the focus on children and young people in his films. Moodysson is a skilful director of children and is often praised as someone who is loyal to the child's perspective. The teenagers in *Show Me Love* deal awkwardly with all the hazards of secondary school, the children in *Together* seem to regard the grown-ups' game-playing with clarity, and Lilya's best and most loyal friend is the young Volodya. In *Mammoth*, as well, it is the children who suffer. Furthermore, as Hansell notes in his article on Moodysson, the children have platonic love relationships based on kindred spirits rather than on sexual attraction (Hansell 2004: 105–7). When Agnes and Elin 'leave the closet' at the end of *Show Me Love*, for all Elin's cocky, 'We're going home to fuck,' they drink chocolate milk, essentially a children's beverage. There is a Christian tendency in Moodysson's works to look for holiness within those who might be regarded as the lowest of the low, the forlorn, the prodigal children and the sinners. In *A Hole in My Heart*, Tess and Erik develop a platonic relationship similar to that of Agnes and Elin, Fredrik and Eva (in *Together*), and Lilya and Volodya.[12] Tess's status as porn performer is sidestepped in a sense by her simultaneous status as victim. In similar fashion, Lilya preserves her childlike innocence through all the abuse and the degrading encounters with clients, praying to the postcard of an angel that she has brought with her to Sweden. Although Tess's victimhood might be more contested (in the beginning of the film, she claims that her dream has always been to be a porn star), she is still depicted as lured by a false dream of fame. Eric, like Volodya, seems to regard the world around him with childlike lucidity.

Furthermore, there is a strong use of religious symbolism in Moodysson's work. Consider, for example, the scene with the baseball bats in *A Hole in My Heart*, interrupted by Eric, who for once leaves his room. Tess escapes from the apartment and there is a brief interlude in the film in which Tess lies down on a pavement in the car park outside a supermarket. There are inserts with close-ups of Eric's face. Suddenly, with rapid editing, Tess is shown outside an entrance to a block of flats with blood streaming from her hands, like a stigma which identifies her with Christ. This type of religious symbolism is not unusual in the work of Moodysson – his second collection of poetry was titled *Evangelium enligt Lukas Moodysson/ The Gospel According to Lukas Moodysson* (1989), and in *Lilya 4-ever* Lilya and Volodya become angels in surreally beautiful sequences. Moodysson himself says that it is practising Christians who are most susceptible to his work because they tend to take life seriously (cited in Gustafsson 2004). But these references also work to uphold an idealised, platonic and quasi-religious view of human relationships that is at odds with Moodysson's reputation as a subversive filmmaker, not to mention as a gender political hero. This seeming contradiction is inherent to a degree in certain strands of Swedish feminist thought, as well as within the anti-porn movement. As I have argued here, the graphic visuals of *A Hole in My Heart*, borrowing their aesthetics from pornography, are seen as justified because of their aim to shock, disgust and disturb the audience into taking a stance against pornography. While the film's combative strategies to destroy visual pleasure are in keeping with that of other new European extreme cinema, my argument here is that it may be necessary as well to sound a cautionary note regarding the apparent subversiveness of Moodysson's filmmaking: the politics as well as the visual excessiveness of his films reveal a strong reactionary tendency in his extreme cinema.

NOTES

1. Seeing the film on its premiere in my hometown, I actually witnessed people leaving. It was reported in the newspapers the day after.
2. The audience numbers were taken from the Swedish Film Institute's webpage in 2005. Since then, however, the webpage has been reorganised and these statistics removed. They are recounted in Mariah Larsson (2006: 245).
3. For information in English on Moodysson and the production company which has produced his films, see Anna Westerståhl Stenport (2010).
4. All quotations from newspaper articles are translated by the author.
5. Dangoule Rasalaite was a victim of trafficking from Lithuania to Sweden, where she was made to work as a prostitute. Her fate became known after she committed suicide by jumping from a bridge in Malmö (in southern Sweden) in early 2000. She was sixteen years old. Mary Mårtensson (2002), 'Här dog Lilja – i verkligheten', *Aftonbladet* 26 August, http://www.aftonbladet.se/wendela/article90756.ab, accessed 30 August 2010.
6. Olof Hedling (2004); Sven Hansell (2004); Mariah Larsson (2006, 2010).
7. 'Rollen som blir för mycket för Flinck' (2004), *Aftonbladet* 4 September; 'Fick andnöd av sin egen äckelscen' (2004), *Expressen* 9 September; 'Varningstext för Moodyssons nya' (2004), *Kristianstadbladet* 9 September.
8. The Big Brother format was created by the Dutch company Endemol and aired for the first time in 1999 in Holland. In Sweden, the show aired for six seasons between 2000 and 2006.
9. For a further discussion of Swedish feminism and its relation to pornography in the early 1970s, see Mariah Larsson (2008).
10. The connection between pornography and snuff films within the American anti-porn movement is discussed by Linda Williams in her study *Hardcore: Power, Pleasure, and the 'Frenzy of the Visible'* (1999).
11. Mulvey's essay has been translated by Anders Åberg as 'Spelfilmen och lusten att se', in Andersson and Hedling (eds) (1995) and by Sven-Olov Wallenstein as 'Visuell lust och narrative film', in Arrhenius (ed.) (2001).
12. These relationships are discussed further in Larsson (2006).

PART IV

Ethics and Spectatorship in the New Extremism

CHAPTER 13

Lars von Trier's *Dogville*: A Feel-Bad Film

Nikolaj Lübecker

Over the last fifteen to twenty years Lars von Trier has firmly established himself as one of the best-known provocateurs in international cinema. This reputation results from a combination of at least three elements. Firstly, the ideas explored: many of von Trier's films combine religious, psychological, sexual and political themes in ways that are bound to provoke. Secondly, the Lars von Trier persona: he is notorious for scandalous remarks at press conferences (referring, for example, to Polanski as 'the midget', himself as 'the greatest director in the world' and George W. Bush [less provocatively?] as 'an asshole') and for performances in a typical avant-garde tradition (at a celebration of one hundred years of filmmaking, von Trier declared 'the death of film', read the Dogme 95 manifesto and then left the stage). Finally, there is the graphic nature of at least some of his films: for instance, the images of unsimulated sex in *The Idiots* (1998) or the female circumcision in *Antichrist* (2009). This last element is perhaps what most obviously ties von Trier to the new extreme as defined by James Quandt (2004), but it is far from being a necessary component in von Trier's provocations. *Dogville* (2003) is a case in point: despite being much less graphic than *The Idiots* and *Antichrist*, the reception of this film clearly demonstrates that, once again, von Trier managed to get under the skin of his viewers: 'anti-humanism!' was the verdict of the Cannes jury.

In the following, I shall analyse how the *Dogville* provocation works, and what von Trier is aiming for through it. I will begin with a distinction between two (not mutually exclusive) approaches to the film. I will then argue that the specificity of *Dogville* develops from the interplay between what would often be seen as two irreconcilable aesthetic systems: Brecht's and the Surrealists'. Finally, I shall make explicit what I mean by the notion of the 'feel-bad' film, and thereby briefly situate *Dogville* within the context of the new extreme.

ANALYSING *DOGVILLE*

For some viewers *Dogville* is a film about Grace (Nicole Kidman). We are in 1932, and she is the beautiful stranger who, under mysterious circumstances, comes to the small town of Dogville at the foot of the Rocky Mountains. The idealist wannabe author of the town, Tom (Paul Bettany), is charmed by her beauty and convinces the citizens of Dogville that by welcoming her they can demonstrate their attachment to the virtues of hospitality and community. Grace makes herself accepted by helping the community, but when both gangsters and police appear to be searching for her the townspeople decide that it is only fair for them to ask 'more' of her. (The film repeatedly manipulates this economic vocabulary.) She thus goes from being a helper and errand girl to a hardworking servant and, eventually, sexual slave, mercilessly exploited by the male citizens of the town. When Grace refuses Tom, the only man who has not turned rapist, he sends for the gangsters, thereby giving her over to what we expect to be her certain death.

But then (after two hours and thirty minutes) the reversal takes place: the gangster boss (James Caan) turns out to be her loving father, and it transpires that the two of them had argued about his ruthless methods and the idealistic daughter had set out to prove the good in human nature. Now that she has failed miserably to demonstrate her point, her father urges her to judge the citizens of Dogville by her own standards: if she had acted like them, she would never forgive herself, and she should therefore not forgive them either. Grace initially protests, but then acquiesces, finally putting the principle to work with a cruelty that surprises even her father: every citizen is killed, the town is burnt down, and Grace and the gangsters leave.

This screenplay has allowed its viewers to engage in very varied discussions of a mainly ethical and political nature. *Dogville* has been regarded as a reflection on the logic of exchange and the elements that escape and challenge the (capitalist) economic sphere – grace, gifts and hospitality (Chiesa 2007; Nobus 2007). The film has been seen as a confrontation between New Testament ethics ('turn the other cheek') and Old Testament ethics ('an eye for an eye'; Fibiger 2003). Encouraged by von Trier's own statements (and a credit sequence composed of documentary photos of American poverty), critics such as Roger Ebert and Todd McCarthy have considered the film as an attack on American society; the film is said to depict a USA in which exploitation and xenophobia are particularly prevalent (for a nuanced discussion see Bainbridge 2007: 142). At the same time, von Trier has also been accused of running errands for George W. Bush by transforming complex political problems into ethical problems of a Manichean character (Rancière 2004). I shall return below to some of these ethical and political discussions, but in order to do so, I will first sketch out a second group of readings that should not, I repeat, be seen as opposed to the first.

For a second group of viewers (to which I belong), this is less a film about Dogville and Grace than a manipulative 'machine' (Horsley 2005: 18) designed to bring out some strong, anti-social drives in the spectator. The central role is occupied not by Grace, but by the spectator.[1] One of the earliest variations of this reading was offered by Adela Abella and Nathalie Zilkha in the *International Journal of Psychoanalysis* in 2004. As these authors explain, von Trier first presents Grace as a victim of the sadism of the citizens of Dogville. The very special *mise-en-scène* (discussed below) 'creates an illusion of transparency and clarity' (Abella and Zilkha 2004: 1521) that lures the spectators into believing they occupy an almost transcendental position in relation to the events. This distance, argue Abella and Zilkha, is likely to make us condemn the citizens of Dogville without questioning our own position. However, with the final reversal we understand that Grace is *not* a simple victim. She has had a choice: she could have sent for her father. Maybe her pride has prevented her from doing this, but maybe she has also been inviting these humiliations, drawing them out of the citizens of Dogville?[2] Suddenly we realise that we have been identifying with a perverse subject. However, this realisation, continue Abella and Zilkha, comes too late to relieve us of our identification with Grace, and at the end of the film we are likely to maintain the identification, deny the perversion, and instead feel relief at the apocalypse:

> owing to the unbearable nature of what we have had to endure while watching the film, we are caught up like Grace in participating emotionally in the final vengeance, experiencing – consciously, unconsciously, openly or covertly – a feeling of relief at the violent destruction of the village which allows us to evade the necessity of thinking. We collude in Grace's perverse destructivity. 'The beast' is lurking in us, too. Lars von Trier has awakened it. (Abella and Zilkha 2004: 1525)

I cannot enter into a detailed discussion of Abella and Zilkha's reading, but I do want to emphasise my agreement with their conclusion: the film is manipulating the spectator, and the aim of these manipulations is to bring out 'the beast' in us.

There are (at least) two clear indications that this film is explicitly concerned with the position of the spectator. The first of these indications is encountered just before the closing credits. It is widely acknowledged that one of the most original elements in *Dogville* is its *mise-en-scène*. The film was shot in a vast hangar formerly used for the construction of locomotives; there is no natural lighting and very few props; houses are chalk lines drawn on the ground, and actors open invisible doors that creak. One way of describing the effect of this *mise-en-scène* is to say that throughout the film von Trier expects his spectators to do the imagining. It is therefore significant that in the very last shots the dog in the town, Moses, suddenly materialises from his chalk lines outside the house of Vera (Patricia Clarkson) and Chuck (Stellan Skarsgård). We see a Rottweiler who rises from the ground and barks in the direction of a camera that descends towards him, before, finally, the screen fades to black. It might be said, then, that the camera movement brings the spectator down to a fusion with the dog. In so far as this shot breaks with the aesthetic of the preceding two hours and forty minutes, it is logical to read it as a meta-shot. The spectator has already seen the way in which 'Dogville bares its teeth' and has just witnessed Grace's horrific yet enthralling revenge. More than that: he or she has helped to produce the images that lead to the long-awaited revenge, and when this revenge is finally performed, with a combination of mathematical logic and unrestricted violence,[3] it is difficult for the spectator not to get carried away. Von Trier capitalises on this, as with the appearance of the dog he takes over and confronts us with the roots of our own imaginary: 'the beast within us has materialised' (Abella and Zilkha 2004: 1525).

Before moving on to the second argument, it is relevant to add a specifically Danish-German interpretation of this shot. In the Danish and German languages there exists the expression 'den indre svinehund'/'der innere Schweinehund' – literally, 'the inner swine dog' or, more idiomatically, 'the inner bastard'. In Denmark this expression became popular in the late 1980s, when it was introduced into debates about immigration and widespread Danish xenophobia. For instance, it is often said – including by von Trier himself[4] – that the very influential Danish nationalist party 'appeals to our inner bastard'. This link between the 'inner bastard' and psychological drives that can be exploited for xenophobic purposes points back to the most famous use of the expression. In 1932 (the year in which Grace comes to Dogville), the German socialist politician Kurt Schumacher debated with Joseph Goebbels in the Reichstag in Berlin. Schumacher – who was soon to be sent to different concentration camps before, post-war, becoming the leader of the Social Democratic Party (SPD) – created a minor scandal by stating that 'the entire national socialist propaganda is a constant appeal to the inner bastard in man' (Iversen 1987: 89). It is this use of the expression that has found its way into the Danish language, and it is this 'inner bastard' – which, psychoanalytically, goes by the name of Thanatos – that 'bares its teeth' in Dogville, in Grace, and finally in us.

Let us turn, then, to the second argument for considering *Dogville* to be a film that explicitly negotiates the relation with the spectator. The idea of using Grace to demonstrate a specific point (such as the omnipresence of the inner bastard) is openly explored by the film itself, as both Tom and von Trier use Grace to construct an argument. When Grace arrives in the town, Tom is giving lectures in the mission house on the topic of hospitality. His approach to lecturing is 'evidence'-based; he works with examples. In this regard, the arrival of Grace seems like a gift from above, and it allows Tom (whose second name is Edison) to pronounce his favourite line: Let me illustrate! Considering the link just mentioned between Tom and von Trier, it is not surprising that Tom's name signals his ties to cinema. (Edison was the major driving force behind the Kinetoscope and the Kinetograph, and as such he was instrumental in the invention of cinema.) This obviously does not mean that Tom simply *is* von Trier; for most of the film, Tom seeks to use Grace to demonstrate the generosity of the citizens of Dogville (and to conceal his own emotional and sexual interest in Grace behind a superficies of intellectualism), whereas von Trier uses her to demonstrate the omnipresence of the death drive. Nevertheless, the close – and self-ironical – link between Tom and von Trier makes it difficult to ignore the often very meta-filmic dimension of the dialogue. An example can be found at the end of the film when Tom, who is trying to save his own life by emphasising the didactic value of Grace's sufferings, utters the following speech:

> although using people is not very charming, I think you have to agree that this specific illustration has surpassed all expectations. It said so much about being human! It's been painful, but I think you'll also have to agree it's been edifying – wouldn't you say?

With such passages, von Trier emphasises the self-reflexive dimension of the film. However, just as with the images of Moses, these moments of self-reflexivity are not moments at which the film folds upon itself, but rather ones at which it speaks directly to the spectator, thereby implicating him or her in the film. Von Trier is making assumptions about our viewing experience, and he is challenging the position that we occupy. I believe these confrontations with the spectator rely on a combination of Brechtian and surrealist aesthetics.

BRECHT AND SURREALISM

Numerous critics have argued that *Dogville* is a Brechtian film. The reasons for making this claim are obvious, and I shall therefore mention them only briefly. Firstly, it is worth noting that von Trier himself has explained that the film borrows a part of its plot from Brecht and Weil's song *Pirate Jenny* from *The Threepenny Opera*. Von Trier originally wanted Nina Simone's version of this song (about Jenny's revenge and the killing of an entire town) to accompany the photomontage at the end of the film, but the idea was discarded because he felt it would have been too obvious. However, this is not von Trier's only reference to Brecht:

> I was also inspired to a degree by Bertolt Brecht and his kind of very simple, pared-down theatre. My theory is that you forget very quickly that there are no houses or whatever. This makes you invent the town for yourself but more importantly, it makes you zoom in on the people. (von Trier cited in Bainbridge 2007: 145)

In light of this remark, it is hardly surprising that the chalk lines and lack of props are generally considered to be instances of *Verfremdungseffekte* (a point to which I will return later). Furthermore, the narrator (John Hurt) offers an ironic framing of the melodramatic story, and thereby imbeds an element of distance within the film. Due to the very written nature of his text (reinforced by literary techniques such as the division of the film into a prologue and nine chapters), the narrator also gives *Dogville* an epic character that (at least initially) prevents the spectator from 'throwing himself into the action like a stone into the river' – as Brecht writes of the kind of drama he seeks to avoid. Add to this the *Lehrstück* dimension that I have already mentioned (the fact that von Trier so clearly and self-consciously presents this film as a didactic engagement with 'the problem of Dogville'), and it seems obvious why Brecht is the most common intertext in studies of *Dogville*. Leaving aside the more technical aspects of Brecht's aesthetic and looking to the ideological motivation that underpins the dramaturgy, we encounter the well-known fact that Brecht's ideas are motivated by a materialist philosophy and a strongly anti-cathartic (anti-Aristotelian) stance. The reason Brecht does not encourage his public to throw themselves into the 'plot-river' is that he seeks intellectual engagement rather than emotional absorption; he wants us to search for political solutions to the conflicts with which the play engages.

We may, though, begin to wonder about the limits of von Trier's Brechtianism. Is von Trier's film not an example of the emotional manipulation about which Brecht is so sceptical? What is the status of catharsis in *Dogville*? If we say that the film manipulates the spectator to a point at which a beast is unleashed (via what is, until ten minutes before the end of the film, an exercise in concealment and mystification), then it is obvious that von Trier's film is far from being a case of orthodox Brechtianism. In order to understand how the *Dogville* 'machine' works, I would therefore like to introduce a very different conceptualisation of the cathartic experience.[5]

Contemporaneous with Brecht (in the mid-1930s), we encounter a theorisation of Dionysian activities, Greek tragedy and catharsis at the margins of the surrealist movement in Paris. Just like Brecht, authors like Antonin Artaud and Georges Bataille were interested in creating a politically progressive aesthetic along (unorthodox) Marxist lines, and in Artaud's case (as in Brecht's) this attempt was tied to a subversion of the naturalist drama. Crucially, however, these authors of surrealist sensibility did not share Brecht's critique of empathy and the cathartic. On the contrary: for Artaud and Bataille the emotional and physical immersion of the spectator was a pre-condition for the production of a new and progressive form of subjectivity; only by appealing to the body of the spectator (by taking a step beyond intellectual appeal) would it be possible to liberate the public:

> Infused with the idea that the masses think with their senses first and foremost and that it is ridiculous to appeal primarily to our understanding as we do in everyday psychological theatre, the Theatre of Cruelty proposes to resort to mass theatre, thereby rediscovering a little of the poetry in the ferment of great, agitated crowds hurled against one another, sensations only too rare nowadays, when masses of holiday crowds throng the streets. (Artaud 1970: 65)

Inspired by rituals from ancient Greece and non-Western cultures, these surrealists attempted to provoke and overwhelm the spectator (or reader) in the hope that he or she would emerge revitalised from the ritualistic experience. In Artaud's famous theorisations of the 'Theatre of Cruelty' and Georges Bataille's writings at the time of *Contre-attaque* (1935–6) and *Acéphale* (1936–9), we thus find a strong belief in a correlation between empathy, transgression and emancipation. A comparable logic can be found in many of von Trier's films.

It is well known that Brecht's aesthetic developed considerably over the years. In *A Short Organum for the Theatre* (1948), for instance, he expresses regret at some of his earlier remarks about discarding the emotional appeal of the theatre. At the same time, Bataille's theorisations developed towards a gradual disappearance of both the anti-rationalist remarks and the dubious celebration of the agitated masses found in some of the earlier texts. Nevertheless, even if Brecht and Bataille are less irreconcilable than one would think, it is undeniable that the Epic Theatre and the surrealist ideas of Cruelty represent two very different aesthetic positions. The specificity of *Dogville*, I believe, is that it holds these incompatible frameworks together and, indeed, derives its tension from the conflictual relation between the two. Needless to say, in combining the epic and the surrealist, von Trier deviates from both of these pre-existing sets of theorisation.

With these two aesthetic systems briefly sketched out, let me now return to the *mise-en-scène*. We saw above the way in which von Trier talks about Brecht's pared-down aesthetic, stressing that it allows spectators to focus on the intersubjective relations in the film (something which could be understood along the lines of a Brechtian prioritisation of the sociological). However, we also saw that he remarks that this pared-down aesthetic 'makes you invent the town for yourself'. Another von Trier quotation goes further in this direction:

in the *Manderlay* DVD extras (a film which uses a similar *mise-en-scène*), he describes the way in which children play, explaining that they can create a world from things that are absent, and that these fantasy universes become more exhilarating than any toy universe could possibly have been. Von Trier thus suggests that the pared-down aesthetic can be used to make the cinematic experience as absorbing as possible. This does not mean that von Trier's minimalist set is not alienating – because it is. However, it is also, and at the same time, engaging.

That *Dogville* very consciously plays this game of distanciation and emotional involvement can be seen in one of its most powerful scenes. When Chuck rapes Grace on the floor of his and Vera's house, the first part of the scene, which leads up to the rape, is filmed primarily as a series of close-ups and with a very mobile handheld camera – like so many other scenes in the film. The intimacy is unbearable, and it is heightened by the whispering voices that highlight the oppressive nature of small-town life. The second part of the scene, the actual rape, is dominated by long shots; Chuck and Grace are in the background but the rape remains clearly visible if we look through the townspeople in the foreground who are unaware of what is happening. A number of zooms link the foreground and the background, thereby communicating the complicity of all the citizens of *Dogville* (see also Laine 2006). The scene thus pushes the spectator from an unbearable intimacy into a number of more 'structural shots' in a way that invites intellectual engagement while remaining excruciating in its emotional charge.

At this point, a clarification is required. On the one hand, I have argued that von Trier often shares the surrealist belief in the correlation between empathy, transgression and emancipation. On the other, I have analysed how *Dogville*'s moment of transgression coincides with the revelation of the beast in all of us. It would thus seem that, whilst at times von Trier advocates the potential of the transgressive experience, at others he warns against such a transgression. Is this a tension that runs through his body of work as a whole? Should we, for instance, say that Karen's 'spassing' in the final scene of *The Idiots* is liberating and authentic, whereas Grace's transgressions (in both *Dogville* and *Manderlay*) are simply destructive?

The short answer is 'yes': *The Idiots* inspires optimism with regard to transgression, whilst *Dogville* and *Manderlay* present more problematic transgressive experiences. At the same time, this answer is also too short. It reduces the complexity of *The Idiots*, in which certain transgressive experiences (such as Stoffer's scene of madness) are far from being idealised, and it overlooks the point I have been trying to make here: although *Dogville* warns against transgression, it also testifies to a very strong belief in the transgressive experience. At the diegetic level, *Dogville* offers a critique of Grace's final revenge. The materialisation of the inner bastard suggests that this is not a film where justice is finally done, and the conversation that precedes the gruesome revenge is therefore no different to the justifications of hideous crimes that we find (for instance) in the Comte de Bressac's rationalisations in the Marquis de Sade's *Justine*. The fact that these explanations (at least to a certain extent) seduce our intellect only demonstrates that we want to be convinced, that our inner bastard is seeking an outlet. At another level, though, *Dogville* testifies to a strong belief in the transgressive experience: it is precisely by putting the spectator through Grace's cathartic experience that von Trier seeks to make his point about the dangers associated with transgression. This demonstrates the importance of maintaining a distinction between artistic and actual transgression (a distinction that many critics of extreme cinema have difficulty observing). Whereas the spectator's transgression is imaginary, Grace's is 'real'. By inviting us to forget this distinction, von Trier puts to work Artaud's idea that 'in our present degenerative state, metaphysics must be made to enter the mind through the body' (Artaud 1970: 77). He is suggesting that we must 'live' these drives in order to control them – and, in the process, he also demonstrates that the drives can be used for intense artistic experiences.

THE FEEL-BAD FILM

The combination of 'inviting the spectator to lose himself' and getting him or her to think about what such a self-loss might mean puts a 'deadlock' on catharsis. Using Brecht's vocabulary, we might say that von Trier invites us to throw ourselves into the action 'like a stone into the river', but that the river turns out to be so shallow that we soon find ourselves bumping against the bed, thereby regaining awareness of ourselves. The manipulative director seems to tease the spectator in accordance with a formula that could be summed up like this: 'So you want catharsis? So you want catharsis? Here you have it! . . . Was it really what you wanted?' This experience originates in a singular collision between the Brechtian aesthetic and the surrealist invitation to immersion whereby these two aesthetics arrest each other; von Trier is drawing the spectator's body into the action, without releasing him or her at the end of the film. On the one hand, we are not given the distance that Brecht recommends; on the other, we are deprived of the cathartic release for which Artaud and Bataille aim. This is the source of what I term the 'feel-bad' experience.

It is possible to offer a psychoanalytic supplement to this analysis of the feel-bad experience. In 'The Fiction Film and its Spectator: A Metapsychological Study', Christian Metz theorises what he calls 'filmic unpleasure' (Metz 1982: 110). According to Metz, this unpleasure arises whenever the spectator's phantasm (which to some extent is generated by the viewing experience) remains unsatisfied by the film. It is true that Metz theorises on the basis of 'narrative' film and that he specifically underlines that the 'impression of reality' (119) plays a key role in the creation of unpleasure. Nevertheless, his theorisations remain pertinent to a formalist work like *Dogville*, since he explains that unpleasure can come from either of two sources. Firstly, it can originate in the 'id', as typically occurs when a film does not nourish our phantasm sufficiently, creating frustration in the spectator, who becomes bored or annoyed. Secondly, it can come from the 'superego', as happens when the satisfaction of the id has been so overwhelming that the superego feels compelled to move in and protect the ego. For instance, the superego might step in and discard certain cinematic experiences (and genres) as being of bad taste.

If we relate these theorisations to *Dogville* it can be argued that a first unpleasure in von Trier's film comes from the id. As Jake Horsley points out in a stimulating analysis (with which I often disagree[6]), von Trier deliberately uses the length of the film to frustrate the spectator. However, as Horsley goes on to explain, whilst this is annoying, it is also absolutely necessary, because 'von Trier needs us to need his apocalyptic ending' (Horsley 2005: 16). To reformulate this in a vocabulary closer to that of Metz: von Trier creates unpleasure first by deliberately 'starving' our id. A second unpleasure is then produced, as we finally get the phantasm that our id has been craving. At this point, when the film turns 'bad taste' by suddenly transforming itself into a Bronson/Eastwood-esque vigilante film, the superego steps in to censor. More precisely, von Trier relieves us of our imaginary duties, takes control, mockingly shows us the manifestation of our inner bastard (our id), and thereby sends us back to our ego. By rephrasing *Dogville*'s feel-bad experience in these psychological terms, it thus becomes clear that the film's ending can be read along the lines of the famous Freudian maxim: 'where id was, there ego shall be.'

This play with catharsis based on a collision between a 'Brechtian' and a 'surrealist' logic can be found in other films sometimes associated with the New Extreme. One of the best examples is Michael Haneke's *Funny Games* (Austria, 1997).[7] Again, critics have tended to stress the Brechtian dimension of the film, but at the same time it is obvious that Haneke constructs an emotional terror machine that aims at the spectator's body before (and, at least as much as) his or her intellect. Even some of the so-called Brechtian moments at which Haneke breaks the fourth wall might best be understood as instances of emotional manipulation. Whereas Brecht's techniques sought to guarantee a critical distance that would allow the theatre-goer to think for himself, Haneke aggressively asserts his dominance by locking the spectator into a sado-masochistic relation. Like *Dogville*, we can therefore consider *Funny Games* to be an exercise in manipulation that works along the aforementioned Artaudian lines: 'In our present degenerative state, metaphysics must be made to enter the mind through the body.' And, like von Trier, Haneke also installs what I have called a deadlock on catharsis. This time the formula is not 'So you want catharsis? So you want catharsis? Here you have it! . . . Was it really what you wanted?', but rather 'So you want catharsis? So you want catharsis? You are NOT going to get it,' or even (if we take the famous rewind sequence[8] into account) 'So you want catharsis? So you want catharsis? Here you have it! . . . No, I was just kidding: you are NOT going to get it!'

In this way *Dogville* and *Funny Games* – despite their many differences – both turn the cinematic experience into a visceral practice that pushes the spectator towards ethical reflection. Some viewers will find that these invitations to reflection are extended in such an aggressive and manipulative way that the directors undermine the message they are striving to put forth. These viewers may even concur with the Cannes jury and consider *Dogville* (and *Funny Games*) to be anti-humanistic. However, the aggression and manipulation not only save the films from facile moralising, but also allow the spectator to engage with the 'inner bastard' in a way more intimate than otherwise possible. Although I have no ambition to make prescribed viewing of *Dogville* and *Funny Games*, it is nevertheless important to insist on the crucial differences between denying the presence of the inner bastard, confronting the spectator with his or her inner bastard, and allowing the (unreflexive) spectator to satisfy the inner bastard. This might very well be the difference between naïve (and dangerous) humanism, enlightened humanism and simple anti-humanism.

NOTES

1. One might think that there is nothing original about this, since directors very often 'use' their characters to get the spectator to respond in a certain way. Nevertheless, I believe *Dogville* does this to an extent that is unusual for a European art film. The fact that von Trier withholds the true identity of Grace until four or five minutes before the end, for instance, is unusual and, no doubt, dishonest to certain viewers. (He similarly hides essential information in *The Idiots* and *Manderlay*.)
2. Grace's status as an ambiguous victim (does she enjoy the suffering?) is one of several good reasons to compare Grace with the Marquis de Sade's *Justine*. Indeed, von Trier himself has pointed up this parallel.
3. Among the key elements constituting this 'mathematical violence' are the fact that Grace has Vera and Chuck's seven children killed in a way that 'rhymes with' cruelties that Grace has had to suffer in an earlier incident, and the fact that Grace personally liquidates Tom in a scene reminiscent of the famous photo of General Nguyen Ngoc Loan executing a Viet Cong prisoner in the streets of Saigon.
4. 'The tone that dominates the debate on immigration is awfully misanthropic. [. . .] [T]his is how the Nazis began – at that point it was the Jews, and today it is the Muslims. There are some easy votes to be had because the inner bastard is lurking just beneath the surface in a part of the Danish population' (von Trier cited in Schultz 2005: 56).
5. At the point of introducing Artaud and Bataille, let me clarify that I am not arguing that von Trier consciously borrows from either of these two authors. The logic I am about to

describe (a logic that links empathy, transgression, catharsis and emancipation) can be found in many of the texts we associate with twentieth-century avant-garde art, and the reader may therefore prefer to substitute *avant-garde* for *surrealism*. If I have chosen to prioritise Artaud and Bataille (and not Jerzy Grotowski or *Tel Quel*, for example), it is because their ideas about art, theatre, cruelty and the Marquis de Sade seem particularly relevant to the study of *Dogville*.

6. For instance, I strongly disagree with Horsley when he describes von Trier as a filmmaker who is 'militant and austere, perhaps the most austere filmmaker that ever was' (Horsley 2005: 12), and when he characterises *Dogville* as a cathartic film (18; I see it as initially pseudo-cathartic – and ultimately 'non-cathartic').

7. Catherine Wheatley's excellent book *Michael Haneke's Cinema* demonstrates that *Funny Games*, *The Piano Teacher* and *Hidden* combine three overlapping frameworks: a 'benign first generation modernism' (which we might associate with Bresson), an 'aggressive second generation modernism' (which might be the Godard of the late 1960s, for instance), and a 'system of generic convention (including the use of stars) that allows for a minimal emotional engagement' (in *Funny Games*, this could be Kubrick) (Wheatley 2009: 153). Although I come to *Dogville* and *Funny Games* with a different set of references, I share with Wheatley the basic idea of an encounter between a Brechtian and a more pro-cathartic tradition, and the belief that this results in a tension which aims to engage the spectator in ethical reflections.

8. After having been tortured and terrorised, the mother of the family finally manages to grab a rifle from her tormentors and shoot one of them. Her other tormentor knocks her back into an armchair, picks up a remote control, and rewinds the film to the point just before this cathartic release, from where the action resumes. This time, when the mother tries to snatch the rifle the tormentors react so quickly that she fails.

CHAPTER 14

A 'Passion for the Real': Sex, Affect and Performance in the Films of Andrea Arnold

Tanya Horeck

What does the idea of the 'new extremism' mean in the context of contemporary British filmmaking? According to the title of a recent article in *The Guardian* newspaper, we are currently witnessing 'The rebirth of the British art film'. Citing a range of films from *Zidane: A 21st Century Portrait* (Douglas Gordon and Philippe Parreno, 2006) and *Hunger* (Steve McQueen, 2008) to *Katalin Varga* (Peter Strickland, 2009), Andrew Pulver writes that these 'visionary' art-house films go beyond the kitchen sink social realism that British cinema is famed for, to offer a 'new filmmaking style'. This new crop of films, while all very different, are characterised by their 'radical spirit of adventure, and a refusal to conform to industry norms' (2009). Although not all of the British art films referred to by Pulver contain the kind of strong images of sex and violence associated with the new extremism, they do share an interest in questions of sensation and embodiment, placing emphasis on 'cinema's intensely tactile quality' (Beugnet 2007a: 3). In this chapter, I want to consider how contemporary British art-house cinema relates to the new extremism and its stylised provocations through an analysis of the films of Andrea Arnold, one of the filmmakers that Pulver associates with the current 'art house bonanza' in the UK (ibid.). My discussion will be focused on the candid depiction of sexuality in her films, a defining feature of what Linda Williams refers to in her book *Screening Sex* as the new breed of European 'hard-core art films', which are 'forging new ways of presenting and visually experiencing cinematic sex' (2008: 23, 295).

The sex in Arnold's films, which to date consists of her Oscar-winning short, *Wasp* (UK, 2003), and her two feature films, *Red Road* (UK, 2006) and *Fish Tank* (UK, 2009), is explicit but simulated. You will not find any 'rivers of viscera and spumes of sperm' (2004) here, to borrow James Quandt's memorable words. Nor will you find her work greeted by the same level of shock and controversy that attended the release of films such as *Intimacy*

(France/UK, 2001), French director Patrice Chéreau's London-set film, where the frisson arose from the 'real' sex that occurred on screen between recognised actors Kerry Fox and Mark Rylance, or *9 Songs* (UK, 2004), British director Michael Winterbottom's film about a love affair told almost entirely through unsimulated sex scenes (interspersed with live rock concert footage). There is an emphasis in these films on the open, intimate and frank nature of the sex depicted. Winterbottom, for instance, has spoken of *9 Songs*, which was awarded the label of the 'most sexually explicit film in the history of British mainstream cinema' (Higgins 2004), as a quest to attain realism:

> I like making films as real as possible. The one exception is that in a love story, the sex can never be real. If you film actors eating a meal, the food is real; the audience know that. But when it comes to sex they know it's pretend. You'd never do that with food and so I started thinking we should make sex real. (cited in Brown 2004)[1]

Like Winterbottom, Arnold is a British filmmaker who has attested to a 'passion for the real' (cited in Lemercier 2009), but I would argue that her brand of cinematic sexual realism, though less explicit, involves the spectator in far more demanding ways. In what follows, I want to explore how Arnold's blend of poetic social realist art cinema engages the spectator in terms of affect, ethics and performance, and how this relates in interesting and possibly unexpected ways, to the more overtly extremist work described by Martine Beugnet as the 'cinema of sensation' (2007a). In 2006, Arnold released her extraordinary debut feature film *Red Road*, a film that is part of something called the 'Advance Party concept', devised by Lars von Trier, in which three directors are invited to shoot three different films using the same characters and locales in Glasgow.[2] It won the Jury Prize at the Cannes Film Festival and received much critical acclaim. The graphic (though simulated) sexual encounter at the heart of *Red Road*, declares Jonathan Romney, is 'the realest sex you'll see in a British film' (2006). Three years later, Arnold released *Fish Tank*, which also won the Jury Prize at Cannes. As with *Red Road* before it, *Fish Tank* is positioned somewhere between British social realism and art cinema or, as Simon Schama and Karl French put it in their review: it is 'the kind of thriller that Ken Loach might make in collaboration with Michael Haneke, a slice of social-realist cinema in which we are never sure what – if anything – is about to happen' (2009). Like Haneke and other directors of the new extremism, Arnold shows a 'disregard for genre boundaries' (Beugnet 2007a: 61), which is designed to unsettle the viewer.

In both *Red Road* and *Fish Tank*, the set piece is a sex scene; in *Red Road* there is an explicit scene of a man performing oral sex on a woman, followed by consensual penetrative sex between the two, which the woman then stages as rape; in *Fish Tank* the sex scene is an illicit encounter between an under-age girl and her mother's boyfriend, which, though consensual, technically constitutes statutory rape. Some critics have suggested that the much talked-about sex scenes in these films are central to their triumph on the film festival circuit. In a letter to the British film magazine *Sight & Sound,* one viewer of *Fish Tank* even goes so far as to accuse Arnold of creating a 'made-for-festivals sex scene, thrown in to give the purposeless script some drive. Frivolous, cheap and not very convincing at all, really' (Pattison 2009). Taking issue with the poetic formalism of Arnold's filmmaking, the same letter suggests that the film 'offers little insight into social relations' because it is not 'grounded in reality' (ibid.).

In keeping with other new extremist films, which work at the level of affect and sensation, Arnold's films do not function as overt 'social problem' movies. But I would suggest that it is precisely through their poetic, affective moments that Arnold's films offer insight into social relations, as they detail the ways in which the female characters respond to the class and gender circumstances in which they find themselves. Furthermore, against a view of the sex in Arnold's work as unnecessary or gratuitous, I want to argue for the affective power of the sexual encounters in her films, which demand an engaged viewer, and which rethink ways of visually depicting female sexuality. In her emphasis on a tactile form of viewing, Arnold's films can be situated as part of a corporeal cinema, which, as Tim Palmer has noted, is of interest for how it 'overhauls the role of the film viewer, rejecting the traditionally passive, entertained onlooker, to demand instead a viscerally engaged experiential participant' (2006b: 172). While the sex scenes in Arnold's films constitute moments of such affective power that they cannot always be readily yoked back to a straightforward causal narrative chain, it is the very way in which they unsettle the narrative terrain, as it were, that makes the viewer engage in an intimate and, indeed, I want to argue, in an *ethical* way, with the bodies on display.[3]

One of the things that apparently sets Arnold's films apart from the new British art films with which she has come to be associated is that, as Robin Gutch asserts, her 'aesthetic is very much about capturing performance, often with a more accelerated pace than the other films' (cited in Pulver 2009). Performance – and movement – are indeed fundamental to Arnold's films, and the kind of affective energy they elicit. Much was made in the press about the intensive power of the performances of the central female leads in her films, especially *Fish Tank,* which features the acting debut of the young Katie Jarvis, who, as was reported in every review of the film, was 'discovered' when she was seen arguing with her boyfriend at a train station. But, following the important work of Deleuzian feminist Elena del Rio, I am more interested in how Arnold's cinema can be understood as what del Rio terms an 'affective-performative cinema', in which gesture and movement play a central role in emphasising 'the ethical and creative potential of the expressive body' (2008:

16). In her book, *Deleuze and the Cinemas of Performance: Powers of Affection*, del Rio explores the 'limits of previous feminist theories of spectacle and performativity' (2008: 18), such as those articulated by Laura Mulvey and Judith Butler, in order to consider the significance of an affective understanding of performance. In her elaboration of what she calls the 'powers of affection', Del Rio 'challenge(s) the notion of the female body as a visual, static fetish by focusing on the body's expressive capacities and their effect upon oppressive structures' (ibid.: 17). In *Red Road* and *Fish Tank*, the gestural and affective force of the female performative bodies confronts us with the complex and often inadequately acknowledged interrelationship between victimisation and agency, and in so doing also significantly reorganises the relationship between viewer and viewed, inviting a form of empathetic spectatorship, or what Jillian Smith has referred to, in a different context, as 'observation without domination' (2008: 120).

With *Red Road*'s opening close-up of a woman's face and hands, we are plunged into immediate proximity with the body. As the film proceeds, we are not given much information to help orientate us in relation to the events we are watching on screen. Instead, we are made to focus on the bodily gestures and movements of the female protagonist, Jackie (Kate Dickie). We do not, for example, know Jackie's motivations; nor can we ever fully account for her actions as they are happening. While some viewers appear to have been frustrated by the withholding of information in *Red Road*, I want to argue that the attempt to immerse us in the moment without any narrative gloss is the source of its critical power. In a recent article about the 'politics of tactility' in Fred Wiseman's 1967 documentary *Titicut Follies*, Jillian Smith discusses Wiseman's decision not to include any descriptive devices: 'He will not state facts, and he will not give us their security and power' (2008: 109). In refusing to give us the comfort that comes from description and explanation, and which 'provides distance between knower and known', Wiseman 'insists that we remain close to the material, affectively engaged' (109). Smith includes a suggestive quotation from Wiseman:

> It's like having a butterfly collection with everything labelled. Whereas if you see somebody and you don't know whether he's an alcoholic or whether he's a rapist or whether he's a murderer or whether he's a psychopath – whatever those terms may mean, if in fact they have any meaning at all – *you* have to decide how you feel about the guy. (cited in Smith 2008: 109)

This quotation from Wiseman is very useful for thinking through the process of watching *Red Road* and *Fish Tank*. As Andrea Arnold has remarked of her films:

I want to make it feel like we've dropped in on some people's lives. With a lot of films, people are sitting on the outside looking in, but I want the audience to get a bit more intimately involved with what's going on, so that they maybe can experience it a little bit more intensely. (cited in Fuller 2010)

In *Red Road* we watch Jackie watching Clyde and we do not know if he is a rapist or a killer or an ex-lover or a boyfriend. We are focused on Jackie's bodily, affective responses, which come before our knowledge of events.

One of the most intriguing moments in *Red Road* occurs early on in the film when Jackie is doing her surveillance work as a CCTV operator. Jackie is initially concerned that she is witnessing a rape but she soon realises that she is watching sex, not violence. 'Sorry, false alarm,' she tells the emergency services she has just called. Here we are in the territory of the Freudian primal scene. Once she realises it is enjoyment not terror on the woman's face, Jackie continues to watch the couple have sex, one hand idly stroking the joystick of the remote control. She is vaguely aroused. Then, suddenly, there is the shock of recognition. She knows this man. Patricia Pisters has noted how in this scene:

> it is [. . .] remarkable how Jackie's body seems to know, before she is conscious of the powerful affects she is about to experience. Her hands are telling: one is tense and 'anxious', the other caressing and 'sexually aroused.' This ambiguity of her emotions is quite remarkable. On an immediate first level, there is an incredible sexual tension between her and this man that at the same time obviously inspires her with fear, disgust or anger. (forthcoming: 16)[4]

We might also point to elsewhere in the film where an explicit correlation is drawn between arousal and disgust, as when Jackie dances with Clyde at his party in a sexually charged scene, only to rush out of the flat to vomit. As Pisters notes, the same kind of 'ambiguous emotions and mixed feelings' are played out in the central sex scene between Jackie and Clyde (ibid.: 18).

In this later scene, Jackie returns with Clyde to his squalid flat. He undresses her and performs oral sex on her. It is a very graphic and (uncomfortably) long scene, which depicts Jackie's sexual arousal and pleasure. The scene of oral sex is followed by a round of boisterous penetrative sex, after which a concerned Clyde asked Jackie if she is all right: 'I was just joining in, I didn't hurt you, did I?' Here Clyde is referring to the use made by the pair of the terms of a rape fantasy, led by a tough-talking Jackie who asks Clyde, 'Do you want to fuck me?' When Jackie further asks, 'What if I say "no"?', Clyde, playing along, responds, 'I'm going to have to force myself on you.'

The idea of performance works on different levels here. Firstly, we have the performative sexual play between Jackie and Clyde, which both reiterates and undoes a familiar, gendered scenario of sexual violence. But what is most remarkable is how this scene works on the level of the affective-performative. To borrow del Rio's language, the sexual entanglement between Jackie's and Clyde's bodies functions as a 'performance (that) involves the expression and perception of affect in the body' (2008: 10). Their bodies react in unexpected and disconcerting ways to the interaction; Jackie is aroused by a man who has killed her family and who she wants to seeks revenge on, and the man who we have had reason to suspect and fear throughout the film assumes the role of the doting and concerned lover. What most interests del Rio about the 'moving body' is 'its power of affection/becoming as a force perpetually in the making. Through moving and gesturing processes, the body emerges as an assemblage of virtual and actual expressions with the capacity to affect and be affected by other bodies' (ibid.: 12). Any clear representational understanding of what is happening in this sex scene in terms of plot and narrative is forestalled here by 'an amorphous, sensory based reality' (Beugnet 2007a: 61), which reconfigures the terms of the viewing experience and reworks understandings of divisions between body and mind, subject and object, and victim and villain.

After the pair have sex, Jackie performs a series of at first inexplicable actions. She goes into Clyde's bathroom, takes sperm from the condom, shoves it up herself, hits her head with a rock and rips her clothes up. She then purposely runs past a CCTV camera and phones the police from a payphone to report a rape. In a reversal of the earlier scene in which Jackie witnessed what she at first assumed was rape but was in fact consensual sex, here it is consensual sex that is staged for the cameras as rape. In this subversion of the rape-revenge drama, the female protagonist is staging a rape scene to entrap a man, who, as we learn at the end of the film, is responsible for the death of her husband and young daughter.

The exceptional power of the sexual encounter in *Red Road* comes from our uncertainty about the motivations that underpin it and how to position ourselves in relation to the seemingly ambiguous and contradictory events we are watching: how do Jackie's sexual fulfilment and pleasure relate to her unease and fear/anger towards Clyde, who she has been anxiously pursuing throughout the film? As Hannah McGill writes in a perceptive review, 'Arnold declines to probe her protagonist's subjective experience or to anticipate her next move. The film's viewers are in the same position as a CCTV camera operative: they can only follow the action, making sense of it as they go' (2006). Once we have gleaned the motivations behind Jackie's actions, we have to return to various events in the film in order to rethink what we have seen and affectively experienced.

In *Fish Tank*, Arnold's more recent film, the question of affectivity and its relation to the performativity of bodies is even more pronounced, focusing as it does on the central figure of fifteen-year-old Mia as a dancer. The film foregrounds Mia's watchful gaze as she observes her mother's new boyfriend, Connor, and his comings and goings. The first meeting between Connor and Mia, occurs, significantly, as Mia is dancing in the kitchen on her own as she watches a hip-hop video on television. Connor enters the kitchen and appraises her dancing, thus setting up a dynamic the film explores between feminine performance, the kind of cultural appraisal and judgement that attend it, and the way the female body – and also the film's body – is able to move against, and away from, such cultural constraints.

There are several key moments in the film before they have sex, where there is close bodily contact between Mia and Connor. These scenes are choreographed in such a way that the speed of the camera changes ever so slightly and everything slows down; the sounds of breathing are amplified, and the tactility of the moment is emphasised (when, for example, Connor carries her sleeping figure to bed). Arnold has said that 'she was constantly trying to find a way to feel what (Mia's) thinking' and that she 'experimented with those moments to try and find that place' (cited in Fuller 2010). The language Arnold uses here is significant: note that she is trying to find a way for us 'to feel' what Mia is thinking, and the emphasis is on what Teresa Brennan calls the 'transmission of affect' (cited in del Rio 2008: 53). As del Rio explains, 'such transmission of affect does not rest on sight alone' but involves the other senses such as hearing and touch (ibid.).

Arnold includes a primal scene in *Fish Tank*, in which Mia watches Connor fucking her mother. The scene begins with an aural cue, as Mia hears sounds of groaning coming from her mother's bedroom. She leaves her room to investigate; the screen goes black for a few seconds as we are invited to concentrate on the sounds of the sex. Transfixed, Mia watches the sex for a few seconds, then becomes disgusted, angry and possibly more than a little sexually jealous, returning to her room and slamming her bedroom door shut. Similar to *Red Road*, the film draws significant connections between this primal scene and the later, central sexual scenario involving the female protagonist.

In the sex scene between Mia and Connor, the choreography of movement between the bodies on screen and our affective relation to the sexual scenario unsettle any easy understandings we may have about the interaction. The sequence begins with Mia dancing alone, at night, in the abandoned flat; the same slowed-down camera speed that is used in the moments of contact between Mia and Connor is also at work in this dance scene, which holds us in proximity to Mia's body in movement. Although the sexual scenario that follows – an 'older man seduces a younger woman' – is very familiar from popular film and television, Arnold shoots it in such a way that clichés are disrupted. After Connor and Mia have sex, a shame-faced Connor, panic in his eyes, hurriedly pulls up his jeans and makes excuses. Previously confident, charming Connor is suddenly flustered, shabby and uncertain how to relate to Mia in the aftermath of their sexual encounter; Mia is breathless and slightly besotted. It is a testament to how closely this scene keeps us with Mia and her perspective that we can see what is 'wrong' about this encounter and feel uncomfortable about it, at the same time as we also see what is powerful about it. The scene resists the temptation to show the encounter according to predetermined ideas about the man as sexual predator and the girl as innocent victim (though it does contain those ideas too). As del Rio writes of the 'expressive event', 'the body does not coincide with a certain subject-position, but rather with the force that pushes boundaries towards a different configuration' (2008: 36).

This reconfiguration also occurs at the level of the film itself; after the sex scene in *Fish Tank* the film shifts tack and becomes a revenge drama in a way that some critics think 'stretches plausibility' (Bennett 2009), but which I think is one of the most remarkable sequences in terms of how the film works on us as viewers. Writing of the 'affective-performative event' as a moment of 'eruption' in film, del Rio notes that 'in the aftermath, we witness a certain wreckage of ideological stability, the debris of a passing storm, as former corporealities and their relations appear profoundly altered or dislocated' (2008: 16). Such a severe dislocation occurs after the sex scene in *Fish Tank* when Mia walks to the new housing estate where Connor lives and finds out that he is a conman – no accident, surely, that his name is Con (her).

Mia crawls into Connor's suburban middle-class house through an unlocked window and begins to explore; she is the proverbial fish out of water (to echo an earlier image from the film). A curious Mia opens a discarded video camera, the same camera Connor loaned her so she could film herself for a dance audition. She presses play and sees a cute little girl in a pretty dress, standing beside her mother in the garden. We hear (but do not see) Connor off camera as he coaches the little girl to sing a song to camera. The song the little girl is singing is Leona Lewis's transatlantic hit 'Bleeding Love', a rather inappropriate song for a six-year-old to be singing really, all about the violence and intensity of sexual love, but none the less wholly in keeping with the film's critique of the way young girls are interpolated into discourses of hollow aspiration in British contemporary culture where women like Jordan and Danielle Lloyd represent the pinnacle of female achievement. Mia's reaction is as immediate as it is violent and visceral; her gaze reels around the room as she takes in all the visual evidence of a female child's presence, the toys, the dollies. She pulls down her pants and pees on the carpet. It is an affective, infantile moment. What so disturbs Mia here, I suggest, is less the realisation that Connor is in a relationship with another woman, but that he is a father; more to the point, it is witnessing Connor playing the role of daddy to a little girl that brings home the unsavoury nature of her relationship to him. Previously, Mia has been at pains to distinguish her relationship with Connor from that of his relationship with her younger sister Tyler. The moment when Mia sees the little girl performing for daddy, the fantasy is punctured: the recognition of the role she has played in Connor's particular fantasies, as another little girl performing for 'daddy', radically alters how she views him and her relationship with him.

It is at this point that the film changes gear and becomes a revenge drama when Mia kidnaps Connor's young daughter, Keira. In the most tense of sequences, Mia takes Keira off into the marshes behind the housing estate, swearing at her and pushing her along roughly, leading her, ultimately, towards the turbulent sea and the possibility of extreme danger and/or death. I would like to suggest that with this thrillingly kinetic genre sequence, which plays upon the viewer's emotions and makes us question our previous understanding of Mia, creating uncertainty in us as to whether or not she will harm the little girl, the film extends the affective encounters explored between Mia and Connor to us. Or to borrow del Rio's words, in this revenge sequence the film (re-)establishes the 'affective links between the film's body and the viewer's body' (2008: 117). In compelling us to question previously held thoughts and feelings, we are made to relate to the film anew.[5] The violent energy expressed by Mia during this sequence relates to the film's radical unsettling of the borders between victimisation and agency and the ever-shifting relations between those two categories. As del Rio notes, 'when a character is not fixed in advance, it can undo itself without warning' (2008: 161), and the surprise or the shock in this sequence come from Mia's change from one state to another, as well as the film's own shift in movement.

It is here that I would like to offer some concluding remarks on the kind of audience engagement solicited by Arnold's 'affective performative cinema'. Despite the fact that the films of the new extremism are frequently viewed as amoral for their sensational content, there is more of an ethical dimension to many of these films than is generally credited. In their explicit address to the spectator and in the way they invite an affective response to the dark events they are depicting, the cinema of sensation confronts the 'often disavowed messiness and ambivalence of ethical response' (Downing and Saxton 2010: 21). As already noted, one of the most remarkable aspects of Arnold's films is that we are asked to suspend moral judgement. Who is Clyde? Is he a rapist, an ex-boyfriend? Who is Connor? Is he a kindly father figure or something more sinister? What tends to go unremarked, is how Arnold does, at the same time, also strategically invite us to make judgements about certain characters and how this relates to the ethical endeavour of her films.[6]

Near the ending of *Fish Tank*, for instance, there is a moving sequence in which the mother and the two daughters, whose fractious relationship has hitherto consisted of relentless sniping at one another, dance together to one of Mia's favourite hip-hop tracks. Throughout the film we have been made to feel a strong antipathy for Mia's mother, who, as in *Wasp*, Arnold's Oscar-winning short film, is filled with heterosexual romantic longings that conflict with her role as a mother and which lead her to neglectful, hurtful behaviour towards her children. As in that earlier film, Arnold uses our inclination to judge others to great effect. As she plays with certain well-worn audience expectations, we are made to feel sympathy for the neglected children and anger towards the mother. Arnold uses certain genre tropes to induce strong emotions in her audience, but, importantly, the production of audience feeling is used to encourage an ethical 'critical engagement' and a 'process of questioning rather than as a positivistic exercise of morality' (Downing and Saxton 2010: 3). There is an important distinction to be made here between affect and sentimentality.[7] What is so compelling about Arnold's films is how she forces us to re-evaluate our preconceptions in a highly reflective way. As reviewer Anthony Quinn notes: 'it's a real skill to present quite unpleasant characters and then reveal them as vulnerable, even loveable' (2009). This is certainly what happens with the figure of the mother in *Fish Tank*; we have been made to feel strongly one way, only for there to be a sudden, unexpected shift in how we are invited to look at her. When we find ourselves moved by the impromptu dance performance at the end of the film it is not out of sentimentality – we are not crying tears of catharsis, in other words – but out of a startling recognition of how we are implicated in what Michele Aaron, following Susan Sontag, calls the 'pain of others' (2007: 116). An empathetic response comes from the way we are suddenly made aware of the connections between the mother's desires and her various limitations/capacities and of how our own hitherto strong judgement feeds into dominant conceptions and beliefs.

The power of both *Red Road* and *Fish Tank* comes not only from their attempts to explore female agency in a context of threat and violation, where lust commingles with fear and disgust, but also, importantly, in their troubling of distinctions between viewer and viewed. Just as in *Red Road*, where Jackie moves out from behind the CCTV cameras she is operating and enters the worlds of those she is watching, thus countering a voyeuristic looking characterised by distance, so too, do *Red Road* and *Fish Tank* invite us to become engaged participants in what we are watching. Arnold's films promote what Lisa Downing and Libby Saxton term an 'ethics of looking', which provokes consideration of how 'ethics is an optics through which we habitually view and conceptualize' (2010: 2). The sex scenes in Arnold's films are key affective moments, which function not as static sexual spectacles but as performative scenarios that actively work to interrogate and rewrite the terms of the heterosexual encounter.

In their concern with shifting the relationship between what del Rio describes as woman's 'state of confinement and her capacities for movement'

(2008: 31), Arnold's sexual revenge dramas have something in common with the 'fiercely engaged sexual politics' (Romney 2004) of the new extremist *grande dame*, Catherine Breillat. Like Breillat, Arnold is concerned with exploring female sexuality in ways that go beyond stark distinctions between an idea of woman as victim and agent, and which present the heterosexual encounter through an ethical optics. While the gritty aesthetic of Arnold's films, with their roots in a tradition of British social realism, could not be further away from the 'ironically sheened images' (Romney 2004) of Breillat's philosophical art porn, the way that both directors use explicit sex scenes as a means of explicating the psychic reality of their female characters is notable. Finally, though British cinema has not typically been discussed as part of a wider tendency towards the extreme in European cinema, my reading of the films of Andrea Arnold suggests ways in which it might be worthwhile to consider how such an arresting reworking of a realist, kitchen sink aesthetic relates to the 'cinema of sensation', where films 'exist first and foremost as affective, sensory experience[s]' (Beugnet 2007a: 47).

NOTES

1. While there was much media discussion regarding Winterbottom's attempt to 'make sex real', it is interesting that the sexual politics of the film is something that is rarely noted. This is a significant omission. As Melanie Williams has argued, 'while *9 Songs* is bracingly radical in some respects, in others it feels surprisingly retrograde' (2006: 62), especially in its treatment of the female character Lisa.
2. See the Sigma films website for a further discussion of this project, http://www.sigmafilms.com/about.php, accessed 21 July 2010.
3. See Martine Beugnet (2007a) who argues that in new extremist films such as Claire Denis's *Trouble Every Day* (France, 2001), 'it is precisely the breakdown of a linear narrative logic and the impossibility of harnessing the shock effects to such a causal chain that give them both affective power and critical edge' (40).
4. See Pister's fascinating discussion of *Red Road* as an 'affective neurothriller' in her forthcoming book *The Neuro-Image: A Deleuzian Film Philosophy of Digital Screen Culture* (Stanford University Press).
5. According to del Rio, in order to understand 'affect as productive of new thoughts or feelings – a certain displacement of familiar beliefs and values is required' (2008: 48).
6. Thanks to Claire Henry for pointing out to me the important role that judgement plays in Andrea Arnold's films.
7. Writing on the cinema of Rainer Werner Fassbinder, del Rio argues that there is 'the need for a theoretical distinction between *sentimentality* and *affect*' (2008: 72). According to del Rio, 'an experience of affect makes the spectator aware of the ways in which he or she bears the ideological or psychic marks of determination sustained by the character,' creating 'a certain distance that allows for examination or contemplation' and thus encouraging empathy rather than the 'sentimental oblivion and vicarious emotion promoted in much of classical Hollywood cinema' (ibid.: 72).

CHAPTER 15

Interrogating the Obscene: Extremism and Michael Haneke

Lisa Coulthard

At the Cannes Festival press conference for *Das Weisse Band/The White Ribbon* in May 2009, Michael Haneke made what is perhaps the most important and yet deceivingly simplistic interpretative comment on his films: 'All my films are about violence.' To anyone familiar with Haneke's œuvre, this is perhaps exceedingly obvious, but this seeming transparency only serves to make the unpacking of the statement more crucial. What does it mean for a film to be about violence and how do Haneke's films do this? While it is necessary to be critical of accepting wholesale interpretive frameworks advocated by the filmmaker himself (for example, his own characterisation of his work as a criticism of postmodern, technologised society and violence-saturated media or as a 'raping' of the spectator), this statement should be taken seriously as a challenge to rethink Haneke's œuvre in terms of violence and to interrogate what exactly film violence means in this context.

Characterised by 'an aesthetics of dread' (Beugnet 2007b: 227), Haneke's films since *Funny Games* (1997; 2007) do not address violence directly so much as they create an environment where one expects violence to erupt any second. Making violence pervasive, as if it is lying in wait, rather than exceptional, intrusive or surprising is crucial to understanding Haneke's violence and the way in which it works as cinematic and ethical critique. In films like *La Pianiste/The Piano Teacher* (2001), *Caché/Hidden* (2005) and *The White Ribbon*, the audience leaves feeling as if they witnessed or were party to acts of brutality and violence, but this feeling becomes more complex when we begin to probe what those acts of violence were and what exactly rendered scenes uncomfortable, shocking or disturbing. In this act of questioning, violence becomes a question or problem, rather than a clear-cut entity, event or action.

To be more precise, in Haneke's films violence is addressed in ways that force us to question our ability to identify and differentiate violence from non-violence. Scenes of seeming non-violence, or at least physical non-violence, are wrought with dread and anxiety (the receipt of a videotape of one's house, the destruction of cabbages, a sexual encounter, forcing a confession from an adolescent boy about his acts of masturbation). The sense of dread and anxiety that infuses seemingly banal or quotidian events indicates the way in which Haneke's films resemble crime scenes that activate a forensic aesthetic; in *Die Siebente Kontinent/ The Seventh Continent* (1989), *The Time of the Wolf* (2003), *Hidden* and *The White Ribbon*, we immediately sense that some crime has occurred or is about to occur as we witness acts and struggle to find a clear and explanatory narrative. In addition to this forensic inquiry, the refiguration of violence as not only physical but psychological is essential to the interrogation of its effects and impact. Examining both extreme and banal forms of psychological cruelty, humiliation and exploitation as forms of violence equally as damaging as any physical blow or wound, Haneke's films query the boundaries of our knowledge and understanding of violence and its sources, effects and impact.

Equally crucial to this troubling of violence as a known entity is the questioning that occurs in fairly clear-cut acts of physical violence (such as murder, rape or suicide), acts that in films like *The Piano Teacher*, *Hidden* and *The White Ribbon* are rendered ambiguous, complex and interrogative. What is the relation of rape to consensual sado-masochistic sex? Is suicide violent, and if so, is it self-violence or can it also be a form of aggression aimed at others? Are children exempt from the guilt that comes with violent action because of ignorance, youth, impressionability? Is self-defence or the covering up of a violent crime a violent action as well? Can animals be murdered or is it merely rationalised slaughter of irrational beings? These are the kinds of questions provoked by Haneke's cinematic inquiries into the definition, construct and understanding of violence as a social, ethical, philosophical and aesthetic category of action. Addressing a range of acts of murder, cruelty, brutality and humiliation, his films trouble our certainty as to what we consider violence and what we exclude.

This querying of violence is frequently missed by many commentators and scholars who consider Haneke's work offensive, extremist or brutally violent; while there are indeed scenes of explicit physical violence in his films, the more troubling dread that Beugnet notes stems less from these moments than it does from a general sense of trauma and fear that pervades even the most innocuous of actions. By focusing on a multitude of actions and reactions, Haneke places acts of physical, interpersonal violence alongside other forms of violence that are less overt, obvious or visible: emotional and psychological abuse and humiliation, the killing of animals, marginalisation and alienation, suicide. The provocation in his work lies in this complex associative relationship between violence and non-violence, a conversation or affiliation that requires one to rethink the separation of the categories themselves. Questioning what differentiates the two, his films probe epistemological and ethical understandings of violence itself: Haneke's true provocation is an interrogation of what is included and excluded within violence's cinematic, philosophical and ethical parameters.

This questioning of violence is tied to what Haneke describes as an essential obscenity in his work:

> I would like to be recognized for making an obscenity, but not a pornographic film. In my definition, anything that could be termed obscene departs from the bourgeois norm. Whether concerned with sexuality or violence or another taboo issue, anything that breaks with the norm is obscene. Insofar as truth is always obscene, I hope that all of my films have at least an element of obscenity. (Haneke in Sharrett 2004)

Obscenity here refers not only to sexually explicit, salacious or shocking material, but also and more importantly to the concepts of repulsion, disgust or offence that result when norms, morals and standards of decency are transgressed or violated. Its relation to transgression and subversion is clear, as is its connection to the idea of ethical truth – a truth that frequently stands against morals and that hurts, disrupts and jars. It is this jarring, this confrontation with truth, that makes Haneke's films both obscene and ethical and it is in the interrogation of violence that I argue this obscenity takes on its most probing and transgressive form. As Alain Badiou notes, truth is not the same as knowledge, but rather violently disruptive of it: 'A truth punches a "hole" in knowledges' (Badiou 2002: 70). This aggressive tearing into what is thought to be known is a good model for approaching the aporetic, ambiguous and sometimes painfully confrontational interrogations of violence that abound in Haneke's cinema and frame his work as truly obscene.

It is crucial to note that, although obscenity works alongside extremism, it is not necessarily itself extreme; it offends, transgresses and violates norms, but it may not, for all of this, be extreme or even excessive in any clear stylistic or aesthetic sense, and this can be considered a positive thing for ethics. In his book *Art and Fear*, Paul Virilio discusses extremist tendencies that focus on bodily violation, pain and the abject in contemporary art and comes to the conclusion that, taken to its limit, transgressive extremism risks insignificance, turning it into a mere 'conformism of abjection' (Virilio 2000: 20). This notion of the potential for conformist safety in art that pushes the limits of extremity – excesses of violence, sex, gore, the body itself – suggests the ways in which some transgressions can operate as inherent transgressions, unable to punch a hole in knowledge because sanctioned. As Slavoj Žižek notes, the inherent transgression is that which appears to violate the system, but that in fact operates as its hidden support. For Virilio extremism runs the risk of becoming this kind of empty, authorised excess and thus of becoming nostalgic and irrelevant or taking refuge in its abjection.

Žižek echoes this same reservation regarding excess's potential as a recuperative, official part of the normative structures and limits its aims to subvert or transgress. Considering recent extremist trends in contemporary art, he notes that 'in postmodernism, the transgressive excess loses its shock value and is fully integrated into the established artistic market' (Žižek 2000: 25). As objects bought, sold, consumed and therefore thoroughly immersed in consumer capitalism, even the most excessive art becomes part of the system that 'feeds on them in order to reproduce itself' (ibid.: 25). Extending this critique beyond the considerations of market capital, Žižek points to the role of the sublime and the sacred in such excesses, whereby trash, excrement and other abject objects fill in the place of the sublime thing, but rather than thereby attaining or even radically emptying sublimity, they in fact reveal a nostalgic yearning for the sacred place of sublimity itself: 'in other words, the problem is no longer that of horror *vacui*, of filling in the Void, but, rather, that of *creating the Void in the first place*' (ibid.: 27).

While both Žižek and Virilio are referring to the abjection, excess and violation of the body found in a certain strain of contemporary art (exemplified but not limited to the British artists associated with the Royal Academy of Art's Sensation exhibit in 1997), their comments on excess are worthwhile to keep in mind when considering European new extremity. In particular, what these critiques of extremist tendencies suggest is the way in which violent excess can work to further conservative, normative and conformist, rather than subversive, transgressive or productively troubling ends. For considerations of the representation of violence this implies the weakness of excess as an interrogative or ethical confrontation of violence. Excess runs the risk of taking refuge in the aesthetics of violence in lieu of critique; that is, by elevating the extreme into a sublime value, one hazards engaging in reductive sacralising or redemptive narratives of violation by assigning transgressive worth to acts that are in fact merely basely violent. In opposition to these risks of extremism, we can think of obscenity in relation to a more ethically directed outrage, a shift that is perhaps best illustrated by a consideration of what is without doubt the most obscene film ever created – Pier Paolo Pasolini's *Salò, Or the 120 Days of Sodom* (1975). Going beyond the merely extreme – and it is most definitely extreme by any definition – *Salò* is able to offend truly because its points of violation extend far beyond the corporal violations that form its surface. Defying nature, God, morality, sexuality, society and even history, *Salò* is a truly offensive and obscene work and it is no coincidence that Haneke has stated that it is his touchstone for all of his film violence – the film that he would most like to remake.

In order to probe this relation between obscenity and violence in Haneke's films, I want to focus on *The Piano Teacher* and *The White Ribbon*, and specifically on the role of intimate, sexual violence in each. Although these films offer an array of abuse, psychological cruelty, perverse sexuality, self-violence and outright physical brutality that articulates the multiplicity of violence and its effects, I will focus my discussion on two key scenes addressing rape and abuse: Erika's rape in *The Piano Teacher* and the Doctor's sexual abuse of his fourteen-year-old daughter in *The White Ribbon*. This focus draws our attention to an essential element in the violence of new extremism and, as I will argue, an essential feature of Haneke's critique of violence – sexual abuse and rape. As Dominique Russell has argued in her introduction to the edited collection *Rape in Art Cinema*, the films of the new extremism have recently placed rape in the cinematic foreground and have done so in ways that demand examination and analysis. This is particularly significant in the films associated with this movement, because, as Russell suggests, art cinema elevates fundamental ambiguity as a thematic, narrational and formal mode – a feature that offers certain provocations to the consideration of the representation of rape. That is, as a consequence of this ambiguity, rape in art cinema 'is at once present and absent, a given, but not quite there' (Russell 2010: 2). This kind of absent presence is similarly analysed in Tanya Horeck's seminal work *Public Rape*, which argues that there has been an intensification of the public visibility of rape in recent years, but that this visibility alone does not constitute any kind of revelatory insight into rape, either in representation or in real life. Put simply, visibility is not equivalent to understanding, inquiry or insight.

These kinds of essential ambiguities are crucial to Haneke's treatment of violence, especially violence as it occurs within the domestic realm. In particular, the sense of dread and anxiety that critics have noted in his work is one that seems to emanate from the familial and that finds precise articulation in the abuse and violence associated with domestic and intimate ties. In particular, both *The Piano Teacher* and *The White Ribbon* highlight the ambiguities of violent action by exploring the problems of witnessing, interpretation and visibility inherent in acts of private, domestic and psychological brutality. Through the isolation of scenes of sexual abuse in these films, we can begin to analyse Haneke's critique of violence as an obscenity of truth, rather than a mere revelling in extremist, abject or excessive limit cases of experience.

The Piano Teacher, and the novel from which it was adapted, concentrate on the cruelty inherent in familial and romantic bonds, through its treatment of a deeply troubled mother–daughter relationship and its connection with a sexual relationship defined by humiliation, alienation and abuse. Telling the story of a piano teacher (Erika), who begins a sexual relationship with an eager, courting student (Walter) that ends in her beating and rape, *The Piano Teacher* is a bleak and harrowing portrait of the psychological distress, cruelty and damage inherent in both romance and the family. In particular, their pending romance is framed in sado-masochistic terms when Erika gives Walter a letter outlining the abuse she would like to receive at his hands, an abuse that resonates with the audience who has witnessed her abusive behaviour towards others, her self-mutilation and her deeply troubled co-dependency with her controlling mother.

Yet for the seeming simplicity of this summary, the film trades in productive and standing ambiguities about Erika and her desires, thoughts and fate. As with all of Haneke's films, there is an avoidance of psychologisation – motives, clear causal explanations, character desire and insight are all intensely restricted. Instead we are shown actions and effects, and are left to fill in the gaps in between. These gaps operate effectively in this film as any quick review of the critical literature attests – there are a wide range of interpretations regarding Erika's desires and her fate. Both Harriet Wrye and Frances L. Restuccia, for instance, downplay the rape as a violent act in favour of seeing it is as evidence of Erika's manipulative madness or as a vehicle for her liberation. In his recent book on Haneke, Peter Brunette goes even further to argue that not only is it possible that Erika desires the rape, thereby erasing the event as rape (Brunette 2010: 100), but that the first sexual encounter can be read as a kind of rape of Walter (ibid.: 98). In contrast to this interpretation is Robin Wood's perceptive '"Do I disgust you?" Or, Tirez pas sur *La Pianiste*' that reads the film as a provocation to the audience to rethink our responses to disgust, perversion and 'normal' sexuality; as he claims, one of 'the film's many brilliant insights is its revelation that the "normal" person [Walter] is capable of a brutality and insensitivity far uglier than the fantasies of the sick' (Wood 2002: 5).

What strikes one in these interpretations is the insistence on retroactive readings of Erika's desires, which in turn lead to a problematic logic claiming that if the rape helps her, it must have been desired and is therefore not rape at all. There is also a relative absence of interrogation into the character of Walter and his cruelty – the underlying assumption seems to be based on a projection of motivations that assert either that Walter is under Erika's influence or that he truly loves her. When considering these critical diversions, it is important to keep in mind that the rape, as well as the final gesture of Erika's stabbing herself in the shoulder, is shown on screen – the ambiguity is not a result of offscreen or darkened action, contrasting versions of an event or its narrative absence. Rather, the ambiguity hinges on the interpretation of Erika herself: she either desires the rape and is cured, desires it and remains so stuck to her desires that she descends into madness, or does not desire it but is cured nonetheless, therefore rendering it a fulfilment of unconscious desires.

In paralleling the rape scene with the other scenes of sexual activity or contact, we note the way in which violence infects them all. Here is where Brunette's analysis, although it goes too far, brings up a crucial point: every sexual encounter in the film is infused with power, humiliation and control. This, combined with Erika's letter and her utter humiliation at the hands of Walter, who responds to this laying bare of her soul with anger, disgust and rejection, sets the stage for the final rape scene that is quite clearly depicted as not what Erika wants; what she does want is a mystery, but, as she says to Walter, this brutality is definitely not it. Haneke's ambiguity then is aimed less at the question of whether a rape and beating occurred, or even whether or not Erika deserved, desired or benefitted from such an act, but rather at the more crucial question of how we differentiate this climactic action from the multiple small acts of violence, power, cruelty and humiliation throughout the text. The camera does not try to give us any characterological insight in the sequence. Rather the act is presented as a fact, an objectified act to which we are privy as viewers, but crucially as uninformed, even ignorant, viewers; the logic of the act is opaque, unclear, radically ambiguous. The very differences in critical interpretations are, in some way then, the crucial point in so far as they represent the struggle to pin down, render transparent and logical, what is an essentially illogical and multidimensional act; this struggle for understanding is meant to resonate and be allowed to stand as an ambiguity, rather than be resolved.

By questioning Walter's brutality, we are forced to question his romance as well, an interrogation that is quite obvious in Elfriede Jelinek's novel that makes his courtship explicitly about power and control from the first moment. Haneke's version is more subtle and it is perhaps one of the reasons that Jelinek calls her text pornographic, while Haneke insists on the obscenity of his. By undermining the romance, we begin to question the norms, conventions and tropes that shape it; rather than a critique of Walter specifically, we are instead invited to interrogate the violence of the construction of the 'lover' pursuing his 'beloved' and to recognise the spectre of rape inherent in courtly, romantic love. As Žižek notes, masochism (as well as its violence) is always already constitutive of courtly love and is its inherent transgression: 'It is only with the emergence of masochism, of the masochist couple, towards the end of the last century that we can now grasp the libidinal economy of courtly love' (Žižek 2000: 150).

This concentration on the couple and its inherent violence takes a different turn in Haneke's recent *The White Ribbon*, in which the narrator tells a tale of his courtship of the sweet, young Eva, as well as the strange goings-on in his village community. As an unusually whimsical centre for a Haneke film, the courtship between Eva and the Teacher seems at first to be a tale of sweetness in the midst of malice; as outsiders to the community and without children of their own, they are to some extent separate from the fear, cruelty and suspicion that dominate village life in this early twentieth-century German town. Yet the role of the Teacher as a part of the established power structures of the village (as indicated by his job-defined naming) and as the problematically unreliable narrator casts a slight shadow on the courtship, as does the cinematography of their courtship scenes themselves: shot in the dark in the schoolhouse scene; shot with a whirling, unsteady camera in the dance sequence; and filmed with an extremely shaky and nausea-inducing handheld camera in the carriage scene. As the precursor to the procreation of children, the formation of the romantic couple is a starting point that is at once exempted from the evil of the village, yet shadowed by the vague sense of dread that pervades all such unions and their fate.

Subtitled 'Eine deutsche Kindergeschichte' ('A German children's story'), *The White Ribbon* drives home this centrality of the family in Haneke's vision of violence. Throughout his films, children (especially pre-adolescents) figure prominently and are frequently framed as occupying a liminal zone – between the pure potential of childhood and the damage of socialisation. As an illustration of the destructive forces of socialisation and its concomitant repressions, alienations and power structures, pre-adolescent youth present a threat in his films, but it is a threat learned from adult example. This opposition is particularly clear in *The White Ribbon*, which features a few young children (under six years of age) who are excluded from the culture of suspicion, scrutiny and misapprehension that takes place both within the story and in our viewing of it. In this evasive whodunit, like in *Hidden*, everyone is under suspicion; the difference is that, in this film, the very young children are not. By addressing children who are not yet part of this system but are in the process of becoming part of it, Haneke sets up a larger attack on the destruction of children wrought by family and society. And like *Hidden*, *Benny's Video* (1992) and *The Piano Teacher*, the parents of the ruined children of *The White Ribbon* are faced with their own crimes and confronted with their actions.

In *The White Ribbon*, this familial structure is echoed in the community, which is organised around the paternal power of the Baron that filters through village life in multiple ways. The villagers fear and respect him (noting that his absence from church must indicate his anger, for instance), and seem resigned to his power. Owning nature, the Baron permits the Teacher to fish in his streams; owning the workers, his rejection of the Farmer's family means their destruction; owning God, or at least the Church, he enlists this sacred place to seek vengeance and restitution for crimes. Within this encompassing familial structure, we are invited in the homes of five families: the Pastor's, the Steward's, the Farmer's, the Doctor's and Eva's (from another village). In each we see the exercise of power, repression, abuse and violence: the beating of children in the Pastor's and the Steward's; disagreement, humiliation and relatively restrained physical violence (the slap) in the Farmer's home; sexual abuse and cruelty in the Doctor's; and a somewhat weaker, albeit still present repression, humiliation and control in Eva's home. Answering Eva's question of who would do such a thing as beat a child, we are forced to note that everyone in the village, aside from the Teacher and Eva perhaps, has shown him or herself capable of such a thing. The slap of a child echoes across the film as the Midwife, the Pastor and the Steward all hit young children and, in the case of the latter two, beat them quite badly.

But the youth are not exempt from this and we see these same actions, as they have acquired them as their own behaviours; their interactions likewise reveal the 'mutual suspicion' mentioned by the narrator, as well as outright violence. Added to this, of course, is the suspicion that the children are connected in some way to the unsolved mysteries of the community – the sense of dread that pervades the film indicating that they have learned their lessons only too well. But beyond this, what this pervasive cruelty, violence and suspicion point to is the unsolved mysteries as unexceptionable, as not constituting major crimes any more than the daily beatings, rapes, cruelties and accidental deaths. This is where the sibling discussion about death takes on significance. Rather than death as a result of old age, severe illness or exceptionally bad accidents, in *The White Ribbon* we see that suicides (threatened and achieved), the impending catastrophe of the war and interpersonal abuse seem more likely to cause death. The fact that the Farmer's wife's accidental death is rendered ambiguous through the eradication of a causal lead-up or cinematic revealing of the act itself adds yet another illustration of this pervasive sense of death by unnatural causes.

This diffusion of violence across the film links directly to the questioning of what constitutes violent action. Why is beating or severely whipping your own child acceptable, but the beating of other children horrific? How do psychological cruelty (outright, as well as the subtle cruelties of repression), and domestic and sexual abuse figure in our understanding of violence as an identifiable crime? How do accidental death through negligence and self-violence from despair fit into these understandings? Further, by severing cause from effect, violence is represented as an objective and isolated fact, rather than an individualised, contextualised or psychologised process. The Farmer's suicided body is discovered but we witness nothing suggesting his intent to kill himself; Rudi is found beaten, as is Sigi, whose battered body we are not even shown; the Farmer's wife dies in an accident but we only glimpse her corpse around a corner or through darkness (and her character did not play a part in the narrative before the event); even Peepsie the bird's murder is presented as objectified result (a corpse), even though we witness its preparation several scenes earlier. Indeed, only the initial scene of the Doctor's fall is shown as an action and, in this instance, the wire is not visible and disappears soon after the accident. In opposition to these invisible actions with visible effects, we have the multitude of scenes of everyday – quite literally 'domestic' – violence that fail to shock or horrify the community itself. These scenes of private, interpersonal violence are played out in some depth and detail, frequently in long takes or at least isolated scenes. For instance, the Doctor's cruelty to his mistress the Midwife and his sexual abuse of his daughter are lengthy, dramatic and weighty scenes, as are the moments of the beating of children (Martin's whipping, the Steward's beating of his son), even though these scenes are played behind closed doors.

The central and perhaps most disturbing scene of abuse is, however, the Doctor's sexual abuse of his fourteen-year-old daughter. Foreshadowed by the Midwife's comment after her humiliation at the hands of the Doctor, this scene addresses the abuse as a visual and acoustic discovery. Having woken afraid, the young boy Rudolph searches in the candle-lit darkness for his sister Anna, whom he detects through the sound of her tears, at which point he opens the door on to the brightly lit scene of abuse. The scene closely resembles a medical examination, with the fully clothed Doctor seated facing his daughter as she sits on the table in her nightdress, and the blinding light adds to the effect. Yet even the very young Rudi knows that something is amiss in this scene as he stands quietly weeping at the door but not crossing the threshold into the room. Through its banality, quotidian nature and narrational perspective, the scene is rendered particularly horrifying. Suggestive of everyday, non-sensationalised and coercive acts of violence, the rape in this instance reveals its own cover-up. As spectators, we too are in the position of Rudi, seeing the events from across the threshold and being told a lie we know is not true. (The subtle but clearly heard gesture of the Doctor doing up his zipper makes this emphatic.) We know abuse is happening, but the evidence is suggestive rather than overt and the way in which the offender and his victim greet discovery with nonchalance renders the abuse that much more acute. Abuse is quite literally just around the corner in the home and the daughter's willingness to collude in the lies to the young Rudi makes the scene even more poignant.

This scene's focus on the threshold of the examination room indicates the way in which doors play a central function in the film, as they construct the domestic space as a private one structured and determined by the patriarch (the offices with closed doors in the Doctor's and the Pastor's homes) and founded upon secrecy, lies and aggression. The fact that closed doors are tied not only to the abuse of children but to the Farmer's suicide, his wife's preparation for internment and the psychological abuse of the Midwife stresses this public/private divide. This is further emphasised in the cinematography of the film that seems to prohibit the crossing of thresholds; characters are either inside or outside rooms or houses and the camera never follows them through any of these spaces. The only time it makes this transition is when the Farmer and his son argue between the pig barn and the outside space, and here the camera moves uncannily through the wall of the barn itself, thus drawing attention to its movement as artifice. This 'behind closed doors' structure is crucial to the film's engagement with the family as a source of violence. By interrogating the question of privacy, the claustrophobia of the family and the issue of evidence, these scenes bring to bear the discourse and history of domestic abuse and family violence. Further, with the added layer of the narrator's unreliable narration and the fact that he could not possibly know what goes on behind those doors, these scenes work to interrogate further our understanding of violence as a known category, experience and issue.

This form of active questioning is insisted upon throughout the film in a multitude of ways. For instance, the cutting is so severe (it starts on action at the last possible moment and cuts away from action at the first possible moment) that every scene ends and begins with a moment of brief confusion, the dialogue is to a large degree interrogative (answering questions with questions is routine among the adults in this village, as the first meeting of the Teacher and Eva illustrates, where her first three lines are 'Why?', 'Who says?' and 'So?'), scenes are shot in almost total darkness and the narrator himself (the first Haneke has ever used) serves to muddy rather than clarify the events (why and when is he telling this story? How could he know of some of the events we are shown?). Further, although the film ends with the certainty of the First World War and its impact (a fact that has been foreshadowed by the line 'the world won't collapse,' said by both Eva's father and the Doctor), the future of the members of this community is as unknown as its history. Although there are certain assumptions made (for instance, the timeline and opening comments place the youth of the village as adults in the Nazi period, a significant relation for understanding the origins of global violence), there are many unanswered questions.

This fundamental ambiguity, aligned with an active questioning, pervades the depiction of parental brutality and sexual abuse in *The White Ribbon*, and as I have shown, it is equally evident in the disturbances to romantic and sexual clichés and tropes that we witness in *The Piano Teacher*. As a form of violence yoked to emotional trauma, intimacy and structures of guilt, shame and humiliation, rape is central to Haneke's interrogation of emotional brutality, cruelty and alienation. In *The White Ribbon*, the trauma of the family and its domestic space are crystallised in the central scene of the discovery of incestuous rape; while in *The Piano Teacher*, it is crystallised in Erika's rape, acoustically witnessed by her mother and perpetrated by her would-be romantic partner.

In his book on violence and masculinity in American cinema, Asbjørn Grønstad places Haneke within a list of productively offensive directors that 'shatter the lull' of violent representations and transfigurations (2008: 11). It is this offensiveness that I connect to Haneke's own terminological definition of his work as obscene; rather than merely excessive or even, like many films of the new extremism, focused on the body in a sensational or abject manner,

Haneke's films explore and extend the parameters of violence itself, and this is what makes them obscene. Disorienting spectatorial expectation and insisting on standing ambiguities, Haneke's films disrupt our knowledge and certainty about violent action. In linking violence to familial and romantic structures, problematising its visibility and diffusing its influence so that it pervades every aspect of the film, Haneke critiques the very question of excess, and the norms it implies, and suggests the obscenity and extremity of the everyday.

CHAPTER 16

On the Unwatchable

Asbjørn Grønstad

> The true mental daring and hardihood are those displayed when the artist simultaneously acknowledges the worth of what is being violated and yet presents unflinchingly its violation. And it *hurts* the reader or viewer to be involved in that process and to feel the broader implications of that violation.
>
> (Fraser 1974: 116)

> [A]ny ethical inquiry into film will need to engage with the destructive and anti-social.
>
> (Downing and Saxton 2010: 2)

> In their affective impact on the spectator, film experiences are real experiences.
>
> (Peucker 2007: 41)

> [T]here is no longer beauty or consolation except in the gaze falling on horror, withstanding it, and in unalleviated consciousness of negativity holding fast to the possibility of what is better.
>
> (Adorno 1974: 25)

In his review of Gaspar Noé's *Irréversible* (France, 2002), celebrated movie critic and connoisseur Roger Ebert begins by observing that the film is 'so violent and cruel that most people will find it unwatchable' (Ebert 2003). Reporting from the Cannes festival six years later, on 17 May 2009, Ebert's writing is wound up, impassioned. He has just come out of a screening of *Antichrist* (Denmark, 2009), the instantly notorious film by Lars von Trier, which he rather glowingly describes as 'an audacious spit in the eye of society' (Ebert 2009a). The director, he raves, 'is not so much making a film about violence as making a film to inflict violence upon us, perhaps as a salutary experience. [. . .] This is the most despairing film I've ever seen' (ibid.). Two days later, on 19 May, Ebert writes another review of the same film. 'I rarely find a serious film by a major director to be this disturbing. Its images are a fork in the eye. Its cruelty is unrelenting. Its despair is profound' (Ebert 2009b). *Irréversible* and *Antichrist*, however, are not exceptional cases of filmic belligerence but may be grasped more adequately as two of the more punishing examples of a roughly decade-long cycle of art films that compel us to rethink the notions of spectatorship, desire and ethics.

My own reframing of the notion of the unwatchable as a film theoretical concept is not inspired by Roger Ebert's use of it above – a serendipitous but none the less elucidatory matter – but by Catherine Breillat, for whom the term is part of the sexual lexicon of her 2001 novel, *Pornocratie*. In this book (from which her 2004 feature *Anatomy of Hell* is adapted), the unwatchable references that which in or despite its sheer visibility eludes visual representation. In the film adaptation, Breillat's heroine pays a gay man to scrutinise her intimate parts, requesting him to watch her where she is unwatchable: 'no need to touch me. Just tell me what you see.' While Merriam-Webster's codification of the term, first recorded in 1886, as 'not suitable or fit for watching' or 'tending to discourage watching' is still worth keeping in mind, it seems to possess an inherent conceptual or even philosophical complexity that requires further examination.

Toward the end of *Seul contre tous*, the debut feature by the Argentinian-born Gaspar Noé from 1998, a title card flashes across the screen with a somewhat unsettling forewarning: 'You have 30 seconds to leave the theatre.' Annoyingly self-conscious as this message might be, on a certain level it is nevertheless genuinely intended. The subsequent scenes are harrowing and pretty hard to sit through. But the insertion of the text into the diegesis of the film captures quite succinctly, I think, the intractable ambivalence at the heart of the everyday phenomenology of watching images that make us uncomfortable. Should I stay or should I go? If I continue watching, what exactly are my motivations? If I leave, what does this protest signify, besides discomfort? What is the nature of the ethical relation by which the viewer and the film are both enveloped? Are some images unwatchable? And if yes, when and under what circumstances? Does the unwatchable have a set of recurring formal characteristics? Finally, is there an aesthetics of the unwatchable? Taking as my point of departure Siegfried Kracauer's statement that 'nothing could be more legitimate than [the cinema's] lack of inhibitions in picturing spectacles that upset the mind,' I want to try to delineate the peculiar scopic psychology that underlies the somewhat oxymoronic notion of an unwatchable cinema (Kracauer 1960: 58). To do this, I introduce the concept of *entropic images* to interpret the self-destructive narratives and the narratives of self-destruction that characterise films such as those of Noé and von Trier. Impossibly violent, they assault their own audience and negate that scopophilic pleasure considered intrinsic to film as an art form. Uncompromising and anti-voyeuristic, they enact a reversal of the relation between film and spectator that historically has defined the cinematic situation – these films compel us to look away.

The history of film is overwhelmingly about the production of aesthetic pleasure in its multiple and various forms. But nested within this history is a parallel and minor tradition, going back at least to the first avant-garde movements, whose crucial project has been to problematise, withhold and sometimes overturn the cinematic pleasure principle. The increased cultural visibility of this tradition since the late 1990s can be evidenced in a steadily growing corpus of films, the focal point for which might have been what James Quandt once dubbed 'the New French Extremity'.[1] Its scope has since proven more global, however, and might be said to include films such as *The Idiots* (von Trier, Denmark, 1998), *The Piano Teacher* (Haneke, France, 2001), *Ken Park* (Clark and Lachman, US, 2002), *The Brown Bunny* (Gallo, US, 2003), *Alexandra's Project* (de Heer, Australia, 2003), *9 Songs* (Winterbottom, UK, 2004), *Anatomy of Hell* (Breillat, France, 2004), *Caché* (Haneke, Germany, 2005), *Battle in Heaven* (Reygadas, Mexico, 2005), *The Wayward Cloud* (Ming-liang, Taiwan, 2005), *Taxidermia* (Pálfi, Hungary, 2006), *Shortbus* (Mitchell, US, 2006) and *Import/Export* (Seidl, Austria, 2007), to name some of the recurring titles associated with this trend. Too long neglected by scholarship in the discipline of film studies, the tradition of transgressive films is an important part of the history of the medium and crucial for a deeper understanding of the effects of cinema and the ontology of looking. In this chapter, I will concentrate on two of the films that might be considered part of the new extremist trend, the difficult and occasionally hyperviolent *Irréversible* and *Antichrist*.

The notion of spectatorship, from the much-discussed and much-criticised 'Screen' theory of the 1970s to the cognitivism-inflected theorising of the last decade and a half, has tended to be theorised from without, in the sense that more or less totalising explanations or narratives about the viewing process have been projected on to the film experience. More often than not, these approaches have originated in other fields such as philosophy and psychology and, when applied to film, have put to work a bundle of concepts that – while illuminating in their own ways – might have deterred the invention and cultivation of ways of understanding spectatorship that are more firmly embedded in cinema history and in the cinematic. When it comes to the difficult topic of transgressive visuality of painful images, we need perhaps to become more attuned to other, more specifically aesthetic conceptualisations of viewing and of the relation between spectator and image. I would suggest, firstly, that the future study of spectatorship might benefit from taking into account what the films themselves have historically had to say about the subject, the assumption being that the protocols for scopic behaviour are in no small measure derived from depictions and narratives intrinsic to the cinema. In one way or another, films are also about viewing, and the ideas about the business of watching images that they sometimes produce might potentially impinge upon, blend into, or in some cases even construct modes of spectatorship. The spectator–film interface is a highly permeable one, in the sense that the activity of watching cannot be sufficiently studied apart from its particular object, just as the analysis of controversial films is largely unfeasible apart from some kind of conceptualisation of the spectator and the viewing process. Spectatorship, in short, cannot adequately be considered independently of the specificity of each individual film. Secondly, I want to explore the notion that some film images may be considered as *incomplete* or *unfinished* tropes, discrete formal entities that carry significational value and that are autopoetical: capable, that is, of engendering a form of conceptual thought that can only be expressed through filmic means but that nevertheless may be paraphrasable by ventriloquistic discourse. Thirdly, it seems to me that a revitalisation of the philosophy of spectatorship – particularly as it pertains to images of pain and painful images – needs to embrace both phenomenology and ethics (as these areas are being revamped for future intellectual discourses), or perhaps more accurately, the epistemological dialectics that will emerge from their encounter.

Throughout the history of cinema, there have been numerous attempts to inflict violence upon the viewer. However, the extensive research on media violence has been preoccupied with the kind of violence that occurs intradiegetically and has rarely, if ever, even acknowledged the existence of a more subterranean history of film violence in which the spectator (rather than other characters in the narrative) is the target of the abuse. It is difficult to overlook the implicit irony here. Generations of scholars, often with a background in sociology rather than aesthetics, have ceaselessly worried about the effects of classical Hollywood violence, a form that is designed to please rather than to appal and that is frequently too formulaic and insipid to cause much unease in the audience. At the same time, this school of research has been pretty much oblivious to the – admittedly select – list of films that deliberately attempt either to make the spectators uncomfortable or to problematise the process of viewing.[2]

The emblematic image for the confrontational cinema strata is the notorious carving of the eyeball in Buñuel and Dalí's *Un Chien andalou* (France, 1929), which Mary Ann Caws has variously referred to both as 'the most aggressive act conceivable' and as a 'supreme gesture' (Caws 1989: 136). Performing an act of ocular mutilation, the sequence has yielded a host of interpretations, many of which have been aptly summarised by Martin Jay. The laceration of the eyeball, he writes, has for instance been read as 'a simulacrum of sexual cruelty against women, a symbol of male castration anxiety, the conception of an infant, [and as] an indication of homosexual ambivalence' (Jay 1993: 258). But he also interestingly points out that critics have tended to neglect the 'literal dimension' of this violence (ibid.). The destruction of the visual organ implies physiological damage that is detrimental to the faculty of vision; as such, the razor's work signifies an assault on the act of viewing. Moreover, for the viewer the scene is almost unbearably painful to watch, probably also because it feels as if it were her own eye that was being cut open.

That the filmic semi-tropes, or half-tropes found in particularly disconcerting or confrontational moments of singular films attain their own kind of theoretical insight regarding spectatorship, is also evident in the fact that they often precede the pronouncements of film theory. When the Screen theorists of the 1970s critiqued the notion of cinematic pleasure, for example, the subject had already been approached aesthetically in films such as Michael Powell's *Peeping Tom* (UK, 1960) and Stanley Kubrick's *A Clockwork Orange* (UK, 1971). The latter's Ludovico Technique, an aversion therapy treatment in which the main character Alex is strapped to his seat and forced to watch graphic and disturbing footage for days on end, is another pertinent fictional expression of the less than affable relation between screen and spectator. In the 1990s, what had previously, and at least since *Un Chien andalou*, been a mere tendency culminated in what very much seemed like a movement, in which entire filmographies (those of Michael Haneke, Catherine Breillat, Bruno Dumont and Lars von Trier, to name a few) apparently were committed to the task of destroying the sensibilities of the viewer. A dirty job, but somebody has to do it.

Branded as scandalous upon their initial release, *Irréversible* and *Antichrist* share a few similarities, although the two films diverge aesthetically and topographically. The frantic suburban netherworld of the former, with its probing, vertiginous point of view and maddening soundscape, springs from a filmic consciousness far removed from the feral, occult verdancy of the latter. But both films are helmed by self-styled rabble-rousers, whose narratives are fuelled by a sense of mounting paranoia.[3] Focusing on relationships in distress, both films feature key scenes involving excessive sexual violence.

The recipient of an anti-award from the ecumenical jury at Cannes, *Antichrist* was shot while its director suffered from a severe depression. Making the film helped him defeat it: one reason, perhaps, why he considers *Antichrist* to be the most important movie of his career and a film that demanded to be made (Sélavy 2009). The narrative charts the downward spiral of a nameless couple whose young son falls to his slow-motion death in the film's stylised opening shots. We are off to the most brutal beginning imaginable, and from there on it will only get worse. Paralysed by grief, the mother (Charlotte Gainsbourg) is hospitalised at first, but before long her therapist husband (Willem Dafoe) persuades her to be treated by him. After a while they retreat to 'Eden', their cabin deep in the woods, so that the woman may confront her worst fears, which again is an essential part of the healing process as devised by her husband. She spent the previous summer at 'Eden' alone with her son, trying to complete her thesis on the topic of gynocide. The whole place is teeming with life, with swarming, crawling, bursting, overwhelming nature. Everything is full of nervous, restless energy. The woods are alive with the sound of a thousand menacing forces. One morning the husband awakes to find leechlike insects attached to his hand. At night the roof of their cabin is showered relentlessly with acorns. A deer is seen giving birth to its seemingly stillborn fawn. Crows are buried alive and a fox eviscerates itself. Nature seems to be in disarray.[4]

A common interpretation of the film among reviewers seems to be that it is based on the premise that nature is inherently evil and, furthermore, that it collapses the distinction between nature (as in 'the wilderness') and human nature.[5] At one point the Gainsbourg character exclaims that 'nature is Satan's church,' a statement which epitomises the general mood of the film. In another scene, the man is approached by a fantastic talking fox, enunciating the message 'chaos reigns.' But whose chaos is this, exactly? Increasingly, it would appear, the anarchic forces in nature become indistinguishable from the nature of female sexuality. For von Trier – and this is a profoundly problematic assumption – nature, violence, (women's) sexuality, madness, suffering, destruction and death are inextricably entwined. This amorphous, undifferentiated mess is enworlded by the film itself; it is built into almost every scene and is part of the reason why watching it is so taxing. The experience of nature in *Antichrist* is a twisted, ironic inversion of the 'perfect exhilaration' someone like Emerson enjoys while roaming the New England forests. 'In the woods, we return to reason and faith,' he writes in his epochal *Nature* (Emerson 1849: 39). Von Trier's conception of nature is closer to that of a Joseph Conrad or a Werner Herzog; the latter's remark concerning nature's 'overwhelming growth and overwhelming lack of order' seems particularly apposite in the context of *Antichrist*.[6]

The conception of nature as Satan's church is certainly not a unique sentiment from a controversial director who has stated that he wanted to subvert the cultural connotations affixed to the serene image of a bucolic cottage by the lake. Historically, the supposition that nature is home to evil and sin was a feature of Puritan thought, as was the persecution of women accused of witchcraft. As Richard Slotkin has argued, from the early European settlements in the colonies in the seventeenth century the wilderness became the conceptual foundation for the formation of Puritan identity. Intending 'to redeem the Satanic forest for Jesus', the colonists were certain that nature was corrupt and in need of regeneration (Slotkin 1978: 52).[7] In more specifically aesthetic terms, *Antichrist* evokes a few intertextual resonances that foreground the terrible darkness of the woods, most salient of which are perhaps Benjamin Christensen's *Witchcraft Through the Ages* (Denmark, 1922), Carl Dreyer's *La Passion de Jeanne d'Arc* (France, 1928), David Lynch's television series *Twin Peaks* (US, 1990), and Daniel Myrick and Eduardo Sánchez's *The Blair Witch Project* (US, 1999). In fact, what makes *Antichrist* such a densely layered film is to some extent its refraction of fragments of a number of discourses concerning both nature and narrative. While a dominant frame of reference in the film, the Puritan alignment of nature with evil is tempered by strong undercurrents of Paganism and Shamanism. In interviews, von Trier, a Catholic convert, has stated that some of the creatures in the film derive from visions he had when on Shamanic journeys.[8] It is also possible, finally, to identify the film's ecological preoccupation, made apparent as a very secular estrangement from nature that is also part of the global psychology engendered by the climate change crisis.

Although *Antichrist* includes some of the most graphic scenes in all of contemporary art cinema, the film is nothing if not cerebral and allusive. It is, for one thing, dedicated to Tarkovsky. The director also references some of his previous films – *Europa* (Denmark, 1991) and *The Kingdom* (Denmark, 1994) – and there seem to be a number of more oblique quotations from horror film classics such as *Rosemary's Baby* (Polanski, US, 1968), *The Exorcist* (Friedkin, US, 1973), *The Omen* (Donner, US, 1976), *Saw* (Wan, US, 2004) and *Pan's Labyrinth* (del Toro, Spain, 2006). Like Claire Denis's *Trouble Every Day* (France, 2001), von Trier's film is a comparatively rare fusion of horror and art cinema. *Antichrist* also arguably inscribes itself into a disparate set of films that converge on the motif of mourning, from *Don't Look Now* (Roeg, UK, 1973) to *In the Bedroom* (Field, US, 2001), *The Son's Room* (Moretti, Italy, 2001), *21 Grams* (Iñárritu, Mexico, 2003) and *The Door in the Floor* (Williams, US, 2004).[9] In addition, the two protagonists in von Trier's psychological drama bring to mind the bickering couple grieving over their dead child in Robert Frost's poem 'Home Burial', where the wife accuses her husband of insensitivity ('you think the talk is all') while he implores her to let him into her grief (Frost 1914).[10]

But the most prominent hypotext in *Antichrist*,[11] thematically as well as philosophically, might be a literary fairy tale written by von Trier's countryman, Hans Christian Andersen. In the film's tragic prologue, where the young boy falls out of an open window while his parents are having sex in an adjacent room, the camera dwells briefly on a couple of toys perched on the child's nightstand. It is an unobtrusive moment, easily missed in the terrifying inevitability of what is already in progress. The source of this visual quotation is *The Steadfast Tin Soldier* (1838), the somewhat fatalistic story about the misfortunes endured by the titular character. Mesmerised by a paper ballerina, the one-legged toy soldier ignores the advice given by a troll not to look at her. The following morning he falls from a windowsill and is found by two boys, who then put him in a paper boat in the gutter. A fish swallows the tin soldier, but someone catches the fish and cuts it open. Released from the belly of the fish, the tin soldier actually manages to see the ballerina again, just before he is thrown into the fire. At the same moment a breath of wind blows the ballerina too into the fire, the soldier melting into the shape of a tin heart. This was Andersen's first wholly original tale and thus indicative of his nascent autonomy as a writer. Over the years the significance of desire, accident, passivity and stoicism to the story has not gone unnoticed. *Antichrist*, in turn, re-appropriates the tale through this intertextual fragment, a subtle but conceptually pregnant gesture that fuses the injunction against looking with an apprehension of the unwatchable. The softly falling snowflakes – in this context again a sign of the evilness of nature – captivate the boy and lure him to the window. His death instantiates the first moment of the unwatchable in the film, emotionally if not graphically. What image could possibly be more painful than that of the death of a child under such circumstances? As spectators, we are already in the grip of trauma as the film begins (which is also the case in *Irréversible*, in which the most shocking scene takes place almost at the start), and the subsequent chapters take us through the progressively more intense stages of grief, pain and despair.

In terms of its aesthetic, the prologue also differs profoundly from what follows it. With its monochrome design, extreme slow-motion cinematography and emotive soundtrack,[12] the sequence comes across as overly stylised – verging almost on kitsch – in fact, as the antithesis of everything that the Dogme movement was about. But the main body of *Antichrist* oscillates between realism and surrealism, interspersed with occasional horror-film segments. There are some handheld shots and a curious proclivity for dorsality, for zooming in on the back of the characters' heads. When the explicit violence occurs it is just as troubling as Ebert's remark above would have us believe. In scenes that borrow from a torture-porn aesthetic the Gainsbourg character drills a grindstone through her husband's leg, and as a prelude she jerks his organ until it ejaculates blood. But the film's most infamous scene comes later, when the woman shears off a part of her labium, an unprecedented moment in contemporary art cinema that appears authentically transgressive while at the same time forging an intertextual connection with Nagisa Ôshima's *In the Realm of the Senses* (Japan, 1976). Our instinctual reaction is to look away. Those who do not, get a fork in the eye.

How, with reference to the spectator, is one to make sense of this ostensibly masochistic penchant for unwatchable images, and how, with reference to the artist and the film, is one to make sense of a poetics which accentuates such an excess? One way would be to consider *Antichrist*, as well as the cinema of the unwatchable of which it forms a part, against the background of a persistent fantasy of modern spectatorship. According to Martin Harries, this is the fantasy of self-destructive viewing. Our past century, he notes, 'had a particular investment in a formal logic that placed the spectator in a spot where that spectator had to contemplate her own destruction' (Harries 2007: 9). The mythical antecedent for this theory is a biblical figure, Lot's wife, who is turned into a pillar of salt as punishment for disobeying the commandment of the angels not to look back at the crumbling cities of Sodom and Gomorrah. Harries, with reference to Artaud, locates this form of self-destructive spectatorship in modernism, and claims that this fantasy carries with it a set of 'narrowly aesthetic and widely political applications' (ibid.: 8, 14). Its foundation is the risk of, and desire for, an 'experience of spectatorship so overwhelming that it destroys the spectator' (ibid.: 14). There are shadings of the sublime in Harries's description of destructive spectatorship, but his theory might more fruitfully be aligned with the kind of masochistic gaze identified by Gaylyn Studlar, who in *In the Realm of Pleasure* contends that cinematic pleasure is closer to masochistic pleasure than to the sadism posited as fundamental to the viewing experience by the film theorists of the 1970s (Studlar 1988: 76).

In *Antichrist*, the power of the self-destructive glance to unravel the mind of the spectator is also intra-diegetically encoded on the level of film form. The ambiguity of the mother's gaze toward the window during the intercourse – did she in fact realise what was about to happen early enough to have intervened? – prefigures her escalating confusion and mental frailty. And the unspeakable horror of having to witness the ensuing accident is what destroys her sense of self and pushes her over the edge of sanity. But there is also a key scene, strangely ignored in the criticism of the film, involving the business of looking at images that contain devastating information. These are the Polaroid snapshots of the son that the Defoe character comes across not long before the relationship with his wife really begins its downward spiral. Examining the photographs (taken by his wife when she was alone with their son at the same cabin the previous summer), he notices that the boy has his shoe on the wrong foot in every picture. His act of looking thus produces a suspicion either that his wife is capable of the same kind of neglect that prevented her from catching the boy before he fell out of the window, or that she is actually acting out a kind of sadistic cruelty developed as a side-effect of her immersion in the history of misogyny. In all these cases, the process of looking proves to be an existentially and psychically harmful act, unmaking the life-world of the protagonists.

In her essay 'The Aesthetics of Silence', Susan Sontag broaches the delicate issue of what she perceives to be the vapidity of much of the art of the 1950s and 1960s: '[t]he art of our time is noisy with appeals for silence. A coquettish, even cheerful nihilism. One recognizes the imperative of silence, but goes on speaking anyway. Discovering that one has nothing to say, one seeks a way to say *that*' (Sontag 1966a: 12). For the artist, the realisation that he has nothing to say – no wisdom to impart or even viewpoints to put forward – generates mostly noise but, according to Sontag, this noise is not without a structure or intention of its own. The recognition that one has brushed up against the limitations of speech also requires an outward manifestation, and the business of giving form to this articulatory impasse then becomes the operating principle which fuels a tradition of aesthetic nihilism. In the visual arts, the deployment of an auditory term – noise – as a descriptive metaphor more often than not invokes the notion of spectacle or variations thereof. Siegfried Kracauer, in the earlier quotation, applauds the very capacity inherent in the medium of film for manufacturing scenes that distress the audience. A striking formulation from a theorist hardly associated with immoderation or excessive declarations, Kracauer's telltale phrase, '[n]othing could be more legitimate,' could be construed as a sanctioning of an aggressive brand of cinema with palpable ties to Eisenstein's concept of the cine-fist and possibly also to Artaud's Theatre of Cruelty.

These two perspectives – Sontag's and Kracauer's – on the topic of violent and ferocious art nicely capture the divergent feelings aroused by the films of Argentinian-born filmmaker Gaspar Noé, unarguably the principal contender for the title of cinema's *enfant terrible* this side of the millennium. His unprecedented and unusually punishing second feature, *Irréversible*, is nothing if not noisy, although not necessarily nihilistic. It does, however, come across as a vicious assault on its own audience, an act of sheer violence that registers even on a physiological level. So uncompromising is this onslaught that it is as if the director was dead set on chasing away the few spectators who possessed the temerity to remain in the theatre after the Godardian warning in his previous feature. You have thirty seconds to leave the theatre, indeed. If the cinema is all about the dissemination of (mindless) pleasure, about watching beautiful bodies move through exquisite spaces in search of ever new adventures – a common assumption that turned into a harsh indictment in the work of feminist critics like Claire Johnston and Laura Mulvey in the 1970s – then *Irréversible* undeniably looks very much like the antithesis of that entire conception of the medium. Noé's universe is one of discomfort and offence, and *Irréversible* – while less sophisticated than *Antichrist* (which replicates the dynamics of the unwatchable on a diegetic level) in its treatment of the ethics of viewing – is possibly the only other film in the modern art cinema tradition to have caused as much media turbulence as von Trier's shocker. A frenzied, hyper-kinetic and disorienting film about revenge narrated in reverse chronological order, *Irréversible* outraged audiences, and during its premiere in Cannes in the spring of 2002, 250 people left the theatre, nauseated. (Intriguingly, its director has admitted to leaving the theatre himself during the rape scene in Sam Peckinpah's *Straw Dogs* [US, 1971] (Brottman and Sterritt 2004: 37).) Critics were offended by what they perceived to be manifestations of misogyny, homophobia and racism in the film, although worst of all was doubtlessly the unprecedented affront to conventional aesthetic sensibilities represented by its unusually visceral style. The unhinged swivelling and gyrating handheld camera movements and the extreme low-frequency sound applied in the first third of the movie induce a level of physical discomfort rarely experienced in the cinema. One senses the onslaught of motion (picture) sickness, an effect attributable to the mechanics of cinematography and point of view alone. *Irréversible* is already almost unwatchable. Violence inheres in the feral, uncontainable gestures of the camera. In the first of thirteen ostensibly uninterrupted segments (following a prologue dominated in part by the philosophical musings of the butcher from *Seul contre tous*) we see two men, the wounded Marcus (Cassel) and the handcuffed Pierre (Albert Dupontel), being escorted out of the S&M nightclub 'The Rectum' by the police.[13] Pierre has just killed a man in the club by smashing his head in with a fire extinguisher,[14] mistakenly believing him to be the rapist Le Tenia.[15] The next segment shows us the performance of this act in all its unimaginable brutality. We come to understand that the assault was a gesture of retribution for the abuse of Marcus's girlfriend (and Pierre's former lover) Alex by the homosexual Le Tenia, who in the film's most notorious scene beats her into a coma after anally raping her. Described by a critic as the 'fulcrum upon which the narrative rests', the sequence is the director's most self-conscious deployment of 'unwatchability' as an aesthetic mode (Cameron 2006: 71). Noé places his camera quite close to the action, and it remains stationary throughout the scene. He shows us the rape in its entire temporal unfolding, a nine-minute continuous segment accompanied by the raw, animal shrieks of the victim. There is little narrative or compositional motivation for showing this kind of cruelty in its actual duration. Hence, it could be maintained that the scene is not about the violence but about the act of looking at painful images. It is another way of asking, in meta-spectatorial terms, how much of this sort of thing we can endure.

Discussing the opening massacre in Peckinpah's *The Wild Bunch* (US, 1969), Richard Slotkin formulates a similar question. The audience, he writes:

> is engaged with an aesthetic equivalent of the ethical problem of violence: How much of this sort of thing are we willing to look at? Is looking somehow a form of 'consent'? [. . .] Are we willing to take responsibility for 'what we see' and for the curiosity – a form of wish or desire to see the unspeakable – that has brought us to this scene? (Slotkin [1998] 1992: 597)

The relatively scant criticism of *Irréversible* has tended to orbit around the film's narrative construction, often inviting comparisons to Chang-dong Lee's *Peppermint Candy* (1999) and Christopher Nolan's *Memento* (2000). Allan

Cameron, for instance, observes that *Irréversible* fits the template of what he calls a 'modular narrative' (Cameron 2006: 65), while Mikita Brottman and David Sterritt suggest that it reveals a corporeal structure that begins in the anal realm (Alex's rape in the underground passageway) and then continues toward the vaginal realm (the pregnancy test near the end of the film) (Brottman and Sterritt 2004: 39). Much has also been made of the subtle embedding within the narrative of an important intertext, *An Experiment with Time* (1927), J. W. Dunne's derided, quasi-scientific treatise on the existence of an alternative temporal reality where past, present and future times merge in a new experiential dimension accessed through dream states and trances (Dunne 1927). As Brottman and Sterritt write, *Irréversible* 'seems characterized by a belief in human helplessness in the face of a future that is as unchangeable as it is unavoidable, since – as Dunne suggests – it is already present' (Brottman and Sterritt 2004: 39). This reading is corroborated by the film's brusque postscript (and also Noé's working title), 'Time destroys everything,' from Ovid's *Metamorphoses* but which also calls to mind Schopenhauer's aphorism '[t]ime is that by virtue of which everything becomes nothingness in our hands and loses all value' (Schopenhauer 1970: 51). Thus situating the film in discourses about time and narrative – which also serves to align it with the kind of temporal self-consciousness found in Modernist literature and film – it is no wonder that more thematic interpretations of *Irréversible* have underscored its existential determinism, its strains of fatalism, apocalypticism, disillusionment and apathy. I would like to suggest, however, that *Irréversible*'s primary concern is neither narrative nor temporality as such, but rather the entropic dimension at work in a particular vein of contemporary art cinema. Here, the entropic as a theoretical concept is meant to convey a certain quality inherent in narratives of exhaustion and disintegration such as *Antichrist* and *Irréversible*, as well as the aesthetic configuration within these works of a trope of viewing. More specifically, the notion of entropic cinema involves the scopic organisation of an unwatchable mode of spectatorship, one that might be sufficiently harnessed – both intellectually and morally – to engage with aesthetic forms that emerge from what Susan Sontag once called 'the frontiers of consciousness' (Sontag 1966a: 45).

As the visual grammar and moral reference points of contemporary art cinema change, so, perhaps, must our ways of looking. Existing theories concerning both medium aesthetics, spectatorship and hermeneutics need to be at least reconsidered, if not altogether thrust aside. While eschewing the oppressive rhetorical power that any 'object' may potentially wield over the critic (in the form of fascination, seduction and so on), if we let it, we should none the less acknowledge the fact that films tend themselves to generate the manifold interpretational contexts – social, political, artistic – into which they are inserted by the critic. Sometimes a film opens up spaces of reflection that are more vital than the film itself. Or, one could say that these discursive spaces really represent an extension of the text, its epistemological determination, and that its aesthetic validation is proportionate to the extent to which it upends culturally hegemonic conventions and expectations. On that view, which would be both pragmatic and modernist in its conception of the function of artistic works, going beyond normativity would not only be an indication of artistic merit but also an integral part of the work's ontology. But this is an old story now, one with which we are all too familiar, and I certainly do not want to propose a reframing of the discussion of transgressive cinema in modernist terms. What I do want to draw attention to, however, is the possibility that some films demand something of the viewer that cannot adequately be provided by resorting to the fine selection of theories already available to her. Although they need not be entirely disposed of, maybe they should be momentarily suspended when one is confronted with new artistic expressions, and maybe one ought to take seriously Leo Steinberg's advice in *Other Criteria* that '[t]he critic interested in a novel manifestation holds his criteria and taste in reserve. Since they were formed upon yesterday's art, he does not assume that they are ready-made for today' (Steinberg 1972: 63). It is my hope that the concepts of entropic cinema and the unwatchable – theoretically situated somewhere between Wimsatt and Beardsley's affective fallacy and Jacques Rancière's (2009) notion of emancipated spectatorship – might provide a rudimentary platform from which to appraise more concisely the contributions of an art cinema of the extreme.

NOTES

1. Important releases within this other, darker French new wave were *Seul contre tous* (Noé, 1998), *Les Amants criminels* (Ozon, 1999), *Romance* (Breillat, 1999), *Baise-moi* (Despentes and Trinh Thi, 2000), *Trouble Every Day* (Denis, 2001), *Irréversible* (Noé, 2002) and *Twentynine Palms* (Dumont, 2003).
2. There is a fine line between, on the one hand, pictorial portrayals of human misery and anguish designed to stir the social consciousness and empathy of the viewers, and on the other, images that seem deliberately composed to make them uncomfortable. In my ongoing monograph project *Cinema and the Unwatchable: Film and the Negation of Pleasure*, I trace the confrontational sensibility of a cinematic tradition that aims sometimes to question, at other times to destroy the sensation of visual pleasure and even to violate the moral or emotional consciousness of the viewer. From Buñuel to Pasolini, von Trier and Noé, the acts of provocation that the images from this tradition perpetrate can be conceptualised as instances of what I have metaphorically termed razorblade gestures, the emotional, psychic and ethical slicing open of the gaze of the spectator. Unlike the images that tend to inflame the religious or political iconoclast, those that appear to enact violence against the viewer do not usually trigger acts of retaliation. Even while redrawing the boundaries for what can be visually imagined and put on display, these offensive images seem impervious to iconoclastic censure. Their taboo-breaking is of

a different order. They challenge the moral integrity of the spectators and put their subjectivity at risk.
3. Such is von Trier's cinematic notoriety that his work was the subject of a 'special report' in the American satirical news publication *The Onion*, 'Denmark introduces harrowing New Tourism Ads directed by Lars Von Trier'. One of the segments shows a deranged mother pursuing her son through the woods, eventually shooting him in the head (*The Onion* 2009).
4. The anthropomorphising of nature seems to be a recurrent motif across a range of cultural artefacts of the noughties, richly evident in the work of the folk ensemble The Handsome Family and in a record such as Neko Case's *Middle Cyclone* (ANTI-, 2009).
5. See, for instance, theauteurs.com.
6. See *Burden of Dreams* (Les Blank, 1982, Flower Films).
7. See also Slotkin [1973] (2000).
8. See, for instance, Hillis (2009).
9. A slew of other intertexts have also been brought up in the criticism on *Antichrist*, from the painting of Hieronymus Bosch and Peter Paul Rubens to Antonioni's *Red Desert* (1964) and the work of Peter Greenaway, Damien Hirst and Robert Flanagan. See Daniel Vilensky (2009).
10. I owe this observation to my colleague Øyvind Vågnes, who first brought up the poem in a conversation about *Antichrist* in Bergen on 23 February 2010.
11. This is Genette's term (1982).
12. The music that plays over the prologue is Georg Friedrich Händel's aria, 'Lascia ch'io pianga', from the Italian opera *Rinaldo* (first performed in London in 1711). Concerning a request to be released from agony, the libretto could be read as a comment on the function of sex in *Antichrist*.
13. This first chapter of the film actually consists of separate shots morphed together digitally in post-production. The episode is made up of roughly thirty fragments joined together seamlessly by a series of hidden cuts.
14. The scene was supposedly inspired by a documentary film in which a man's face is blasted off in an execution in Lebanon.
15. This motif of mistaken identities and violence is also present in Noé's *Carne* (1991), in which the butcher protagonist revenges himself on the wrong man.

Afterword

CHAPTER 17

More Moralism from that 'Wordy Fuck'

James Quandt

'Flesh and Blood: Sex and Violence in Recent French Cinema' began as a brief review of Bruno Dumont's then latest film, *Twentynine Palms* (France, 2003). Shocked by *Palms* in all the wrong ways, and feeling betrayed by a director whose early work I had taken considerable stock in, even the largely disparaged *L'Humanité* (France, 1999), I intended to puzzle out the reasons for Dumont's descent into gore and hard core, whether it was a mere exaggeration of the brute corporeality of his previous cinema, or something more disturbing: a submission to fashion. With its stilted, unconvincing performances, delivered largely in a language (English) Dumont avoided in interviews because he lacked mastery, and set in a landscape at once alien and unoriginal, *Twentynine Palms* felt like a forced anomaly, a freakish excursion into the unknown. But to what end? Was it sheer coincidence that *Palms* followed a spate of self-styled transgressive French films by Beineix, Breillat, Ozon, Noé and, most unlikely of all, Claire Denis, whose vampire nocturne, *Trouble Every Day* (France, 2001), seemed a radical departure from her earlier films, even those dealing with such 'extreme' subjects as cockfighting and serial killers? This most distant of observers – I do not follow French intellectual life with any assiduity, frustrated by the vague responses of Gallic film critics about the emergent trend (something about a crisis of the relationship between the image and the body was the generally nebulous response to questions I posed by email), felt a primitive need to 'explain' this development, or at least to question its cause and intention. Encouraged by my editor at *Artforum* to expand the review into a full-scale essay to explore this 'certain tendency', I was initially concerned about the spoiler fetishists who would take objection to my revealing all the violent surprises of *Twentynine Palms* in the article's opening paragraph, then quickly realised they were the least of my worries.

Parking 'new' in front of any purported development in cinema, thematic, national or otherwise, is a venerable tack, and by naming this development the 'New French Extremity', the article appeared to give form to an apparent but hitherto unspecified affinity. (To mistake it for a movement would be a step too far, as that term implies a communal consciousness and coherency that the disparate New French Extremity obviously lacked.) Published just before the world premiere of Catherine Breillat's *Anatomy of Hell* (France, 2004), the film that would mark the apotheosis and nadir of the trend in its ludicrous combination of the Holy Trinity, Home Hardware and assorted orifices – though Jean-Claude Brisseau's self-exculpatory *Les Anges exterminateurs/The Exterminating Angels* (France, 2006) would soon offer close competition – the article seemed both premature and instantly outdated. But it quickly travelled the internet, inciting mockery, outrage, abuse, beleaguered accord and, sometimes, a degree of relief that the forbidden had finally been broached. Derided by *The Guardian*, attacked in all manner of blogs and listserves as prudish or moralistic, twice quoted in *The New York Times*, and finally assigned its own Wikipedia site, the article took on a life never intended, with often-uncomfortable results.

Superficially read and frequently misconstrued, 'Flesh and Blood' became a lesson in the dangers of online apprehension, with the distressing effect of relegating complex artists to a false or constricting taxonomy: 'Claire Denis is also considered to be one the representatives of the New French Extremity, a term coined by James Quandt to designate transgressive films made by French directors at the turn of the 21st century,' reads Denis's faculty biography on the website for the European Graduate School (EGS 1997–2010). That my article discussed only one of Denis's films, citing it as something of an aberration in her career, seems a subtlety lost on anyone intent on making her an agent of a movement. Similarly Ozon, whose work had departed from the shock tactics of *See the Sea* (France, 1997) before the article even appeared. Indeed, the coastal title of his emphatically 'mature' *Sous le sable/Under the Sand* (France, 2000) seemed something of a deliberate acknowledgement that *the Sea* was long behind him.[1] No matter: that same EGS faculty list blithely includes Ozon among the prime purveyors of the 'style':

> Gaspar Noé's films are associated with the New French Extremity, a style of filmmaking featuring violence and perversion which questions the boundary separating the psychotic and the socially acceptable. Other directors who are part of the New French Extremity include François Ozon, Bruno Dumont, and Catherine Breillat. (ibid.)

Critical distance allowed by half a decade – an eternity in contemporary culture – reveals some of the article's obvious faults, including its confusion of the specific genre of French horror, which quickly established its own distinctive sanguinary *terroir*, with its art-house confraternity, an understandable imprecision further complicated by the recent release of such films as Pascal Laugier's *Martyrs* (France, 2008) and Alexandre Bustillo and Julien Maury's *À l'intérieur* (France, 2007). The transglobal nature of extreme cinema also could have been cited, particularly its origins in the cinema of Michael Haneke, although he seems less an antecedent of New French Extremity than a manifestly Austrian case, inheritor of a tradition that extends from the Calvary carnage of early Tyrolean art to the bodily abasement of Viennese Actionism and the traumatics of Ingeborg Bachmann and Elfriede Jelinek. (If ever there were an illustration of the commonplace that repression breeds sadism, Austrian culture is it.) Matters of degree, style and tone also differentiate such avatars of extreme cinema, largely subsequent to the appearance of the article, as Swedish Lukas Moodysson (*A Hole in My Heart*, 2004), Greek Yorgos Lanthimos (*Dogtooth*, 2009), Austrian Ulrich Seidl (*Dog Days*, 2001; *Import/Export*, 2007), Filipino Brillante Mendoza (*Serbis*, 2008; *Kinatay*, 2009) and, most famously, the depressive Dane Lars von Trier (*The Idiots*, 1998; *Antichrist*, 2009), from the New French Extremity. Avoiding the philosophical affectations of the French extremists, some of these directors, particularly Mendoza, employ shock cinema, like Fassbinder and Pasolini before them, to confront audiences with grim societal facts.

Two frequently repeated criticisms of the article were predictable in their 'circle the wagons' way: for its deliberate avoidance of theory – no mention of Kristeva's 'abject', obligatory references to Deleuze, or forging of neologisms ending in 'ivity' or 'ality' – and its nostalgia for the transgressors of the cinematic past (Fassbinder et al.). Why a preference for artists who truly risked all with their impassioned critiques of society automatically qualifies as conservative remains a mystery to me; our times, perhaps even more than Pasolini's, cry out for the voice of the heretic who declared, 'The first duty of an artist is not to fear unpopularity.' As backward-looking as a desire for the authentically subversive appears, to choose the incisive, committed visions of genuine rebels over the miasmic, apolitical and posturing ones of the largely bourgeois artists of the New French Extremity seems to me the very opposite of reactionary. Can one really claim that *Irréversible* (Gaspar Noé, France, 2002) marks any kind of advance – aesthetic, political, social, sexual – on *In a Year of 13 Moons* (Rainer Werner Fassbinder, Germany, 1978)?

Indeed, my full-bore attack on Noé's homophobic farrago proved the most contentious of the article's positions, unsurprisingly, given his status as *monstre sacré*; if Claire Denis enjoys secular sainthood amongst cinephiles, Noé's following has a fanboy fervour that views all naysayers as tremulous enemies. 'Quandt is a wordy fuck who – on this issue – is hiding his head up his ass for fear of the raw humanity these films illustrate,' declared one online commentator. 'Apparently to save himself from the horrors of the worst humanity has to offer he'd like to see all terrible acts illustrated as "ideas" as opposed to the very real and very brutal events' (MUBI 2008–10). (That 'thwock' you hear is the removal of said head from ass, along with the Tom Wolfe bow tie.) Until Noé's *Enter the Void*, which confirms the director's infantile fixation on the womb, emerged at the 2009 Cannes Film Festival, the New French Extremity had begun to look like an already archaic notion, as if naming it had also educed its death knell, annunciation and surcease in short order. The increasingly global nature of 'extreme' cinema seemed to have rendered the Frenchness of the New Extremity passé or partial, until Noé reasserted national dominion with his druggy trawl through a Tokyo in which guns are Texas-prevalent, verisimilitude rendered irrelevant in the director's spatially and temporally distorted hyper-vision of hell. (Spurious realism and the lack of the actual are central to my critique of the New French Extremity, but for those who take violence for veracity – oh, the raw humanity! – the greater the brutality, the more authentic the director's vision. It is the obverse-cohort of the glib slippage from 'humane' to 'human', which turns the latter into a signifier of empathy, tolerance, kindness, when the contrary should surely apply.)

Enter the Void, whose title's double-entendre on birth-giving vaginal canal and death-dealing nightclub – Eros and Thanatos, the hole and *le néant* – aptly captures Noé's latest puerile bid for profundity, may prove the last stand of the New French Extremity. The other directors discussed in 'Flesh and Blood' have largely moved on to more refined or mature work, or returned to home ground, though the violent denouement of Claire Denis's *White Material* (France, 2009) feels like an unconvincing flash of the old extremity, and Bruno Dumont's *Hadewijch* (France, 2009) culminates in an act of mass killing that the director suggests is a consequence of intense spiritual isolation. (Dumont's latest film, essentially *Mouchette sauvée des eaux*, exhibits a shocking disregard for social reality, more ideational than actual in its description of contemporary Paris.) Philippe Grandrieux, whose adepts passionately objected to my political and philosophical disdain for his 'visionary' cinema and who shares more with Noé than first appears, has retreated from the *lustmord* of *Sombre* (France, 1998) and *La Vie nouvelle* (France, 2002) to the Tarkovskian aura of *Un Lac* (France, 2008), with its snowy, fairy-tale forest, emblematic horse and Schubert *Lied*. Though one cannot blame an artist for his followers (least of all the grand Russian master, who spawned countless Tarkclones), the morally stunted tenor of Grandrieux's initial films can certainly be grasped from this exchange between two of his admirers: 'I think his films have amazing cinematography and sound design. But ultimately, I think the guy is a little too obsessed with killing prostitutes,' someone writes, paying homage to Grandrieux on Harmony Korine's website, to which another replies: 'You can never be too obsessed with killing prostitutes' (Harmony Korine Forum 2007). Godard and Fassbinder also dispatched hookers – Mieze's murder in *Berlin Alexanderplatz* (Germany, 1980) is one of the most traumatising moments in the latter's cinema – but it seems unthinkable that their work would elicit such callow, callous reaction. Though the 'new extremism' has perforce rejected humanism as false piety, pitilessness should not be mistaken for truth or courage, an error too often made by its reflexive defenders.

What, then, *was* the New French Extremity? A manifestation of cultural and political impasse, an anxious reaction to *fin de siècle* and the late capitalist condition the French call *la précarité*? A short-lived resurgence of the violational tradition of French culture, also reflected in contemporaneous literature (e.g. Michel Houellebecq, Catherine Millet, Marie Darrieussecq, Jonathan Littell)? The wilful imposition of thematic pattern on a disparate and disconnected group of films? In the waning days of the phenomenon, the answer appears no clearer, but many of its films have quickly come to look like desperate artefacts.

NOTE

1. The parallels between Ozon and Christophe Honoré, whose *Ma Mère* (France, 2004) was conscripted by many critics for the New French Extremity, are striking; both their recent films, *Le Refuge* (France, 2009) and *Non ma fille, tu n'iras pas danser* (France, 2009), seem to imply that heterosexuality and parenthood are imperatives of 'growing up', though Honoré's latest work, *Homme au bain*, named after a Caillebotte painting and featuring scalp-tattooed gay porn star François Sagat, is intended to counter what Honoré calls 'a return of homophobia in the movie business' (Honoré 2010, translation mine). Interestingly enough, Sagat's first non-porn film appearance was in that most extremist of franchises, *Saw VI* (Bousman, US, 2007).

Notes on Contributors

Neil Archer is Lecturer in Film Studies at Anglia Ruskin University. His work on French and transnational cinema has appeared in a number of journals, and he is currently preparing a monograph on the French road movie. He is the editor of *Adaptation: Studies in French and Francophone Culture* (Peter Lang, forthcoming 2011).

Martin Barker is Research Professor at Aberystwyth University. He has researched and published on a wide range of issues, across comic books, the history and ideology of censorship campaigns, methods of film analysis, and film audiences of many kinds. A running theme through much of his research is the gap between claims about what audiences might do, and what actual research into audiences reveals. In 2003 he directed the international study of the audiences for the film of *The Lord of the Rings*. In 2006 he oversaw a major research project for the British Board of Film Classification, from which his contribution to this volume derives, into the nature of audience responses to screened sexual violence.

Martine Beugnet is Professor in Film Studies and heads the Film Studies section at the University of Edinburgh. To date, she has written *Sexualité, marginalité, contrôle: cinéma français contemporain* (L'Harmattan, 2000), *Claire Denis* (Manchester University Press, 2004) and, together with Dr Marion Schmid, *Proust at the Movies* (Ashgate, 2005). Her fourth book, entitled *Cinema and Sensation: French Film and the Art of Transgression*, was published by Edinburgh University Press in 2007. She has written articles and essays on a wide range of contemporary cinema topics.

Jenny Chamarette is a Research Fellow in French at Fitzwilliam College, University of Cambridge. Her research specialisms are in French and

European cinema and lens-based media (including photography, video and installation art) and twentieth-century French phenomenological thought. She is the co-editor of *Guilt and Shame: Essays in French Literature, Thought and Visual Culture* (Peter Lang, 2010), and has published a number of articles on analogies of temporality and early cinema, and on contemporary French filmmakers, in the Peter Lang series *Modern French Identities*. She has written on visual ellipsis in the critical theory journal, *Paragraph*, and contributed annotations to *Senses of Cinema*. She curated the *Light Up!* Short Film Festival in 2009 and regularly assists in film selection at the Cambridge Film Festival.

Lisa Coulthard is Associate Professor of Film Studies in the Department of Theatre and Film at the University of British Columbia. She has published on European cinema, visual arts, film violence and theory, and is currently completing a book on sound and music in the films of Quentin Tarantino.

Michael Goddard is Lecturer in Media Studies at the University of Salford. His current research centres on East European cinema and media culture, particularly in Poland from the 1960s to the present, as well as on radical media in the spheres of film and video, radio, post-punk musics and cyberculture. His research into radical media is connected to his contribution to the paradigms of media archaeology and especially media ecologies, and this approach underlies his sabbatical project on radical media ecologies of the 1970s. He has also done substantial research into Deleuze's aesthetic and film theories, which has resulted in a number of publications. Another strand of his research concerns Italian post-autonomist political thought and media theory, particularly the work of Antonio Negri and Franco Berardi (Bifo). Recently, he completed a manuscript for publication by Wallflower Press on the cinema of the Chilean-born filmmaker Raúl Ruiz.

Asbjørn Grønstad is a film scholar and Professor of Visual Culture in the Department of Information Science and Media Studies, University of Bergen, where he is also the Director of the Nomadikon centre and the research project 'New Ecologies of the Image'. His most recent books are *Coverscaping: Discovering Album Aesthetics* (co-edited with Øyvind Vågnes, Museum Tusculanum Press, 2010) and *Transfigurations: Violence, Death and Masculinity in American Cinema* (Amsterdam University Press, 2008). Grønstad is also a founding editor of *Ekphrasis: Nordic Journal of Visual Culture*.

Daniel Hickin is a PhD researcher at the University of Southampton, where his thesis examines British film censorship since 1998. With the support of *Screen*, he co-organised the 2008 international symposium and 2009 seminar series on 'Transnational East Asian Cinema since 1997'. He has been published by *The Velvet Light Trap*.

Tanya Horeck is Senior Lecturer in Film Studies at Anglia Ruskin University. She has published essays in a number of journals and is the author of the book *Public Rape: Representing Violation in Fiction and Film* (Routledge, 2004). Her research interests include film theory and violence, documentary theory and film, affect and spectatorship. She is currently working on a second monograph, *Capturing Crime: Reality, Fiction, Film*.

Tina Kendall is Senior Lecturer in Film Studies at Anglia Ruskin University, where she is also Pathway Leader for the undergraduate Film Studies degree. Her research interests include theories of spectatorship, affect and unpleasure, especially as these relate to contemporary European cinema. She has published on questions of stillness, intermediality and the new materialism in film. She is editor of a special issue of *Film-Philosophy* on Disgust and Spectatorship, and is currently preparing a monograph on the cinema of Bruno Dumont.

Mariah Larsson is currently working on a research project dealing with the exhibition of pornographic film in Malmö in the 1970s. She also teaches at Malmö University, where she is the Programme Coordinator of the Masters programme in Sexology. Her publications include her dissertation *Skenet som bedrog: Mai Zetterling och det svenska sextiotalet [Deceptive Glow: Mai Zetterling and the Swedish 1960s]* (2006), and a number of articles and book chapters on film and sexuality, as well as on pornographic film. She is the co-editor (with Anders Marklund) of *Swedish Film: An Introduction and Reader* (2010).

Nikolaj Lübecker is a Tutorial Fellow in French at St John's College, University of Oxford. His latest monograph, *Community, Myth and Recognition in 20th Century French Literature and Thought*, is a study of the notion of community in writings by André Breton, Georges Bataille, Jean-Paul Sartre and Roland Barthes (Continuum, 2009); other publications concern Stéphane Mallarmé, Surrealism, Paul Nizan and Claire Denis. He is currently preparing a book on *The Contemporary Feel-Bad Film*.

James Quandt is Senior Programmer at TIFF Cinematheque in Toronto, where he has curated internationally touring retrospectives of the films of Mikio Naruse, Kenji Mizoguchi, Robert Bresson, Shohei Imamura, Kon Ichikawa and Nagisa Ôshima. A frequent contributor to *Artforum* magazine, he has edited monographs on Bresson, Imamura, Ichikawa and Apichatpong

Weerasethakul. The revised edition of the anthology on Robert Bresson will be published in early 2011.

Catherine Wheatley is a Lecturer in Film Studies at King's College, London. Her books include *Je t'aime, moi non plus: Anglo-French Cinematic Relations* (Berghahn, 2010, co-edited with Lucy Mazdon) and *Michael Haneke's Cinema: The Ethic of the Image* (Berghahn, 2009). Her next book, *Sex, Art and Cinephilia: French Cinema in Britain*, will be published by Berghahn in 2011, and she is currently writing a short guide on the film *Hidden* for the BFI Film Classics series. Catherine is also a regular contributor to *Sight & Sound*.

Leila Wimmer is Senior Lecturer in Film Studies at London Metropolitan University. She is the author of a monograph on *Cross-Channel Perspectives: the French Reception of British Cinema* (Peter Lang, 2009).

Works Cited

Aaron, Michele (2007), *Spectatorship: The Power of Looking On*, London: Wallflower.
Abella, Adela and Nathalie Zilkha (2004), '*Dogville*: A Parable on Perversion', *International Journal of Psychoanalysis* 85, pp. 1519–26.
Åberg, Anders (1995), 'Spelfilmen och lusten att se', in Lars Gustaf Andersson and Erik Hedling (eds), *Modern filmteori 2*, Lund: Studentlitteratur.
Adorno, Theodor W. (1974), *Minima Moralia: Reflections From Damaged Life*, trans. E. F. N. Jephcott, London: NLB.
Agamben, Giorgio [1995] (1998), *Homo Sacer: Sovereign Power and Bare Life*, trans. Daniel Heller-Roazen, Stanford: Stanford University Press.
—(2004), *The Open: Man and Animal*, trans. Kevin Attell, Stanford: Stanford University Press.
Alexander, James R. (2003), 'Obscenity, Pornography, and the Law in Japan: Reconsidering Oshima's *In the Realm of the Senses*', *Asian-Pacific Law and Policy Journal* 4:1, pp. 148–68.
Amour Fou Production Company (2007), 'Interview with Christophe Honoré', Press Release, http://www.amourfou.at/subs/filme/mere/pdf/Entretien-Anglais.pdf, accessed 17 July 2009.
Ang, Ien (1985), *Watching Dallas: Soap Opera and the Melodramatic Imagination*, London: Methuen.
Angelo, Adrienne (2010), 'Sexual Cartographies: Mapping Subjectivity in the Cinema of Catherine Breillat', *Journal for Cultural Research* 14:1, pp. 43–55.
'*Antichrist*' (2008–10), *The Auteurs*, http://www.theauteurs.com/topics/6030, accessed 31 March 2010.
Artaud, Antonin [1938] (1970), *The Theatre and its Double*, London: Calder & Boyars.
Assouline, Florence (2000), '*Baise-moi*, un film dégueulasse', *L'Evènement du jeudi* 21 July, n.p.
Attali, Danielle (2000), '*Baise-moi*', *Le Journal du dimanche* 2 July, n.p.
Augé, Marc (1995), *Non-Places: Introduction to an Anthropology of Supermodernity*, trans. John Howe, London: Verso.
Authier, Christian (2002), *Le Nouvel Ordre sexuel*, Paris: Bartillat.
Badiou, Alain (2002), *Ethics: An Essay on the Understanding of Evil*, trans. Peter Hallward, London: Verso.
Bainbridge, Caroline (2004), 'The Trauma Debate: Just Looking? Traumatic Affect, Film Form, and Spectatorship in the Work of Lars von Trier', *Screen* 45:4, pp. 391–400.
—(2007), *The Cinema of Lars von Trier: Authenticity and Artifice*, London: Wallflower.

Balibar, Étienne (2007), 'Uprising in the *Banlieues*', *Constellations* 14.1, pp. 47–71.
Barker, Martin (2005, 2006), 'Loving and Hating *Straw Dogs*', *Participations: Online Journal of Audience and Reception Studies* Part 1, 2:2, November and Part 2, 3:1, December, http://www.participations.org/Volume%205/Issue%201%20-%20special/5_01_selfe.htm, accessed 6 January 2009.
Barker, Martin, Jane Arthurs and Ramaswami Harindranath (2001), *The Crash Controversy: Censorship Campaigns and Film Reception*, London: Wallflower.
Barker, Martin, Kate Egan, Ernest Mathijs, Jamie Sexton, Ross Hunter and Melanie Selfe (2007), 'Audiences and Receptions for Sexual Violence in Contemporary Cinema', Report to the BBFC, http://www.bbfc.co.uk/classification/downloads, accessed 6 January 2009.
Barker, Martin and Ernest Mathijs (eds) (2008), *Watching* Lord of the Rings*: Tolkien's World Audiences*, New York: Peter Lang.
Basu, Feroza (2006), 'Confronting the "Travel" in Twentieth-Century Travel Literature in French', in Charles Forsdick, Feroza Basu and Siobhán Shilton (eds), *New Approaches to Twentieth-Century Travel Literature in French: Genre, History, Theory*, New York: Peter Lang, pp. 131–200.
Bataille, Georges (1961), *The Tears of Eros*, trans. Peter Connor (1989), San Francisco: City Lights.
—(1966), *Ma mère*, Paris: J.-J. Pauvert.
—(1970), *Œuvres complètes vol. I*, Paris: Gallimard.
Baudrillard, Jean (1986), *Amérique*, Paris: Grasset.
—(1988), *America*, trans. Chris Turner, London: Verso.
—(2001), 'The Spirit of Terrorism', *Le Monde* 2 November, http://www.jiscmail.ac.uk/lists/cyber-society-live.html, accessed 11 March 2010.
Baudry, Jean-Louis (2004), 'The Apparatus: Metapsychological Approaches to the Impression of Reality in Cinema', in Leo Braudy and Marshall Cohen (eds), *Film Theory and Criticism* (6th edn), Oxford: Oxford University Press, pp. 206–23.
BBFC (British Board of Film Classification) (1999a), '*Romance* Press Release', http://www.bbfc.co.uk/news/press/19990729.html, accessed 16 February 2010.
—(1999b), '*Seul contre tous* Press Release', http://www.bbfc.co.uk/news/press/19990101.html, accessed 16 February 2010.
—(1999c), 'BBFC Annual Report 1999', http://www.bbfc.co.uk/downloads/pub/BBFC%20Annual%20Reports/BBFC_AnnualReport_1999.pdf, accessed 16 February 2010.
—(2002a), '*Irréversible* Press Release', http://www.bbfc.co.uk/news/press/20021021.html, accessed 16 February 2010.
—(2002b), 'BBFC Annual Report 2002', http://www.bbfc.co.uk/downloads/pub/BBFC%20Annual%20Reports/BBFC_AnnualReport_2002.pdf, accessed 16 February 2010.
—(2009a), '*In the Realm of the Senses*', http://www.bbfc.co.uk/website/Classified.nsf/c2fb077ba3f9b33980256b4f002da32c/12f831f5611a0b41802566c80042f0a0?OpenDocument, accessed 3 March 2010.
—(2009b) 'BBFC Guidelines 2009', http://www.bbfc.co.uk/downloads/pub/Guidelines/BBFC%20Classification%20Guidelines%202009.pdf, accessed 16 February 2010.
—(2010), Statistics, http://www.bbfc.co.uk/statistics/index.php, accessed 16 February 2010.
Bellour, Raymond (2005), 'Bords Marginaux', in Nicole Brenez (ed.), *La Vie nouvelle/Nouvelle Vision*, Clamecy: Nouvelle Imprimerie Laballery, pp. 16–17.
Bennett, Ray (2009), '*Fish Tank*', *The Hollywood Reporter*, 14 May, http://www.hollywoodreporter.com/hr/film-reviews/fish-tank-film-review-1003973214.story, accessed 15 July 2010.

Bernstein, J. M. (2004), 'Bare Life, Bearing Witness: Auschwitz and the Pornography of Horror', *Parallax* 10:1, pp. 2–16.
Best, Victoria and Martin Crowley (2007), *The New Pornographies: Explicit Sex in Recent French Fiction and Film*, Manchester: Manchester University Press.
Betz, Mark (2003), 'Art, Exploitation, Underground', in Mark Jancovich (ed.), *Defining Cult Movies: The Cultural Politics of Oppositional Taste*, Manchester: Manchester University Press, pp. 202–22.
Beugnet, Martine (2004a), 'French Cinema of the Margins', in Elizabeth Ezra (ed.), *European Cinema*, Oxford: Oxford University Press, pp. 283–98.
—(2004b), *Claire Denis*, Manchester: Manchester University Press.
—(2005), 'Evil and the Senses: Philippe Grandrieux's *Sombre* and *La Vie Nouvelle*', *Studies in French Cinema* 5:3, pp. 175–84.
—(2007a), *Cinema and Sensation: French Film and the Art of Transgression*, Edinburgh: Edinburgh University Press.
—(2007b), 'Blind Spot', *Screen* 48:2, pp. 227–31.
Beugnet, Martine and Elizabeth Ezra (2010), 'Traces of the Modern: An Alternative History of French Cinema', *Studies in French Cinema* 10:1, pp. 11–38.
Blackman, Lisa and Couze Venn (eds) (2010), 'Affect' [Special Issue], *Body and Society* 16:1.
Bonitzer, Pascal (1976), 'L'Essence du pire', *Cahiers du cinéma* September–October, pp. 48–52.
Bordwell, David [1979] (2002), 'The Art Cinema as a Mode of Film Practice', in Catherine Fowler (ed.), *The European Film Reader*, London: Routledge, pp. 94–102.
Boujut, Michel (2000), 'Pourquoi se faire baiser?', *Charlie Hebdo* 5 July, n.p.
Bourcier, Marie-Hélène (2005), *Sexpolitiques. Queer Zones 2*, Paris: La Fabrique.
Bousé, Derek (2000), *Wildlife Films*, Philadelphia: University of Pennsylvania Press.
Bowles, Brett (2004), '*La Vie de Jésus*', *Film Quarterly* 57:3, pp. 47–55.
Bradshaw, Peter (2003), '*Irréversible* Review', *The Guardian*, 31 January, p. 16.
—(2005a), '*Ma Mère*' [Review], *The Guardian*, http://film.guardian.co.uk/News_Story/Critic_Review/Guardian_review/0,,1429798,00.html, accessed 3 March 2010.
—(2005b), '*9 Songs*', *The Guardian* 11 March, http://film.guardian.co.uk/News_Story/Critic_Review/Guardian_Film_of_the_week/0,4267,1434764,00.html, accessed 15 July 2010.
—(2008), '*Import/Export*', *The Guardian* 3 October, http://www.guardian.co.uk/film/2008/oct/03/drama.importexport, accessed 11 March 2010.
Brecht, Bertolt (1964), *Brecht on Theatre: The Development of an Aesthetic*, John Willett (ed.), London: Methuen.
Breillat, Catherine (2001), *Pornocratie*, Paris: Denoël.
Brenez, Nicole (2003), 'The Body's Night: an Interview with Philippe Grandrieux', *Rouge* 1, www.rouge.com/au/1/grandrieux, accessed 01 July 2008.
—(ed.) (2005), *La Vie nouvelle/Nouvelle Vision*, Paris: Léo Scheer.
Brooks, Xan (2009) '*Antichrist* – A Work of Genius or the Sickest Film in the History of Cinema?', *The Guardian* 16 July, http://www.guardian.co.uk/film/2009/jul/16/antichrist-lars-von-trier-feminism, accessed 5 October 2010.
Brottman, Mikita and David Sterritt (2004), Review of *Irréversible*, *Film Quarterly* 57:2, pp. 37–42.
Brown, James (2004), 'Lights, Camera, Explicit Action', *The Independent* 13 May, www.independent.co.uk/arts-entertainment/films/features/lights, accessed 16 July 2009.
Brunette, Peter (2010), *Michael Haneke*, Urbana: University of Illinois Press.
Bruyn, Oliver de (2000), 'Le Marécage porno', *Le Point* 23 June, n.p.

Burch, Noël (2007), *De la beauté des latrines. Pour réhabiliter le sens au cinéma et ailleurs*, Paris: L'Harmattan.
Burt, Jonathan (2002), *Animals in Film*, London: Reaktion.
Burt, Martha R. (1980), 'Cultural Myths and Supports for Rape', *Journal of Personality and Social Psychology* 38, pp. 217–30.
Cameron, Allan (2006), 'Contingency, Order, and the Modular Narrative: *21 Grams* and *Irréversible*', *The Velvet Light Trap* 5, pp. 65–78.
Camy, Gérard and Albert Montagne (2002), '*Baise-moi*', *Cinémaction* 103, pp. 217–21.
Carter, Angela (1979), *The Sadeian Woman: An Exercise in Cultural History*, London: Virago.
Cartwright, Lisa (2008), *Moral Spectatorship: Technologies of Voice and Affect in Postwar Representations of the Child*, Durham, NC: Duke University Press.
Caws, Mary Ann (1989), *The Art of Interference: Stressed Readings in Verbal and Visual Texts*, Cambridge: Polity Press.
Chauvin, Jean-Sébastien (2001), 'Au-delà des genres', *Cahiers du cinéma* 559, pp. 77–8.
Chiesa, Lorenzo (2007), 'What is the Gift of Grace? On *Dogville*', *Film-Philosophy* 11:3, pp. 1–21.
Chrisafis, Angelique (2002), 'Rape Scene Tests Censors Nerve', *The Guardian*, 17 August, p. 9.
Christopher, James (1999), '*Seul contre tous* Review', *The Times* 18 March, p. E7:1.
Copperman, Annie (2000), 'Un Faux Événement', *Les Échos* 28 July, n.p.
Crowley, Martin (2004), 'Bataille's Tacky Touch', *MLN* 119:4, pp. 766–80.
Cumberbatch, Guy (2002), ' "Where Do you Draw the Line?": Attitudes and Reactions of Video Renters to Sexual Violence in Film', Report prepared for the BBFC, http://www.bbfc.co.uk/classification/downloads, accessed 6 January 2009.
Danquart, Didi, Sabine Fröhlich, Gass Henrik Lars, Eva Hohenberger, Werner Ružička et al. (1996), 'How Provocative Can You Get? A Round Table Discussion on the Films of Austrian Director Ulrich Seidl', *Dox: Documentary Film Quarterly* 10, pp. 34–7.
Del Rio, Elena (2008), *Deleuze and the Cinemas of Performance: Powers of Affection*, Edinburgh: Edinburgh University Press.
Deleuze, Gilles (1988), *Le Pli: Leibniz et le baroque*, Paris: Minuit.
—(1989), *Cinema 2: The Time-Image*, trans. Hugh Tomlinson and Robert Galeta, Minneapolis: University of Minnesota Press.
—(2002), *Francis Bacon: Logique de la sensation*, Paris: Seuil.
Deleuze, Gilles and Félix Guattari (1972), *L'Anti-Œdipe: Capitalisme et schizophrénie*, Paris: Seuil.
Derrida, Jacques (2008), *The Animal That Therefore I Am*, ed Marie-Louise Mallet, trans. David Wills, New York: Fordham University Press.
Douin, Jean-Luc (2000), 'Cinéma: le retour de la censure', *Le Monde* 15 July, n.p.
—(2009), '*Un Lac*: fantasmagorie sensuelle', *Le Monde* 17 March, http://www.lemonde.fr/cinema/article/2009/03/17/un-lac-fantasmagorie-sensuelle_1168844_3476.html, accessed 30 March 2010.
Downing, Lisa (2004), 'French Cinema's New "Sexual Revolution": Postmodern Porn and Troubled Genre', *French Cultural Studies* 15:3, October, pp. 265–80.
Downing, Lisa and Libby Saxton (2010), *Film and Ethics: Foreclosed Encounters*, London: Routledge.
Dufreigne, J. P. (2000), 'Je tue, ils, elles ...', *L'Express* 29 June, n.p.
Dunne, J. W. (1927), *An Experiment With Time*, London: A. & C. Black.
Ebert, Roger (2003), '*Irréversible*', *Chicago Sun-Times* March 14, http://rogerebert.suntimes.

com/apps/pbcs.dll/article?AID=/20030314/REVIEWS/303140303/1023, accessed 31 March 2010.
—(2009a), 'Cannes #5: Even Now Already is it in the World', Roger Ebert's Journal, 17 May, http://blogs.suntimes.com/ebert/2009/05/for_even_now_already_is_it_in.html, accessed 31 March 2010.
—(2009b), 'Cannes #6: A Devil's Advocate for Antichrist', Roger Ebert's Journal, 19 May, http://blogs.suntimes.com/ebert/2009/05/a_devils_advocate_for_antichri.html, accessed 31 March 2010.
Elsaesser, Thomas (2005), *European Cinema: Face to Face with Hollywood*, Amsterdam: Amsterdam University Press.
Emerson, Ralph Waldo (1849), *Nature*, Boston: James Munroe.
European Graduate School [Online] (1997–2010a), 'Claire Denis – Biography', http://www.egs.edu/faculty/claire-denis/biography/, accessed 30 March 2010.
—(1997–2010b), 'Gaspar Noé – Biography', http://www.egs.edu/faculty/gaspar-noe/biography/, accessed 30 March 2010.
Falcon, Richard (1999), 'Reality is Too Shocking', *Sight & Sound* 9:1, pp. 10–14.
—(2002), 'Cruel Intentions', *Sight & Sound* 12:9, 1 September, pp. 52–3.
—(2005), '*Twentynine Palms*', *Sight & Sound* 15:8, pp. 75–6.
Fassin, Eric (2003), 'The Politics of *PaCs* in a Transatlantic Mirror: Same-Sex Unions and Sexual Difference in France Today', in Roger Celestin et al. (eds), *Beyond French Feminism. Debates on Women, Politics, and Culture in France, 1981–2001*, New York: Palgrave Macmillan, pp. 27–38.
Ferguson, Frances (2004), *Pornography, the Theory: What Utilitarianism Did to Action*, Chicago: University of Chicago Press.
—(2006), 'Eine Umfrage zur Pornografie', *Texte zur Kunst*, December, pp. 109–12.
Fibiger, Bo (2003), 'A Dog not Yet Buried – Or *Dogville* as a Political Manifesto', *P.O.V.: A Danish Journal of Film Studies* 16, pp. 51–5.
'Fick andnöd av sin egen äckelscen' (2004), *Expressen*, 9 September, n.p.
Fleckinger, Hélène (2005), 'Expérience érotique et transgression', in Nicole Brenez (ed.), *La Vie nouvelle/Nouvelle Vision*, Clamecy: Nouvelle Imprimerie Laballery, pp. 104–10.
Flitterman-Lewis, Sandra (1996), *To Desire Differently: Feminism and the French Cinema*, New York: Columbia University Press.
Foucault, Michel (1976), *La Volonté de savoir*, Paris: Gallimard.
Franco, Judith (2004), 'Gender, Genre and Female Pleasure in the Contemporary Revenge Narrative: *Baise-moi* and *What It Feels Like For a Girl*', *Quarterly Review of Film and Video* 21:1, pp. 1–10.
Fraser, John (1974), *Violence in the Arts*, London: Cambridge University Press.
French, Phillip (1999), 'One Man's Meat', *The Observer*, 21 March 1999: 6.
Frey, Mattias (2003), 'A Cinema of Disturbance: The Films of Michael Haneke in Context', *Senses of Cinema*, http://archive.sensesofcinema.com/contents/directors/03/haneke.html, accessed 05 June 2010.
Frost, Robert (1914), 'Home Burial', North of Boston, London: David Nutt.
Fuller, Graham (2010), 'Social Realism in a Poetic Lens', *The New York Times* 17 January.
Gaffez, Fabien (2005), 'Carnet de bord. Notes et contre-notes d'une incubation cinéphile', in Nicole Brenez (ed.), *La Vie nouvelle/Nouvelle Vision*, pp. 26–34.
Garcin, Jérome (2000), 'Un entretien avec les deux héroïnes de *Baise-moi*: "Le Porno, c'est du viol"', *Le Nouvel Observateur* 22 July, n.p.
Garrard, Greg (2004), *Ecocriticism*, London: Routledge.
Genette, Gérard (1982), *Palimpsestes: La Littérature au second degré*, Paris: Seuil.

Gentele, Jeanette (2003), 'Lilja 4-ever visas i duman', Svenska Dagbladet 6 May.
Gentleman, Amelia (1999), 'Explicit Euro-Sex Test for Censors', The Guardian, 22 February, p. 5.
Gianorio, Richard (2000), 'Baise-moi: Vices et sévices compris', France-Soir 28 June.
Girard, René (1977), Violence and the Sacred, trans. Patrick Gregory, Baltimore: Johns Hopkins University Press.
Glaister, Dan (1998), 'Sins of the Flesh', The Guardian, 19 August 1998, p. 14.
Godard, Jean-Luc (1972), Godard on Godard, Jean Narboni and Tom Milne (eds), trans. Tom Milne, New York: Da Capo.
Gorin, François (2000), 'Baise-moi', Télérama 28 June, n.p.
Gormley, Paul (2005), The New-Brutality Film: Race and Affect in Contemporary Hollywood Cinema, Bristol: Intellect.
Golsan, Richard (Joseph) (2000), Vichy's Afterlife: History and Counterhistory in Postwar France, Lincoln, NB: University of Nebraska Press.
Grandrieux, Philippe (2000), 'Sur l'horizon insensé du cinéma', Cahiers du cinéma hors série: Le Siècle du cinema November, pp. 90–3.
Grandrieux, Philippe, Antoine de Baecque and Thierry Jousse (1999), 'Le Monde à l'envers : Entretien avec Philippe Grandrieux', Cahiers du cinéma 532, p. 39.
Grønstad, Asbjørn (2006), 'Abject Desire: Anatomie de l'enfer and the Unwatchable', Studies in French Cinema 6:3, pp. 161–9.
—(2008), Transfigurations: Violence, Death and Masculinity in American Cinema, Amsterdam: Amsterdam University Press.
Gržinić, Marina (2008), Re-Politicising Art, Theory, Representation and New Media Technology, Vienna: Schlebrügge.
Gustafsson, Annika (2004), 'Moodysson går hem i kyrkan', Sydsvenska Dagbladet, 29 September, n.p.
Hagman, Hampus (2007), ' "Every Cannes Needs its Scandal": Between Art and Exploitation in Contemporary French Film', Film International 5:5, pp. 32–41.
Hainge, Greg (2007), 'Le Corps concret: Of Bodily and Filmic Material Excess in Philippe Grandrieux's Cinema', Australian Journal of French Studies 44:2, pp. 153–71.
Hansell, Sven (2004), '—Du är inte normal! Kön, norm och frihet i Lukas Moodysson's filmer', Kvinnovetenskaplig tidskrift 1–2, pp. 99–112.
Hardt, Michael and Antonio Negri (2000), Empire, Cambridge, MA: Harvard University Press.
Harmony Korine Forum [Online] (2008), 'Philippe Grandrieux', accessed 30 March 2010.
Harries, Martin (2007), Forgetting Lot's Wife: On Destructive Spectatorship, New York: Fordham University Press.
Hawkins, Joan (2000), Cutting Edge: Art Horror and the Horrific Avant-Garde, Minneapolis: University of Minnesota Press.
Hayles, N. Katherine (1993), 'The Materiality of Informatics', Configurations 1:1, pp. 147–70.
Hayward, Susan (1992), 'A History of French Cinema: 1895–1991: Pioneering Filmmakers (Guy, Dulac, Varda) and their Heritage', Paragraph 15:1, pp. 19–37.
Hedling, Erik and Ann-Kristin Wallengren (eds) (2006), Solskenslandet: svensk film på 2000-talet, Stockholm: Atlantis.
Hedling, Olof (2004), 'Om Lilja 4-ever – en svensk film', in Bibi Jonsson, Karin Nykvist and Birthe Sjöberg (eds), Från Eden till damavdelning. En vänbok till Christina Sjöblad, Lund: Absalon, pp. 323–34.
Higgins, Charlotte (2004), 'Cannes Screening for most Sexually Explicit British Film', The Guardian 17 May, http://www.guardian.co.uk/uk/2004/may/17/cannes2004.film, accessed 5 October 2010.

Hillis, Aaron (2009), 'Sexual Perversity in Denmark: An Interview with Lars von Trier', *IFC*, 21 October, http://www.ifc.com/news/2009/10/lars-von-trier.php, accessed 31 March 2010.
Hills, Matt (2005), *The Pleasures of Horror*, London: Continuum.
Hirsch, Marianne (2008), 'The Generation of Postmemory', *Poetics Today* 29:1, pp. 103–28.
Holden, Stephen (2005), 'A Young Man's Education in Mom's Hedonistic Ways', *New York Times* 13 May, http://query.nytimes.com/gst/fullpage.html?res=9E01E5D71030F930A25 756C0A9639C8B63&sec=&spon=, accessed 3 March 2010.
Holmes, Diana (1996), *French Women's Writing 1848–1994*, London: Athlone.
Honoré, Christophe (2010), 'François Sagat redéfinit la notion de virilité', *Yagg* [Online], http://yagg.com/2010/02/15/christophe-honore-francois-sagat-redefinit-la-notion-de-virilite/, accessed 30 March 2010.
Horeck, Tanya (2004), *Public Rape: Representing Violation in Fiction and Film*, London: Routledge.
Horsley, Jake (2005), *Dogville vs. Hollywood: The War between Independent Film and Mainstream Movies*, London: Marion Boyars.
Iordanova, Dina (2003), *Cinema of the Other Europe*, London: Wallflower.
Iversen, Gunnar (1987), *Den indre svinehund: Essays om fred og fordragelighed*, København: Nyt Nordisk Forlag.
Jacobsen, Kirsten (2003), *Dagbog fra Dogville*, København: Gyldendal.
James, N. (2002), '*Irréversible* Cannes Report', *Sight & Sound* 12:7, pp. 12–16.
Jansson, Malena (2004), Review of *A Hole in My Heart*, *Svenska Dagbladet*, 17 September.
Jay, Martin (1993), *Downcast Eyes: The Denigration of Vision in Twentieth-Century French Thought*, Berkeley: University of California Press.
Joffrin, Laurent (2000), 'Pornographie, violence: La Liberté de dire non', *Le Nouvel Observateur*, 22 June, n.p.
Jordan, Shirley Ann (2004), *Contemporary French Women's Writing*, Oxford: Peter Lang.
Joyard, Olivier (2000), 'X le retour', *Cahiers du cinéma* 548, July–August, pp. 16–17.
J. P. D. (2000), '*Baise-Moi*', *L'Express*, 29 June, n.p.
Kermode, Mark (2001), 'Left on the Shelf', *Sight & Sound* 11:7, 26.
Klossowski, Pierre [1970] (1994) *La Monnaie vivante*, Paris: Joëlle Losfeld.
Kracauer, Siegfried (1960), *Theory of Film: The Redemption of Physical Reality*, London: Oxford University Press.
Krämer, Peter (1998), 'Post-Classical Hollywood', in John Hill and Pamela Church Gibson (eds), *The Oxford Guide to Film Studies*, Oxford: Oxford University Press, pp. 289–309.
Kristensen, Lars (2007), 'Divergent Accounts of Equivalent Narratives: Russian-Swedish *Interdevochka* Meets Swedish-Russian *Lilya 4-ever*', *PORTAL Journal of Multidisciplinary International Studies* 4:2, http://epress.lib.uts.edu.au/ojs/index.php/portal/article/view/488, accessed 30 August 2010.
Krzywinska, Tanya (2006), *Sex in the Cinema*, London: Wallflower.
Kuhn, Annette (1988), *Cinema, Censorship and Sexuality, 1909–1925*, London: Routledge.
Laderman, David (2002), *Driving Visions: Exploring the Road Movie*, Austin: University of Texas Press.
Laine, Tarja (2006), 'Lars von Trier, *Dogville* and the Hodological Space of Cinema', *Studies in European Cinema* 3:2, pp. 129–41.
Larsson, Mariah (2006), 'Om kön, sexualitet och moral i *Ett hål i mitt hjärta*', in Erik Hedling and Ann-Kristin Wallengren (eds), *Solskenslandet: svensk film på 2000-talet*, Stockholm: Atlantis, pp. 245–66.

—(2008), 'Långt ner i 1973: Kvinnlig njutning enligt kvinnorörelsen och porrfilmen', in Marie Cronqvist, Lina Sturfeldt and Martin Wiklund (eds), *1973 – en träff med tidsandan*, Lund: Nordic Academic Press, pp. 85–100.
—(2010), 'Representing Sexual Transactions: A National Perspective on a Changing Region in Three Swedish Films', in Erik Hedling, Olof Hedling and Mats Jönsson (eds), *Regional Aesthetics*, Stockholm: Royal Library, pp. 21–41.
Lawrence, Michael (2010), 'The Death of an Animal and the Figuration of the Human', in Brian Price and John David Rhodes (eds), *On Michael Haneke*, Detroit: Wayne State University Press, pp. 63–84.
Lemercier, Fabien (2009), 'Cannes 2009, Interview with Andrea Arnold', *CineEuropa* 14 May, http://cineeuropa.org/interview.aspx?documentID=108559, accessed 15 July 2009.
Lewis, Jon (2009), 'Real Sex: the Aesthetics and Economics of Art-house Porn', *Jump Cut* Spring, www.ejumpcut.org/archive/jc51.2009/index.html, accessed 5 Sept 2010.
Lindblad, Helena (2009), Review of *Mammoth*, *Dagens Nyheter* 23 January, n.p.
Lockwood, Dean (2009), 'All Stripped Down: The Spectacle of "Torture Porn"', *Popular Communication* 7:1 January, pp. 40–8.
Longworth, Karina (2005), 'Von Trier Cuts Controversial Donkey', *Cinematical* 4 March. Available from http://www.cinematical.com/2005/03/04/von-trier-cuts-controversial-donkey/, accessed 10 March 2010.
Lowenstein, Adam (2005), *Shocking Representation: Historical Trauma, National Cinema and the Modern Horror Film*, New York: Columbia University Press.
Luckett, Moya (2003), 'Sexploitation as Feminine Territory: The Films of Doris Wishman', in Mark Jancovich et al. (eds), *Defining Cult Movies. The Cultural Politics of Oppositional Taste*, Manchester: Manchester University Press, pp. 142–56.
McCann, Ben (2008), 'Pierced Borders, Punctured Bodies: The Contemporary French Horror Film', *Australian Journal of French Studies* 45:3, pp. 225–37.
McGill, Hannah (2006), 'Preview: *Red Road*', *Sight & Sound* November, http://www.bfi.org.uk/sightandsound/feature/49329, 10 December 2008.
MacKenzie, Scott (2002), '*Baise-moi*, Feminist Cinemas and the Censorship Controversy', *Screen* 43:3, pp. 315–24.
—(2010), 'On Watching and Turning Away: Ono's *Rape*, *Cinéma Direct* Aesthetics, and the Genealogy of *Cinéma Brut*', in Dominique Russell (ed.), *Rape in Art Cinema*, New York: Continuum, pp. 1–12.
McNair, Brian (2002), *Striptease Culture: Sex, Media, and the Democratization of Desire*, London: Routledge.
Marks, Laura U. (2000), *The Skin of the Film: Intercultural Cinema, Embodiment, and the Senses*, Durham, NC: Duke University Press.
Mårtensson, Mary (2002), 'Lukas Moodysson: "Jag läste att hon hade hoppat från en bro"' *Aftonbladet* 26 August, n.p.
Martin, Florence (2006), '*Cléo de 5 à 7*', in Phil Powrie (ed.), *The Cinema of France*, London: Wallflower, pp. 113–23.
Marx, Leo (1964), *The Machine in the Garden: Technology and the Pastoral Ideal in America*, New York: Oxford University Press.
Massumi, Brian (2002), *Parables for the Virtual: Movement, Affect, Sensation*, Durham, NC: Duke University Press.
Matheou, Demetrios (2005), 'Vanishing Road', *Sight & Sound* 15:8, pp. 16–18.
Maxwell, Richard (2000), 'Picturing the Audience', *Television and New Media* 1:2, pp. 135–57.
Mazierska, Ewa and Laura Rascaroli (2006), *Crossing New Europe*, London: Wallflower.
Mérigeau, Pascal (2000), 'La haine du monde', *Le Nouvel Observateur* 22 June, n.p.

Merriam-Webster Dictionary, http://www.merriam-webster.com/dictionary, accessed 31 March 2010.
Metz, Christian [1977] (1982), *Psychoanalysis and Cinema: The Imaginary Signifier*, London: Macmillan.
Morrey, Douglas (2002), 'Textures of Terror: Claire Denis' *Trouble Every Day*', *Belphegor* 3:2, http://etc.dal.ca/belphegor, accessed 11 March 2010.
Mouton, Jane (2001), 'From Feminine Masquerade to *Flâneuse*: Agnès Varda's *Cléo in the City*', *Cinema Journal* 40:2, pp. 3–6.
MUBI [Online] (2008–10), 'About the New French Extremity', accessed 30 March 2010.
Mulvey, Laura [1975] (2009), 'Visual Pleasure and Narrative Cinema', in Laura Mulvey, *Visual and Other Pleasures* (2nd edn), Basingstoke: Palgrave Macmillan, pp. 14–30.
Muray, Philippe (2000), 'Et voilà pourquoi votre film est muet', *Le Débat* 110, pp. 122–35.
Neyrat, Cyril (2009), '*La Terre tremble*: *Inland* de Tariq Teguia', *Cahiers du cinéma* 644, pp. 10–11.
Nichols, Bill (1991), *Representing Reality: Issues and Concepts in Documentary*, Bloomington: Indiana University Press.
Nobus, Dany (2007), 'The Politics of Gift-Giving and the Provocation of Lars von Trier's *Dogville*', *Film-Philosophy* 11:3, pp. 23–37.
Noé, Gaspar (1999), 'I'm Happy Some People Walk Out', *The Guardian* 12 March, http://www.letempsdetruittout.net/gasparnoe/index.asp?v=50, accessed 14 October 2010.
Norman, Neil (2002), 'The New French Shocker', *Evening Standard*, 16 May, p. 31.
Orpen, Valerie (2007), *Cléo de 5 à 7*, London: I. B. Tauris.
Orr, John (2004), 'New Directions in European Cinema', in Elizabeth Ezra (ed.), *European Cinema*, Oxford: Oxford University Press, pp. 299–312.
O'Shaughnessy, Martin (2010), 'French Cinema and the Political', *Studies in French Cinema* 10:1, pp. 39–56.
Palmer, Tim (2006a), 'Style and Sensation in the Contemporary French Cinema of the Body', *Journal of Film and Video* 58:3, 1 October, pp. 22–32.
—— (2006b), 'Under Your Skin: Marina de Van and the Contemporary French *cinéma du corps*', *Studies in French Cinema* 6:3, pp. 171–81.
Pattison, Michael (2009), 'Fish Stank', Letter to the Editor, *Sight & Sound* 19:12.
Pellecuer, David (2005), 'La Vue nouvelle', in Nicole Brenez (ed.), *La Vie nouvelle/Nouvelle Vision*, Paris: Léo Scheer, pp. 81–92.
Petit, Chris (2008), 'Germany and England/England and Germany', *Vertigo* 4:1, pp. 40–2.
Peucker, Brigitte (2007), *The Material Image: Art and the Real in Film*, Stanford: Stanford University Press.
Ph. R. (2000), 'La Pornographie comme véritable piège', *La Croix*, 28 June, n.p.
Pisters, Patricia (forthcoming), *The Neuro-Image: A Deleuzian Film Philosophy of Digital Screen Culture*, Stanford: Stanford University Press.
Plantinga, Carl (2009), *Moving Viewers: American Film and the Spectator's Experience*, Berkeley: University of California Press.
Powrie, Phil (2007), 'French Neo-Noir to Hyper-Noir', in Andrew Spicer (ed.), *European Film Noir*, Manchester: Manchester University Press, pp. 56–83.
Pulver, Andrew (2009), 'Rebirth of the British Art Film', *The Guardian* 24 July, http://www.guardian.co.uk/film/2009/jul/24/rebirth-of-british-art-film, accessed 4 May 2010.
Quandt, James (2004), 'Flesh and Blood: Sex and Violence in Recent French Cinema', *Artforum* February, http://www.artforum.com/archive/id=6199&search=james%20quandt, accessed 5 September 2010.
Quinn, Anthony (2009), '*Fish Tank*', *The Independent* 11 September, http://www.

independent.co.uk/arts-entertainment/films/reviews/fish-tank-15-1785099.html, accessed 6 January 2010.
Radway, Janice (1984), *Reading the Romance: Women, Patriarchy and Popular Literature*, Chapel Hill, NC: University of North Carolina Press.
Raissinger, Catherine (2002), 'The Racial and Sexual Politics of Civil Unions in France', *Radical History Review* 83, Spring, pp. 73–93.
Rancière, Jacques (2004), *Malaise dans l'esthétique*, Paris: Galilée.
—(2009), *The Emancipated Spectator*, trans. Gregory Elliott, London: Verso.
Rauger, Jean François (2000), 'Virginie Despentes, ses acteurs et ses hardeurs', *Le Monde* 7 June, n.p.
Rayns, Tony (1999), '*Seul contre tous* review', *Sight & Sound*, 9:2, p. 58.
Rees-Roberts, Nick (2008), *Queer French Cinema*, Edinburgh: Edinburgh University Press.
Restuccia, Frances L. (2005), 'Jouissance and Desire in Michael Haneke's *The Piano Teacher*', *American Imago* 62:4, Winter, pp. 453–82.
Revolver Entertainment (2004), 'Interview with Director Christophe Honoré', in *Ma Mère* [DVD Extras].
'Rollen som blir för mycket för Flinck' (2004), *Aftonbladet* 4 September, n.p.
Rollet, Brigitte (2005), 'Cultural Exception(s) in French Cinema', in Emmanuel Godin and Tony Chafer (eds), *The French Exception*, Oxford: Berghan, pp. 167–78.
Romney, Jonathan (1999), 'Blood Simple', *The Guardian*, 19 March, p. 8.
—(2000), '*L'Humanité*: Rapture or Ridicule?', *Sight & Sound* 10.9, pp. 22–5.
—(2002), 'Cannes Report', *Independent on Sunday*, 26 May, p. 10.
—(2004), 'Le Sex and Violence', *The Independent*, 12 September, http://www.independent.co.uk/arts-entertainment/films/features/le-sex-and-violence-546083.html, accessed 6 September 2010.
—(2006), '*Red Road*: Sealed with a Glasgow Kiss', *The Independent* 29 October, http://www.independent.co.uk/arts-entertainment/films/reviews/red-road-18-422116.html, accessed 4 March 2009.
Rosenberg, Tiina (2002), *Queerfeministisk agenda*, Stockholm: Atlas.
Ross, Kristin [1996] (1999), *Fast Cars, Clean Bodies: Decolonization and the Reordering of French Culture*, Cambridge, MA: MIT Press.
Russell, Dominique (2010), 'Introduction: Why Rape?', in Dominique Russell (ed.), *Rape in Art Cinema*, New York: Continuum, pp. 1–12.
Schama, Simon and Karl French (2009), 'Surfeit of the Sweetest Things', *The Financial Times* 9 September, http://www.ft.com/cms/s/2/ce8e695e-9d5d-11de-9f4a-00144feabdc0.html, accessed 6 January 2010.
Schiappa, Edward (2008), *Beyond Representational Correctness: Rethinking Criticism of Popular Media*, New York: State University of New York Press.
Schoenbach, Klaus (2001), 'Myths of Media and Audiences', *European Journal of Communication* 16:3, pp. 361–76.
Schopenhauer, Arthur (1970), *Essays and Aphorisms*, sel. and trans. R. J. Hollingdale, London: Penguin.
Schultz, Laura Luise (2005), 'Når den røde lampe lyser er helligånden til stede' [Interview with Lars von Trier], *Ud og Se* May, pp. 46–58.
Scott, D. (2004), *Semiologies of Travel: From Gautier to Baudrillard*, Cambridge: Cambridge University Press.
Sélavy, Virginie (2009), 'Interview with Lars Von Trier', *Electric Sheep*, 3 July, http://www.electricsheepmagazine.co.uk/features/2009/07/03/antichrist-interview-with-lars-von-trier/, accessed 31 March 2010.

Selfe, Melanie (2008), 'Inflected Accounts and Irreversible Journeys', *Participations* 5:1, May, http://www.participations.org/Volume%205/Issue%201%20-%20special/5_01_selfe.htm, accessed 6 January 2009.
SFI's webpage http://www.sfi.se/sv/varastod/Beviljade-stod/Produktionsstod-2007/, accessed 1 April 2010.
Sharkey, Alix (2002), 'Scandale! The Story Behind *Baise-moi*', *The Observer* 14 April, http://www.guardian.co.uk/film/2002/apr/14/filmcensorship.features, accessed 16 April 2002.
Sharrett, Christopher (2004), 'The World That is Known: Michael Haneke Interviewed', *Kinoeye: New Perspectives on European Film* 4:1, 8 March, www.kinoeye.org/04/01interview01.php, accessed 28 June 2010.
Shaviro, Steven (1993), *The Cinematic Body*, Minneapolis: University of Minnesota Press.
—(2005), 'Come, Come, Georges: Steven Shaviro on Georges Bataille's *Story of the Eye* and *Ma Mère*', *Artforum* 1 May, http://www.thefreelibrary.com/Come,+come,+Georges%3A+Steven+Shaviro+on+Georges+Bataille's+Story+of...-a0132554947, accessed 27 July 2009.
—(2006), 'Why Porn Now?', *Pinocchio Theory* 9 November, http://www.shaviro.com/Blog/?p=526, accessed 9 July 2009.
—(2010), 'Post-Cinematic Affect: On Grace Jones, *Boarding Gate*, and *Southland Tales*', *Film-Philosophy* 14:1, pp. 1–102.
Sherry, Kate (2002), 'Censor's Betrayal as He Passes "Sick" Rape Film', *Daily Mail*, 22 October, p. 8.
Shin, Chi-Yun (2008), 'Art of Branding: Tartan "Asia Extreme" Films', *Jump Cut: A Review of Contemporary Media* 50, Spring, http://www.ejumpcut.org/archive/jc50.2008/TartanDist/text.html, accessed 1 October 2010.
Shohat, Ella and Robert Stam (1994), *Unthinking Eurocentrism: Multiculturalism and the Media*, London: Routledge.
Short, J. Rennie (1991), *Imagined Country: Society, Culture and Environment*, London and New York: Routledge.
Singh, Anita (2009), 'Cannes 2009: *Antichrist* Horror Film Headed for Britain', *The Daily Telegraph*, 24 May, http://www.telegraph.co.uk/culture/film/cannes-film-festival/5374834/Cannes-2009-Antichrist-horror-film-headed-for-Britain.html, accessed 6 October 2010.
Slotkin, Richard [1973] (2000), *Regeneration Through Violence: The Mythology of the American Frontier, 1600–1860*, Norman: University of Oklahoma Press.
—(1978), 'Dreams and Genocide: The American Myth of Regeneration Through Violence', in Jack Nachbar, Deborah Weiser and John L. Wright (eds), *The Popular Culture Reader*, Bowling Green: Bowling Green University Popular Press.
—[1998] (1992), *Gunfighter Nation: The Myth of the Frontier in Twentieth-Century America*, Norman: University of Oklahoma Press.
Smith, Alison (1998), *Agnès Varda*, Manchester: Manchester University Press.
Smith, Jillian (2008), 'The Politics of Tactility: Walter Benjamin Materialized by Way of Frederick Wiseman's *Titicut Follies*', *Studies in Documentary Film* 2:2, pp. 103–22.
Sontag, Susan (1966a), 'The Aesthetics of Silence', in *Styles of Radical Will*, New York: Farrar, Straus & Giroux.
—(1966b), 'The Pornographic Imagination', in *Styles of Radical Will*, London: Secker & Warburg.
—(1977a), *Illness as Metaphor*, New York: Picador.
—(1977b), *On Photography*, Harmondsworth: Penguin.

Spoiden, Stéphane (2002), 'No Mans Land: Genres en question dans *Sitcom, Romance*, et *Baise-Moi*', *Esprit Créateur* 42:1, pp. 96–106.
Staiger, Janet (1992), *Interpreting Films: Studies in the Historical Reception of American Cinema*, Princeton, NJ: Princeton University Press.
—(2000), *Perverse Spectators: The Practices of Film Reception*, New York: New York University Press.
Starr, Peter (1995), *Logics of Failed Revolt*, Stanford: University of Stanford Press.
Steinberg, Leo (1972), *Other Criteria: Confrontations with Twentieth-Century Art*, London: Oxford University Press.
Stenport, Anna Westerståhl (2010), 'A New Swedish Model? Memfis Film and Lukas Moodysson', in Mariah Larsson and Anders Marklund (eds), *Swedish Film: An Introduction and Reader*, Lund: Nordic Academic Press.
Studlar, Gaylyn (1988), *In the Realm of Pleasure: Von Sternberg, Dietrich and the Masochistic Aesthetic*, Urbana: University of Illinois Press.
Tarr, Carrie and Brigitte Rollet (2001), *Cinema and the Second Sex: Women's Filmmaking in France in the 1980s and 1990s*, London: Continuum.
Taylor, David (2002), 'Film with Nine-Minute Rape Cleared', *Evening Standard*, 21 October 2002, p. 17 The Onion (2009), 'Denmark Introduces Harrowing New Tourism Ads Directed by Lars von Trier', 24 February, http://www.theonion.com/video/denmark-introduces-harrowing-new-tourism-ads-direc,14403/, accessed 31 March 2010.
Thomas, Kevin (2005), 'Degrading, Disgusting, Depressing', *Los Angeles Times* 13 May, http://articles.latimes.com/2005/may/13/entertainment/et-mere13, accessed 3 March 2010.
Tookey, Chris (1999), '*Seul Contre Tous* Review', *Daily Mail*, 19 March, p. 44.
—(2002), 'This Danger to Society', *Daily Mail*, 24 October, p. 12.
—(2003), '*Irréversible* Review', *Daily Mail*, 31 January, pp. 52, 53.
Trinity Distributors (2008), Press Notes for *Import/Export*, www.importexport.ulrichseidl.com, accessed 11 March 2010.
'Varningstext för Moodyssons nya' (2004), *Kristianstadbladet*, 9 September.
Vicari, Justin (2006), '*Dog Days*', *Film Quarterly* 60:1, pp. 40–5.
Vilensky, Daniel (2009), '*Antichrist*: Chronicles of a Psychosis Foretold', *Senses of Cinema* 53, http://www.sensesofcinema.com/2009/feature-articles/antichrist-chronicles-of-a-psychosis-foretold/, accessed 31 March 2010.
Vincendeau, Ginette (2000), '*Baise-moi*', *Positif*, September, n.p.
—(2001), 'Sisters, Sex and Sitcom', *Sight & Sound* December, www.bfi.org.uk/sightandsound/feature/91/, accessed 6 January 2009.
—(2005), '*Ma Mère*', *Sight & Sound* 15.3, p. 3.
—(2007), 'The New French Extremism', in Pam Cook (ed.), *The Cinema Book*, 3rd edn, London: BFI, p. 205.
Virilio, Paul (1989), *War and Cinema: The Logistics of Perception*, trans. Patrick Camiller, London: Verso.
—(2000), *Art and Fear*, trans. Julie Rose, London: Continuum.
Walker, Alexander (1999), '*Seul Contre Tous* Review', *Evening Standard*, 18 March, pp. 29, 30.
—(2002a), 'A Filthy Business', *Evening Standard*, 9 August, p. 29.
—(2002b), 'Who's Exploiting Whom', *Evening Standard*, 20 September, p. 31.
—(2003), '*Irréversible* Review', *Evening Standard*, 30 January, p. 46.
Wallach Scott, Joan (2004), 'French Universalism in the Nineties', *Differences: A Journal of Feminist Cultural Studies* 15:2, pp. 32–53.

Wallenstein, Sven-Olov (2001), 'Visuell lust och narrative film', in Sara Arrhenius (ed.), *Feministiska konstteorier*, Stockholm: Konsthögskolan.
Weiner, Susan (2001), 'Terre à terre: Toqueville, Aron, Baudrillard and the American Way of Life', *Yale French Studies* 100, pp. 13–24.
Wennö, Nicholas (2003), 'Moodysson kritisk till debatten efter *Lilja 4-ever*', *Dagens Nyheter* 20 February.
Wheatley, Catherine (2008), 'Europa Europa', *Sight & Sound* 18:10, 1 October, pp. 46–9.
—(2009), *Michael Haneke's Cinema: The Ethic of the Image*, Oxford/New York: Berghahn.
Whittam Smith, Andreas (2002), 'How to Survive Years of Drugs, Sex and Violence', *The Independent*, 5 August, p. 15.
Wiberg, Charlotte (2006), 'Filmkritik i svensk dagspress', in Erik Hedling and Ann-Kristin Wallengren (eds), *Solskenslandet: svensk film på 2000-talet*, Stockholm: Atlantis, pp. 267–302.
Wilder, Thornton [1938] (2000), *Our Town and Other Plays*, London: Penguin.
Williams, James (2009), 'His Life to Film: The Extreme Art of Jacques Nolot', *Studies in French Cinema* 9:2, pp. 177–90.
Williams, Linda [1989] (1999), *Hardcore: Power, Pleasure, and the 'Frenzy of the Visible'*, Berkeley: University of California Press.
—(2008), *Screening Sex*, Durham, NC: Duke University Press.
Williams, Linda Ruth (2009), '*Antichrist*: A Work of Genius or the Sickest Film in the History of Cinema?', *The Guardian* 16 July, http://www.guardian.co.uk/film/2009/jul/16/antichrist-lars-von-trier-feminism, accessed 20 July 2010.
Williams, Melanie (2006), '*9 Songs*', *Film Quarterly* 59:3, pp. 59–63.
Williamson, James (2003), '*Trouble Every Day*', *Sight & Sound* 13:1, p. 56.
Wimmer, Leila (2009), *Cross-Channel Perspectives: The French Reception of British Cinema*, Oxford: Peter Lang.
Wimsatt, W. K. and M. C. Beardsley (1949), 'The Affective Fallacy', *The Sewanee Review* 57:1, pp. 31–55.
Wolfe, Cary (1998), 'Old Orders for New: Ecology, Human Rights, and the Poverty of Humanism', *Diacritics* 28:2, pp. 21–40.
Wood, Robin (2002), '"Do I Disgust You?" or, Tirez pas sur *La Pianiste*', *CineAction* 22 March, pp. 54–61.
Wrye, Harriet Kimble (2007), 'Perversion Annihilates Creativity and Love: A Passion for Destruction in Haneke's *The Piano Teacher*', *Psychoanalytic Inquiry* 27:4, pp. 455–66.
Žižek, Slavoj (2000), *The Fragile Absolute*, London: Verso.

Index

À l'intérieur, 211
À ma sœur!
   audience preconceptions, 110, 111
   and BBFC, 105–6, 107
   Critics/Embracers, 13, 111–15
   ending of, 111, 113–14
   sex in, 117
   Vincendeau on, 106
À nos amours, 24
Aaron, Michele, 8, 150, 178
abasement, 19, 20–1, 211
Abella, Adela, 159, 160
abject
   body, 29, 88, 149
   conformism of, 182
   confronted, 34
   dehumanisation, 74
   dystopian, 32
   Eastern Europe, 82
   Eros, 96
   excess, 183
   feminine, 33
   humanness, 4
   Kristeva, 211
   subjectivity, 74–5
Acéphale, 163
Act-Up, 134
Adorno, Theodor, 80, 192
Advance Party concept, 170
aesthetics
   avant-garde, 45, 57, 85, 157, 194
   body, 24, 39
   Brecht, 165
   of dread, 180, 181
   of excess, 40n4
   of expenditure, 29, 40n4
   of impurity, 47, 52
   and politics, 6–7
   of restraint, 40n4
affect
   body, 70, 174
   Body and Society, 7–8
   cultural theory, 7–8, 16–17n2, 52–3
   del Rio, 175, 179n5
   fallacy, 204
   Fish Tank, 174–5
   Horeck on, 15
   image, 70, 85–6
   performativity, 171–2, 174, 176, 177
   Representation, Identity, Body reading group, viii
   sensation, 92
   sentimentality, 179n7
   sex, 171
   transmission of, 175
African mask motif, 35–6, 41n21
Agamben, Giorgio
   ethics, 80
   exclusion/inclusion, 74–5, 78
   and Grandrieux, 78, 79–80
   Homo Sacer, 75, 76, 78
   as influence, 12
   The Open, 75, 99–100
   Remnants of Auschwitz, 80
   subjectivity, 74, 75
   wargus, 70, 75, 78, 79
Aï no Corrida see *In the Realm of the Senses*
Aja, Alexandre, 21
Alexandra's Project, 194
Algerian war, 30–1, 35, 36, 40n6, 41n18
alienation
   Baudrillard, 58
   Eastern Europe, 82, 85
   Haneke, 181, 184, 187, 190
   Marxism, 146
   Seul contre tous, 6, 120
Almroth, Björn, 146
Althusser, Louis, 7–8
American model, 30, 32, 56, 138
American Psycho, 50–1, 54n3
Ameur-Zaïmeche, Rabah, 39
Anatomy of Hell, 20, 95, 193, 194, 210
Andersen, Hans Christian: *The Steadfast Tin Soldier*, 198–9
Anderson, Rafaëlla, 130, 137
Ang, Ien, 116n10
Angelopoulos, Theo, 20
Les Anges exterminateurs, 210
animals
   and humans, 99–100
   killing of, 96–8, 101n4, 181
   as non-humans, 101n5
   violence against, 101n3
Antichrist
   Brooks on, 16n1
   Danish tradition, 211

INDEX

Antichrist (cont.)
  Ebert on, 192–3
  female circumcision, 157
  intertextuality, 198, 199, 205n9
  and *Irréversible*, 196–7
  promotional campaign, 4
  spectators, 53n1
  The Steadfast Tin Soldier story, 199
  Surrealism, 199
  unwatchable, 15
anti-obscenity laws, 69, 80n1
anti-porn movement, 14, 147
Antonioni, Michelangelo, 24, 56, 205n9
apparatus theory, 7–8
Archer, Neil, 11
archetypes
  Beugnet, 81n7
  Grandrieux, 12
  Sombre, 12, 69–70, 73–4, 75–7
  storytelling, 71–2
  subjectivity, 81n7
Arendt, Hannah, 74, 75
L'Argent, 24
Aristotle, 75
Arnold, Andrea, 169–70
  clichés disrupted, 175–6
  genre tropes, 178
  new extremism, 14–15
  sexual revenge dramas, 179
  sexuality, 169
  social realism, 170–1, 179
  spectators, 172–3
  Wasp, 169, 178
  see also *Fish Tank*; *Red Road*
Artaud, Antonin, 162–3, 165, 166, 200, 201
Artforum, 209
art-house films
  auteurs, 29, 43
  BBFC, 125
  Britain, 169
  experimentation, 29
  French, 110, 111, 113, 210–11
  porno-chic, 24–5
  pornography, 131
  reception of, 1
Arvanitis, Yorgos, 20
Asia Extreme cinema, 1
Assayas, Olivier, 6, 29, 33
Attali, Danielle, 136
Au hasard Balthazar, 22
audience response, 8, 9–10, 106–7, 109
  affective performativity, 177
  BBFC survey, 107
  and critical response, 142
  Critics/Embracers, 110–15
  rape, 12–13
  see also reception studies; spectators; spectatorship
Augé, Marc, 85
Austria, 89, 90, 93, 211
auteurs
  and art-house films, 29, 43
  Beugnet on, 8on3
  Dumont, 24, 55
  Moodysson, 143, 146, 151
  new extremism, 16
  Noé, 120
  shock tactics, 43–4
  universal values, 135
Authier, Christian, 132
authorship, 56–7
avant-garde aesthetics, 45, 57, 85, 157, 194

Bach, Karen, 130, 137
Bachmann, Ingeborg, 211
Bacon, Francis, 19, 76, 81n10
Badiou, Alain, 182
Baise-moi
  American model, 33
  and BBFC, 107, 123, 124
  beur actors, 133
  as cult film, 140
  and *Dans ma peau*, 20–1
  gender politics, 134, 137
  identity politics, 138–9
  national identity, 125, 131, 133, 137, 139, 140–1
  as neo-*noir*, 130, 132
  pornography, 130
  rape-revenge story, 32, 95–6, 125, 130
  and *Romance*, 145
  scandal of, 135–7
  sex and violence, 5, 32, 107, 117
  socio-politics, 133, 139–40
  X-certificate, 130–1, 135–6
Balibar, Étienne, 138
banlieue, 131, 132
Barber, Samuel, 49
Barker, Martin, 9, 13, 117–18, 121
Basu, Feroza, 58–9
Bataille, Georges
  aesthetics of expenditure, 29, 40n4
  and Artaud, 162–3
  and Beugnet, 53
  as influence, 2, 18, 44
  Ma mère, 45, 47–8
  sex and transgression, 11
Battle in Heaven, 194
Baudrillard, Jean
  alienation, 58
  Amérique, 58, 63–4
  death of animals, 97–8
  simulacra, 59, 64
Bava, Mario, 2, 18
BBFC (British Board of Film Classification)
  À ma sœur!, 105–6, 107
  audience response survey, 13, 107, 115–16n8
  guidelines, 118, 128n6
  liberalisation, 117–18, 126–7, 128
  The Lord of the Rings, 115n4
  In the Realm of the Senses, 80n1
Beardsley, M. C., 204
Beau Travail, 19
Beineix, Jean-Jacques, 209
Bellour, Raymond, 69, 85–6
Bellucci, Monica, 21
Benjamin, Walter, 74
Benny's Video, 97, 187
Bentham, Jeremy, 100
Berlin Alexanderplatz, 212
Bernstein, J. M., 80
Bertolucci, Bernardo, 20, 43
Best, Victoria, 44
Bettany, Paul, 158
Betz, Mark, 125
Beugnet, Martine
  abjection, 88
  on archetypes, 81n7
  and Bataille, 53
  Cinema and Sensation, 3, 10–11, 82, 86
  cinema of expenditure, 29
  cinema of sensation, 3, 170
  dehumanisation, 70–1
  extreme cinema, 127
  and Ezra, 6–7, 29, 40n4

genre subverted, 56
on Grandrieux, 69
haptic experience, 96
shock tactics, 29, 95
on *Sombre*, 80n3
'Traces of the Modern', 40n4
transgression, 94
biopolitics, 85, 89–90, 91, 92
biopower, 89–90
The Blair Witch Project, 198
Blier, Bertrand, 24
body
  abasement, 211
  abjection, 29, 88, 149
  aesthetics, 24, 39
  affect, 70, 174
  commodification, 87
  decommodified, 33
  discipline, 90
  ethics, 171
  Grandrieux, 76
  image, 70
  resistance, 90, 91–2
  sensation, 7, 8
  see also female body
Bonello, Bertrand, 19, 24, 123
Bonitzer, Pascal, 69
Borowczyk, Walerian, 18
Bosch, Hieronymus, 205n9
Bourcier, Marie-Hélène, 140–1
Bourdieu, Pierre, 109
Bousé, Derek, 97, 101n2
Bråding, Sanna, 146
Bradshaw, Peter, 46, 98, 99, 100, 101, 127
Brecht, Bertolt, 7–8, 157, 161–5
Breillat, Catherine
  Bataille as influence, 44
  Critics, 112
  Fat Girl, 20
  female sexuality, 179
  feminine abject, 33
  Fillette, 20
  new extremism, 1, 2, 29, 117
  Pornocratie, 193
  provocation, 20
  sexual politics, 6
  transgression, 18, 209
  violence, 95
  see also À ma sœur!; *Anatomy of Hell*; *Romance*
Brenez, Nicole, 69, 85, 88
Brennan, Teresa, 175
Bresson, Robert, 22, 24, 97
Brisseau, Jean Claude, 24, 210
British Board of Film Classification *see* BBFC
British filmmaking, 169; *see also* Arnold, Andrea
Brooks, Xan, 16n1
Brottman, Mikita, 203
The Brown Bunny, 194
Brunette, Peter, 185–6
Buñuel, Luis, 6, 18, 62–3, 96, 195
Burch, Noël, 137
Burt, Jonathan, 97
Burt, Martha, 106, 107–8
Der Busenfreund, 93
Bush, George W., 157, 158
Bustillo, Alexandre, 211
Butler, Judith, 172

Caan, James, 158
Caché see Hidden
Cameron, Allan, 202–3

cannibalism, 2, 18, 19–20, 87
capitalism, 74, 87, 147, 148
Carax, Leos, 23, 120
Carne, 21, 96, 120, 205n15
Carter, Angela, 131
Cartwright, Lisa, 7–8
Casar, Amira, 20
Cassel, Vincent, 21, 202
catharsis, 14, 162, 163, 165–7, 168n8
Caws, Mary Ann, 195
Céline, Louis Ferdinand, 21, 24
censorship, 13–14
  classification, 118, 128
  France, 35, 41n19, 117, 119–23
  global filmmaking, 69
  Staiger on, 126–7
  see also BBFC
Chamarette, Jenny, 12
La Chatte à deux têtes, 24
Chauvin, Sébastien, 38
Chéreau, Patrice, 19, 123, 170
Un Chien andalou, 96, 195, 196
Chiennes de garde, 134
Chocolat, 19
Choses secrètes, 24
Chrisafis, Angelique, 124
Christensen, Benjamin, 198
Christopher, James, 122
citizenship/ethnicity, 131
Clark, Larry, 194
Clarkson, Patricia, 160
class/gender, 131, 133, 171
classification, 118, 128
Clay, Thomas, 4
Cléo de 5 à 7, 31, 32–7
A Clockwork Orange, 196
Clouzot, Henri-Georges, 18
Cold War aftermath, 82, 83, 85, 92
colonial history, 11, 30–1, 34–5, 41n21, 138
commodification, 41n21, 45, 74, 87, 146, 147, 149
Conan, Eric, 40n5
Conrad, Joseph, 74, 81n8, 197
Container, 142, 143, 151
Cooper, Dennis, 54n3
corporeality, 33, 39, 70–4; *see also* body
Les Côtelettes, 24
Coulthard, Lisa, 15
Courbet, Gustave, 23
courtly love, 186
Crash, 20, 122, 123
Creed, Barbara, 41n10
crime fiction, 132
Criminal Lovers, 19, 204n1
Critics/Embracers, 13, 110–15, 116n10, 142
La Croix, 136
Cronenberg, David, 20, 146
Crowley, Martin, 11, 44, 46, 52, 53
Cruelty, Theatre of, 163, 201
cultural theory, 7–8, 16–17n2, 52–3

Dafoe, Willem, 197
Dali, Salvador, 195
Dalle, Béatrice, 19
Dans ma peau, 19–20, 32, 33
Dante Alighieri, 85
Daquin, Louis, 41n19
Darrieussecq, Marie, 213
de Heer, Rolf, 194
de Van, Marina
  Dans ma peau, 19–20, 32, 33
  innovation/style, 3

de Van, Marina (*cont.*)
  new extremism, 29
  stylised violence, 95
death
  of animals, 96–8, 101n4, 181
  as taboo, 95, 98
Debord, Guy, 18
decommodification of body, 33
degradation of women, 146, 149
dehumanisation, 70–1, 74
del Rio, Elena
  affect, 175, 179n5
  affective performativity, 171–2, 174, 176
  confinement/movement, 178–9
  Deleuze and the Cinemas of Performance, 172
del Toro, Guillermo, 198
Deleuze, Gilles, 8
  body without organs, 74
  Cinéma I – L'image-mouvement, 81n7
  fold, 41n14
  Francis Bacon, 76, 81n10
  as influence, 211
  Italian neorealism, 85
Deliverance, 24
Demonlover, 6, 33
Demy, Jacques, 56
Denis, Claire
  Beau Travail, 19
  Chocolat, 19
  law reform petition, 130
  new extremism, 29, 210
  No Fear, No Die, 19
  violence in shadow, 95
  White Material, 212
  see also Trouble Every Day
Denmark, 160, 211; *see also* von Trier, Lars
Deodato, Ruggero, 107
Derrida, Jacques, 100
desert landscape, 61–2, 63–4
Despentes, Virginie, 93, 132, 138, 139; *see also Baise-moi*
The Devils, 122
Diamond, Cora, 101n4
Dickie, Kate, 172
Dirty Diaries, 151
discipline of body, 90
disease motif, 34, 36, 38
distanciation, 7–8, 164
Djordjevic, Mladen, 4
documentary techniques, 49, 93
Dog Days, 93, 94–5, 99, 123, 211
Dogme 95 edict, 95, 150, 157
Dogtooth, 211
Dogville
  analysis of, 158–61
  anti-humanism, 157
  as Brechtian film, 161–2
  camera shots, 164
  catharsis, 162
  distanciation, 164
  inner bastard concept, 164–5
  meta-shot, 160
  mise-en-scene, 159, 163–4
  provocation, 157–8
  spectators, 14
Donner, Richard, 198
Don't Look Now, 198
The Door in the Floor, 198
Douin, Jean-Luc, 136
Downing, Lisa, 8–9, 177, 178, 192
dread, 180, 181
The Dreamers, 43

Dreyer, Carl, 198
Duchamp, Marcel, 23, 36–7
Dumont, Bruno
  American way of life, 33
  auteurism, 24, 55
  classic neorealism, 25
  Flandres, 60
  Hadewijch, 212
  landscape, 23
  new extremism, 1, 2, 29
  non-professional actors, 95
  off-screen violence, 95
  Quandt on, 209
  redemptive concept, 64–5
  and Seidl, 93
  on spectators, 6, 24
  transgression, 18
  see also L'Humanité; Twentynine Palms; La Vie de Jésus
Dunne, J. W, 21, 203
Dupontel, Albert, 202
Duval, Robin, 118, 128n5
dystopian vision, 32, 72, 84, 87

Eastern Europe
  abjection, 82
  alienation, 82, 85
  biopolitics of, 85
  feminine submission, 87–8
  Import/Export, 88–9
  Marxist-Leninism, 84
  migration, 4
  monstrosity, 82, 83–4
  primitivism, 82, 83
  as setting, 12, 22, 72, 83
Ebert, Roger, 158, 192–3, 199
Eden, postlapsarian, 23–4, 61, 62, 64, 197
ego-identification, 105, 106
Ellis, Bret Easton, 50–1, 54n3
Elsaesser, Thomas, 4
Embracers *see* Critics/Embracers
Emerson, Ralph Waldo, 197
emotional engagement, 7, 17n2
empathy, 163, 178, 204n2
Enter the Void, 212
Epic Theatre, 163
Eros, 94–6, 212
Esprit, 41n13
ethics
  Agamben, 80
  bodies, 171
  film studies, 8
  of filmmaking, 91
  humanity, 12, 70
  image, 9
  of looking, 178
  New/Old Testament, 158
  non-humans, 70
  obscenity, 182
  sexual tourism, 50
  spectators, 7–16, 170, 178, 193, 195, 201
ethnic cleansing, 86
ethnicity, 131, 138, 139
Ett hål i mitt hjärta see A Hole in My Heart
Eurocentrism, 57, 63–4
Europa, 198
European filmmakers, 1
  American models, 56, 57, 61, 197–8
  Baudrillard, 63, 64
  Cold War, 83
  critical mirror, 90, 92

cultural values, 62
marketing of, 125
provocation, 4, 5, 6, 13, 119, 120, 128
see also Eastern Europe; new extremism
European Union, 84
Eustache, Jean, 24
Evian agreement, 41n18
exception, states of, 75
excess, 29, 31, 40n4, 56, 183
exclusion, 32, 74–5, 76, 78, 84
The Exorcist, 130, 131, 198
expenditure, aesthetics of, 40n4
exploitation, 32, 84, 89, 91, 98–9, 100–1, 158, 181
exploitation films, 2, 18, 125, 131
Ezra, Elizabeth, 6–7, 29, 40n4

Falcon, Richard, 4, 6, 96, 119–20, 127
Fassbinder, Rainer Werner, 6, 19, 179n7, 211, 212
Fat Girl, 20
feel-bad film, 14, 157, 165–7
female agency, 178
female body, 172, 175
female circumcision, 157
femininity, 33, 87–8, 140
feminism, 14, 110, 132, 134, 137, 147, 150
feminist filmmaking, 140
Ferguson, Frances, 5, 50–1, 54n3
Ferman, James, 118, 128n4
Feuillade, Louis, 29, 36
Field, Todd, 198
Le Figaro, 136
Fillette/A Real Young Girl, 20, 36
film maudit tradition, 3, 19, 21–2
filth/cleanliness, 33
Fish Tank
  affectivity, 174–5
  father role, 176–7
  mother role, 177–8
  performative bodies, 172
  revenge narrative, 176, 177
  sex scenes, 15, 169–71
Flandres, 60
Fleckinger, Hélène, 86–7
Flinck, Thorsten, 145, 146
Ford, John, 60
Fortress Europe, 84, 92
Foucault, Michel, 75
Fox, Kerry, 170
France
  censorship, 35, 41n19, 119–23
  colonialism, 11, 30–1, 34–5, 139
  culture, 131
  genres, 44
  history, 39–40
  New Extremity, 1–4, 5, 10, 11, 18, 19, 21, 24, 44
  post-industrial, 133
  see also French national identity; new extremism
Franco, Judith, 132–3
Franju, Georges, 18, 21, 31, 36, 40n4, 96
Fraser, John, 192
French, Karl, 170
French, Philip, 122, 123
French national identity
  citizenship, 131, 137
  and difference, 138
  ethnicity, 133, 139
  minority groups, 140, 141
  universalism, 14, 134, 140
Freud, Lucian, 19
Friedkin, William, 131, 198
Frost, Robert, 198

Fucking Åmål see *Show Me Love*
Funny Games, 120, 166–7, 168n7, 180

Gaffez, Fabien, 81n6
Gainsbourg, Charlotte, 196–7, 199
Gallo, Vincent, 19, 194
Garrel, Louis, 43
gaze
  children's, 73, 77
  corruption of, 148, 149
  destabilising, 86
  masochistic, 200
  spectators, 204n2
  tactile, 34
gender
  Baise-moi, 134
  class, 131, 133, 171
  ethnicity, 131, 138, 139
  French films, 134, 135
  power, 133
  repression, 137–9
  and sexuality, 14, 133, 139–40
  Sweden, 145
  violence, 64, 174
  see also femininity; masculinity
gender politics, 14, 132, 137, 143–4, 152
genres
  American-style, 32, 33, 56, 57, 61–2
  Arnold, 177, 178
  of excess, 29, 31, 39
  French filmmaking, 44
  horror as, 5, 17, 26, 29, 38, 82, 131, 198, 210
  manipulated, 11
  noir, 132
  pornography as, 51, 95, 110, 145
  subverted, 56
  Trouble Every Day, 36, 38
Gentleman, Amelia, 120–1
gesture, 76, 81n10, 172
Gianorio, Richard, 136
Glaister, Dan, 120
global consumer capitalism, 43, 45
global filmmaking, 69
Godard, Agnès, 19
Godard, Jean-Luc, 18, 41n19, 95, 96–7, 130, 212
Goddard, Michael, 12
Godeau, Philippe, 130
Goebbels, Joseph, 160
Golsan, Richard, 30–1, 40n5
Golubeva, Katia, 23–4
Gordon, Douglas, 169
Goupil, Romain, 130
Grandrieux, Philippe
  and Agamben, 78, 79–80
  archetypes, 12
  Beugnet on, 69
  body, 76
  and Conrad, 81n8
  corporeality, 70–4
  experimentalism, 3
  Un Lac, 69, 80n2, 81n5, 212
  new extremism, 1, 2, 29
  on spectators, 81n11
  transgression, 1
  violence in shadow, 95
  see also *Sombre*; *La Vie nouvelle*
The Grapes of Wrath, 60
Grégoire, Ménie, 41n13
Grien, Hans Baldung, 36
Grønstad, Asbjørn, 15–16, 33–4, 190–1, 204n2
Grupp 8, 147

Gržinić, Marina, 83, 84, 87–8
Gutch, Robin, 171
Guyana, 36

Hadewijch, 212
haebophiles, 105
Hagman, Hampus, 43–4
Hainge, Greg, 69, 70–2, 79
Handel, Georg Friedrich, 205n12
handheld cameras, 20, 50, 51, 143, 144, 164, 187, 199, 202
Haneke, Michael
  alienation, 181, 184, 187, 190
  Bataille as influence, 44
  Benny's Video, 97, 187
  death of animals, 96
  Funny Games, 120, 166–7, 168n7, 180
  Hidden, 168n7, 180, 181, 187, 194
  non-violence, 180–1
  offensiveness, 190–1
  provocation, 4, 181, 182
  rape of spectators, 6
  restraint, 5, 40n4
  The Seventh Continent, 181
  The Time of the Wolf, 181
  Viennese Actionism, 211
  violence, 15, 95
  see also The Piano Teacher; The White Ribbon
Hansell, Sven, 144, 151–2
Hardt, Michael, 89
Harewood, Lord, 118, 128n1
Harries, Martin, 200
Haute Tension, 21
Hayles, N. Katherine, 40
Hayward, Susan, 41n19
Hedling, Olof, 144
Heidegger, Martin, 100
Herzog, Werner, 197
Hickin, Daniel, 13
Hidden, 168n7, 180, 181, 187, 194
Hills, Matt, 31, 41n10
Hirsch, Marianne, 31
Hohenberger, Eva, 100–1
Holden, Stephen, 47
A Hole in My Heart
  audience response, 14
  critical response to, 145–6
  degradation of women, 149
  destruction of visual pleasure, 147–52
  food metaphor, 149, 150
  linear narrative lacking, 142
  new extremism, 145–7, 211
  porn film subject matter, 142
  provocation, 142–3
  religious symbolism, 152
  snuff sequence, 147, 148, 149
  soundtrack, 146
  surgery scenes, 142, 146, 148, 149–50
Holmes, Diana, 134
Holocaust, 75, 101n4
Homme au bain, 213n1
homophobia, 202, 211–12, 213n1
Honoré, Christophe
  on Bataille, 48
  documentary techniques, 49
  Homme au bain, 213n1
  innovation/style, 3
  Ma mère, 11, 43, 45–53, 53n1, 213n1
  new extremism, 53–4n2
  Non ma fille, tu n'iras pas danser, 213n1
Horeck, Tanya, 14–15, 108, 139, 184

horror films
  French, 210–11
  as genre, 5, 17, 26, 29, 38, 82, 131, 198, 199
  Hollywood, 18
  and Lowenstein, 7
  mutilation, 24
  pornography, 40n2, 80
  quotations from, 198
  shock tactics, 3, 7
  studies of, 41n10
  Trouble Every Day, 19, 33, 34, 36
  wargus, 70, 75, 78, 79
Horsley, Jake, 166, 168n6
Hostel, 82, 91
Houellebecq, Michel, 213
House on the Edge of the Park, 107
Human Rights Act (1998), 118, 119
human-centrism, 11–12
L'Humanité
  Bresson as influence, 18, 23
  critical response, 55
  mobility, 60
  as new extremist film, 120
  non-professional actors, 95
  Quandt on, 209
  Romney on, 53n1
humanness, 4, 11–12, 21–2, 75, 99–100
Hunger, 169
Huppert, Isabelle, 43, 44, 47
Hurt, John, 162
hyperrealism, 64, 95

I am curious, 146
I Spit on Your Grave, 131
I Stand Alone see *Seul contre tous*
Ichi the Killer, 107
identity politics, 138–9; see also national identity
The Idiots
  BBFC, 119, 120, 122, 128n7
  explicit shots of genitals, 142
  final scene, 164
  members of public, 95, 211
  new extremism, 194, 211
  transgression, 164
  unsimulated sex, 117, 128n8, 157
image
  abject, 151
  affect, 70, 85–6
  body, 70
  counter-image, 4
  entropic, 193–4
  and ethics, 9
  forbidden, 23
  see also visceral
immigration, 167n4
Import/Export
  Eastern Europe, 88–9
  ethics, 91–2
  exploitation of real people, 89, 91, 98–9
  new extremism, 194
  prostitute, 99
  real, 94–5
  Seidl on fiction, 93, 211
  training scenes, 89–91, 99
  transgression, 101
  and *La Vie nouvelle*, 12, 82–3
impurity, aesthetics of, 47, 52
In a Year of 13 Moons, 211
In My Skin see *Dans ma peau*
In the Bedroom, 198
In the Realm of the Senses, 69, 80n1, 199

Iñárritu, Alejandro González, 198
inclusion, 75, 78, 84
Independent, 124
inhumanity, 79, 80
inner bastard concept, 160, 164–5
Interdevochka, 144–5
International Journal of Psychoanalysis, 159
intertextuality
  Antichrist, 198, 199, 205n9
  Dogville, 162
  Irréversible, 203
  Ma mère, 46
Intimacy, 19, 123, 169–70
Iordanova, Dina, 83
Irréversible
  and *Antichrist*, 196–7
  and BBFC, 13, 107, 117, 124, 126–7
  camera shots, 202
  classification, 123–8
  Ebert on, 192
  and *In a Year of 13 Moons*, 211
  intertextuality, 203
  misogyny, 201–2
  modular narrative, 203
  national identity, 125–6
  press coverage, 124–5
  rape and revenge narrative, 124
  rape scene, 125, 126
  released in Britain, 128
  reviews of, 127
  shock tactics, 21–2
  transgression, 124, 127
  unwatchableness, 15, 201
Italian neorealism, 85

Jarl, Stefan, 143
Jarvis, Katie, 171
Jay, Martin, 195–6
Jelinek, Elfriede, 186, 211
Joffrin, Laurent, 138
Johnston, Claire, 201
Jordan, Shirley Ann, 132

Kane, Sarah, 54n3
Katalin Varga, 169
Ken Park, 194
Kendall, Tina, 11
Kermode, Mark, 125
Kidman, Nicole, 158
Kinatay, 211
kineticism, 3, 177, 201
The Kingdom, 198
Klossowski, Pierre, 87
Könskriget, 150–1
Kracauer, Siegfried, 193–4, 201
Kristensen, Lars, 144
Kristeva, Julia, 211
Krzywinska, Tanya, 135
Kubrick, Stanley, 196
Kuhn, Annette, 117, 118, 119

LA Times, 47
Labrune, Jeanne, 130
Un Lac, 69, 80n2, 81n5, 212
Lachman, Edward, 194
Laderman, David, 62
Lalanne, Jean-Marc, 41n23
Land Without Bread, 62–3
Lanthimos, Yorgos, 4, 211
Larsson, Mariah, 14
Last House on the Left, 125, 129n12

Last Tango in Paris, 20
Laugier, Pascal, 211
Lee, Chang-dong, 202
lesbian and gay issues, 134
lesbian love, 142, 143
Die Letze Männer, 93
Lewis, Leona, 176
Life of Jesus see *La Vie de Jésus*
Lilya 4-ever
  gender politics, 143–4
  narrative, 145
  religious symbolism, 152
  sex slave trade, 142
  subjective camera, 151
Littell, Jonathan, 213
Lolita, 110, 122
long shot, extreme, 63, 64
looking, ways of, 203–4
The Lord of the Rings, 115n4
Lowenstein, Adam, 7, 38–9
Luckett, Moya, 140
Ludovico Technique, 196
Lynch, David, 83, 198

Ma mère, 53n1
  Canary Islands, 11, 45, 49
  critical responses, 46–7
  music, 47, 49
  and Ozon, 213n1
  placelessness, 47, 48–9
  promotional poster, 43
  sex tourism, 50, 51
  tackiness, 46, 50, 51, 52, 53
  transcendence/sexuality, 45–6
  transgression, 43
Ma mère (Bataille), 11, 45, 46, 47–8
McCarthy, Todd, 158
McGill, Hannah, 174
MacKenzie, Scott, 3–4, 131
McQueen, Steve, 169
Mammoth, 142, 151
Manderlay, 96, 97, 101n3, 164
manipulation of spectators, 159–60, 162
Marjanovic, Goran, 146
Marks, Laura U., 96
Marshall, Tony, 130
Martin, Florence, 35
Martyrs, 211
Marx, Leo, 62
Marxism, 84, 146
masculinity, 131–4, 140, 190–1
masochism, 15–16, 186
Massumi, Brian, 16–17n2, 31, 41n11
Mathijs, Ernest, 9
Maury, Julien, 211
Mazierska, Ewa, 83
Memento, 202
Mendoza, Brillante, 211
Merleau-Ponty, Maurice, 86
Metz, Christian, 165–6
migration, 83
Miike, Takashi, 107
Millet, Catherine, 213
Ming-liang, Tsai, 194
misogyny, 71, 81n5, 93, 132, 133, 200, 201–2
Mit Verlust ist zu Rechnen, 94
Mitchell, John Cameron, 194
Model Shop, 56
Models, 93, 94
modernisation, 30, 32, 34, 39–40
modernism, 75, 203

monstrosity, 82, 83–4, 85–6
montage, 35–6, 37, 60, 146
Moodysson, Lukas
  as *auteur*, 143–5, 146, 151
  children in films, 151–2
  Container, 142, 143, 151
  gender politics, 14, 143–4, 152
  hand-held cameras, 143, 144
  Mammoth, 142, 151
  new extremism, 1, 4, 14, 211
  poetry collections, 152
  as political radical, 143–4
  provocation, 4
  Show Me Love, 142, 143, 151, 152
  Terrorists – The Kids They Sentenced, 143
  Together, 142, 143, 151, 152
  see also *A Hole in My Heart*; *Lilya 4-ever*
Moretti, Nanni, 198
The Mother and the Whore, 24
Mouchette sauvée des eaux, 212
Mulvey, Laura, 147, 148, 153n11, 172, 201
Muray, Philippe, 57
mutilation, 19–20, 52, 195–6
Muybridge, Eadweard, 101n2
Myrick, Daniel, 198

Nabokov, Vladimir, 110
national identity
  Baise-moi, 125, 131, 133, 137, 139, 140–1
  Dumont, 56, 58
  Irréversible, 125–6
  Noé, 21
  universalism, 14
nature
  anthropomorphising of, 205n4
  Antichrist, 199
  as corrupt, 197–8
  Hobbesian state, 78
  The White Ribbon, 187–8
  wilderness, 62, 197
Negri, Antonio, 89
neorealism, 25, 93–4
new extremism, 1–4, 14, 211
  contextualisation attempts, 29
  emergence of, 120
  examples of films, 194
  marketability, 43–4
  real in, 12–13, 93–4
  second wave, 13, 123
New French Extremity
  Archer on, 2, 3, 10, 11
  Baise-moi, 5, 21
  Dumont, 22, 24, 55
  excess, 183
  A Hole in My Heart, 142
  in literature, 213
  Noé, 210
  Ozon, 19
  Quandt on, 2, 18, 120, 194, 210–13
  Seul contre tous, 21
  Virilio on, 182
Neyrat, Cyril, 39
Nichols, Bill, 57–8
Nietzsche, Friedrich, 74
nihilism, 21, 127, 200–1
9 Songs, 170, 179n1, 194
No Fear, No Die, 19
Noé, Gaspar, 1, 29
  as *auteur*, 120
  Bataille as influence, 44
  BBFC, 13
  Carne, 21, 96, 120, 205n15
  confrontational films, 4, 117
  as *enfant terrible*, 201
  Enter the Void, 212
  kineticism, 3
  New French Extremity, 210
  nihilism, 127
  politics, 6
  Quandt on, 211–12
  and Seidl, 93
  spectators, 6, 123
  stylised violence, 95
  transgression, 2, 18, 209
  see also *Irréversible*; *Seul contre tous*
Nolan, Christopher, 202
Nolot, Jacques, 24
Non ma fille, tu n'iras pas danser, 213n1
non-humans, 70, 100, 101n5
Nouvelle Vague, 34, 36

obscenity, 5, 15, 182, 183–4, 190–1
Observer, 122
offensiveness, 190–1
The Omen, 198
The Onion, 205n3
Orpen, Valerie, 36, 41n22
Orr, John, 95
Ōshima, Nagisa, 69, 80n1, 199
Ovid, 203
Ozon, François, 2
  confrontational films, 4
  Criminal Lovers, 19, 204n1
  and Honoré, 213n1
  New French Extremity, 210
  provocation, 19
  Le Refuge, 213n1
  See the Sea, 19–20, 210
  Sitcom, 19, 120
  Sous le sable, 19, 210
  transgression, 18, 209
  violence and sex, 19

Pálfi, György, 4, 194
Palmer, Tim, 3, 93, 171
Pan's Labyrinth, 198
Papon, Marcel, 30
Paris, Texas, 56
Parreno, Philippe, 169
Pasolini, Pier Paolo, 6, 146, 211
  Salò, 2, 18, 22, 25, 85, 183
Passe ton bac d'abord, 22
The Passenger, 24
La Passion de Jeanne d'Arc, 198
patriarchy, 147, 148
Pattison, Michael, 171
Peckinpah, Sam, 201, 202
Peeping Tom, 196
Pellecuer, David, 76
Peppermint Candy, 202
Perec, George, 32
performance, 91, 175
performativity, 171–2, 174, 176, 177
Perrot, Michele, 134
Petit, Chris, 60
Le Petit Soldat, 41n19
Peucker, Brigitte, 192
Pialat, Maurice, 22–3, 24
The Piano Teacher
  critics on, 185–6
  Jelinek's novel, 186
  mother-daughter relationship, 184–5

new extremism, 194
provocation, 185
rape/abuse, 184–5
sado-masochism, 185
as second-wave, 123
violence, 15, 180
Wheatley on, 168n7
Pisters, Patricia, 172–3, 179n4
Plantinga, Carl, 8
pleasure principle, 193, 194; see also unpleasure
Pola X, 23, 120
Polanski, Roman, 20, 157, 198
politics, 6–7, 44, 142–3
The Pornographer, 19, 24, 123–4, 129n10
pornography
  and art-house films, 131
  Baise-moi, 130
  degradation of women, 146
  Ferguson on, 50–1, 54n3
  as genre, 51, 95, 110, 145
  hard-core, 119
  A Hole in My Heart, 14
  and horror, 40n2
  internet, 91
  in mainstream cinema, 135
  niche marketing, 44–5
  politics, 142–3
  and rape, 137
  in *Seul contre tous*, 120
  snuff films, 153n10
  stars, 20–1
  torture, 1, 147
  violence, 147
Powell, Michael, 196
power, 75, 133
power relations, 89–90, 91, 186
primitivism, 82, 83
prostitutes, killing of, 212
provocation, 2, 4, 204n2
  Arnold, 169
  art-house films, 18, 184
  and BBFC, 119, 123
  Breillat, 20
  Dogville, 157–8
  Dumont, 24
  European filmmakers, 4, 5, 6, 13, 119, 120, 128
  French cinema, 4, 39
  of guilt, 90
  Haneke, 4, 181, 182
  A Hole in My Heart, 142–3, 150
  irréversible, 125
  Moodysson, 4
  Ozon, 19
  The Piano Teacher, 185
  Seidl, 4, 93
  von Trier, 157
Psycho, 24
psychological cruelty, 188
Pulver, Andrew, 169
Puritanism, 197–8

Quandt, James
  new extremism, 16, 57, 70, 157
  New French Extremity, 2, 3, 6, 10, 18–25, 120, 194, 209, 210–13
Quinn, Anthony, 178

race, 19, 139; see also ethnicity
racism, 133, 202
Radway, Janice, 116n10
Raissinger, Catherine, 138–9

Rak, Ekaterina, 91
Rampling, Charlotte, 19
Rancière, Jacques, 204
rape
  anal, 21, 56–7, 202
  audience response, 4, 12–13
  car theft analogy, 32
  ethnicity/class, 139
  Irréversible, 125, 126
  of male, 18, 64
  myth of, 106, 108
  pornography, 137
  public visibility of, 184
  representation/real, 107, 108
  and revenge narrative, 32, 95–6, 124, 125, 130, 131
  sado-masochistic sex, 181
  sex/violence, 95–6
Rasalaite, Dangoule, 144, 153n5
Rascaroli, Laura, 83
Rayns, Tony, 123
real, 12–13, 52–3, 93–4, 96–8, 101
reception studies, 1, 115n6
Red Desert, 205n9
Red Road, 169–70
  performative bodies, 172
  Pisters on, 179n4
  sex scenes, 15, 170–1, 173–4
  spectatorship, 173–4
  voyeurism, 178
Rees-Roberts, Nick, 44, 46, 47, 50
reflection, 14, 16; see also self-reflexivity
Le Refuge, 213n1
Règle du jeu, 96
religious symbolism, 152
Renoir, Jean, 96
repression, 118–19, 137–9
Repulsion, 19–20
resistance, bodily, 90, 91–2
restraint, aesthetics of, 5, 40n4
Restuccia, Frances L., 185
revenge narrative, 130, 176, 177, 201
  for rape, 32, 95–6, 124, 125, 130, 131
reverse-shot, 77–8
Reygadas, Carlos, 194
road movies, 11, 33, 55–6, 57, 58, 60, 62, 71
Robbe-Grillet, Alain, 38
Roeg, Nicolas, 198
Rollet, Brigitte, 130, 131, 133
Romance
  and *Baise-moi*, 145
  BBFC, 119, 122
  genital shots, 142
  and *A Hole in My Heart*, 145
  inclusion, 95
  scandal, 135
  self-discovery, 20
  sex scenes, 117
Romney, Jonathan
  on Arnold, 179
  on *Baise-moi*, 5
  extremism, 6, 56
  on *L'Humanité*, 53n1
  innovation, 3
  on *Irréversible*, 124
  on *Red Road*, 170
  on *Seul contre tous*, 122
  Surrealism, 101n1
Rosemary's Baby, 198
Ross, Kristin, 11, 29–30, 31, 32–4, 38, 41n12
Roth, Eli, 82
Rothko, Mark, 19

Rousso, Henry, 40n5
Rubens, Peter Paul, 205n9
Russell, Dominique, 3, 184
Rylance, Mark, 170

Sade, Marquis de, 2, 18
    Justine, 85, 165, 167n2
sado-masochism, 95, 181, 185
Sagat, François, 213n1
Salò, 2, 18, 22, 25, 85, 183
Sánchez, Eduardo, 198
Le Sang des bêtes, 21, 96
Saw, 198
Saxton, Libby, 8–9, 177, 178, 192
Schama, Simon, 170
Schlöndorff, Volker, 22
Schopenhauer, Arthur, 203
Schumacher, Kurt, 160
scopic psychology, 193, 194, 195
Screen theory, 194–5, 196
See the Sea, 19–20, 210
Seidl, Ulrich, 1
    documentary/fiction, 12–13
    Dog Days, 93, 94–5, 99, 123, 211
    exploitation of real people, 98–9, 100–1
    fiction/non-fiction, 93
    Mit Verlust ist zu Rechnen, 94
    Models, 93, 94
    neorealism, 93–4
    provocation, 4, 93
    quasi-documentary technique, 91
    real, 101
    shock tactics, 94
    see also Import/Export
self-destructiveness, 181, 185, 193–4, 200
self-reflexivity, 1–2, 4, 115, 161, 178
sensation, 7, 8, 92
sensation, cinema of, 3, 170
Serbis, 211
Seul contre tous
    alienation, 6, 120
    BBFC, 13
    censorship, 119–23
    clip in *Baise-moi*, 21
    dark heart of France, 127
    and *Irréversible*, 202
    optical softening, 122
    politics of extreme right, 6
    press release, 121–2
    released in Britain, 128
    reviews, 122–3
    transgression, 119, 121, 123
    unsimulated sex, 117
    unwatchableness, 193–4
The Seventh Continent, 181
Severance, 82
sex
    affect, 171
    art values, 135
    discursive explosion, 44–5
    and gender, 4, 133, 139–40
    perversion/transcendence, 45–6
    revenge dramas, 179
    unsimulated, 20–1, 95–6, 117–18, 119, 128–9n8, 157, 170
    violence, 5, 19, 32, 44, 56–7, 95–6, 107, 108–9, 117, 136
sex slave trade, 142, 144
sex wars, American cinema, 143, 147
sex-as-commodity, 50, 51, 52
sexual tourism, 46, 49, 50, 142

sexuality
    Arnold, 169
    female, 179
    performativity, 174
    tackiness, 46
    and transgression, 11, 45
Shamanism, 198
Shaviro, Steven, 16–17n2, 44, 45, 53
Sherry, Kate, 126
shock tactics
    auteurism, 43–4
    Baise-moi, 136
    Beugnet, 29, 95
    excess, 29
    Irréversible, 21–2
    Ozon, 210
    Quandt, 2, 3, 18, 19
    Seidl, 94
Shocking Truth, 150
Shohat, Ella, 61
Shortbus, 194
Show Me Love, 142, 143, 151, 152
Siffredi, Rocco, 145
Sight & Sound, 106, 123, 171
Simone, Nina, 161
simulacra, 59, 64
Sitcom, 19, 120
Sjöman, Vilgot, 146
Skarsgård, Stellan, 160
Slotkin, Richard, 197–8, 202
Smith, Christopher, 82
Smith, Jillian, 172
snuff films, 147, 149, 153n10
social realism, 170–1, 179
socio-politics, 133, 139–40
Sombre
    American model, 33
    archetypes, 12, 69–70, 73–4, 75–7
    Beugnet on, 80n3
    camera shots, 77–8, 79
    Chamarette on, 12
    consciousness of rapist/murderer, 22
    darkness of human soul, 74
    diegesis as fairy tale, 72, 74
    gesture, 76
    lustmord, 212
    sensual affect, 71
    setting, 72
    subjectivity, 74–5
    Tour de France scene, 77–8
The Son's Room, 198
Sontag, Susan, 38, 178, 200–1, 203
Sous le sable, 19, 210
spectators
    Antichrist, 53n1
    Arnold, 172–3
    Baise-moi, 132
    Critics/Embracers, 13
    del Rio, 9
    Dogville, 14
    Dumont on, 6, 24
    empathy, 204n2
    ethics, 7–16, 170, 178, 193, 195, 201
    gaze, 204n2
    Grandrieux, 81n11
    Haneke on, 6
    identifying with history, 7
    id/superego, 166
    manipulation, 159–60, 162
    moral considerations, 8–9
    Noé, 6, 123

self-reflexivity, 1–2, 4, 115, 161, 178
subjectivity, 163
transgression, 101
unpleasure, 8
Vincendeau, 106
violence, 195
visceral aspects, 1, 3–4, 8, 44, 167, 171
voyeurism, 4
spectatorship
   Dogme 95 edict, 150
   Red Road, 173–4
   reflection, 16
   sado-masochism, 95
   Screen theory, 194–5, 196
   self-destructiveness, 200
   tackiness, 11, 52, 53
Staiger, Janet, 115n6, 118–19, 121, 126–7
Stam, Robert, 61
Steinberg, Leo, 204
Steir, Pat, 19
Sterrit, David, 203
Straw Dogs, 201
Strickland, Peter, 169
Studlar, Gaylyn, 200
subjectivity
   abject, 74–5
   Agamben, 74, 75
   archetypes, 81n7
   Beugnet, 86
   Grandrieux, 76
   Sombre, 12, 73–4
   spectators, 163
   Staiger, 121
   La Vie nouvelle, 46
subversion
   Artaud, 162
   Beugnet, 56
   cinematic, 6
   Moodysson, 146
   obscenity, 182
   Red Road, 174
   Shaviro, 53
suffering, 97, 100
suicide, 45, 52, 188
Surrealism, 19, 101n1, 157, 161–5, 199
Sweden
   anti-porn movement, 147, 151
   feminism, 14
   film criticism, 145–6
   gender, 145
   pornography/politics, 142–3
Swedish Film Institute, 151, 153n2

taboo
   allure of, 45
   breaking, 2, 5, 18, 43, 46, 97, 132, 204–5n2
   death, 95, 98
   obscenity, 182
   sexual, 48
   transgressed, 52
   unbroken, 95
tackiness, 46, 50, 51, 52, 53
tactile aesthetics, 33–4, 175
tactility, politics of, 172
Tarkovsky, Andrei, 198, 212
Tarr, Carrie, 130, 131, 133
taste, 109, 134, 140, 166, 204
Tati, Jacques, 40n4
Taxi Driver, 123
Taxidermia, 194
Teguia, Tariq, 39

Terrorists – The Kids They Sentenced, 143
Thanatos, 94–6, 160, 212
Thelma and Louise, 136
theriomorphosis, 98–101
Thomas, Kevin, 47
Thomas, Quentin, 124, 125, 129n11
The Threepenny Opera, 161–2
Tierische Liebe, 93
Tillsammans, 142
The Time of the Wolf, 181
The Times, 122
Titicut Follies, 172
Todorovski, Piotr, 144–5
Together, 142, 143, 151, 152
Tookey, Christopher, 123, 126
torture porn, 1, 147
transgression
   artistic, 5
   Baise-moi, 136
   Bataille, 44, 46, 53
   Beugnet, 94
   Breillat, 18, 209
   cathartic, 52
   determined, 2–3
   Dogville, 164, 165
   Dumont, 18
   Eastern Europe, 82
   empathy, 163
   excess, 183
   films, 194, 199, 204, 209, 210
   global consumer capitalism, 43
   Grandrieux, 18
   The Idiots, 164
   Import/Export, 101
   Irréversible, 124, 127
   Ma mère, 43
   Noé, 2, 18, 209
   obscenity, 182
   Ozon, 18, 209
   Seul contre tous, 119, 121, 123
   sex, 45
   spectators, 101
   tackiness, 51
   wilful, 2, 18
travel films, 57–8, 59–60
Trinh Thi, Coralie, 33, 95–6, 107, 117, 130; *see also Baise-moi*
Trouble Every Day
   and *Antichrist*, 198
   cannibalism, 19
   classification, 123
   and *Cléo 5 à 7*, 10–11, 31, 32–4, 36–9
   fold, 41n14
   genres, 36, 38
   linear narrative breakdown, 179n3
   sensuous camera work, 38
   staircase sequence, 37–8
   vampires, 209
21 Grams, 198
Twentynine Palms
   camera shots, 56, 58, 60, 63, 64
   cultural framing, 62
   Edenic motif, 23–4, 61, 62, 64
   Hummer car, 60–1
   indexical quality, 59
   music in soundtrack, 62–3
   opening scene, 55
   Quandt on, 209
   as road movie, 11, 33
   violence, 18

Under the Sand, 19, 210
universalism, 14, 131, 134, 135
unpleasure, 8, 15, 165–6

vampirism, 87, 209
Varda, Agnès, 10–11, 31, 32–6, 37
Vega, Alan, 22
Vicari, Justin, 99
Vichy Syndrome, 30–1, 40n5
La Vie de Jésus, 18, 22–3, 55, 59, 95
La Vie nouvelle
  aesthetics of, 19
  American model, 33
  commerce in bodies, 87
  critical response, 69
  Eastern European setting, 72, 77
  ethics, 91–2
  experimentalism, 3
  geopolitics, 85
  image/body, 70
  and *Import/Export*, 12, 82–3
  lustmord, 212
  materiality of image, 71–2
  misogyny claims, 81n5
  monstrosity, 85–6
  Orpheus and Eurydice myth, 22
  subjectivity, 46
  visceral, 88
La Vie nouvelle, book of (Brenez), 85
Vincendeau, Ginette, 3, 4, 50, 51, 106
Vinterberg, Thomas, 4
Violence
  American cinema, 24
  Breillat, 95
  desert, 61–2
  domestic, 188–9
  gender, 64, 174
  Haneke, 15, 95
  hyperreality, 95
  masculinity, 190–1
  mathematical, 167n3
  non-violence, 181–2
  obscenity, 182, 183–4
  off-screen, 95
  physical, 57
  pornography, 147
  sex, 19, 44, 56–7, 95–6, 107, 108–9, 136
  in shadow, 95
  on spectators, 195
  stylised, 95
  women as perpetrators, 132–3, 137
Virilio, Paul, 61, 182–3
visceral
  aesthetics of, 31
  Eastern Europe, 12
  Fish Tank, 176
  French extremism, 6, 7, 10, 52–3
  Irréversible, 202
  Lowenstein, 38–9
  new extremism, 40, 44

spectators, 1, 3–4, 8, 44, 167, 171
La Vie nouvelle, 88
visual pleasure, destruction of, 147–52, 204n2
von Trier, Lars
  Advance Party concept, 170
  Bataille as influence, 44
  on Brecht, 161–2
  confrontational films, 4
  Dogme 95 edict, 95
  Ebert on, 192–3
  Europa, 198
  immigration, 167n4
  information withheld, 167n1
  The Kingdom, 198
  Manderlay, 96, 97
  new extremism, 1, 211
  as provocateur, 157
  subversion, 146
  see also *Antichrist*; *Dogville*; *The Idiots*
voyeurism, 4, 178

Walker, Alexander, 122, 123, 125, 126, 127
Wan, James, 198
wargus, 70, 75, 78, 79
Wasp, 169, 178
The Wayward Cloud, 194
Weekend, 25, 96–7
Weil, Kurt, 161
Wenders, Wim, 56
Wheatley, Catherine, 12–13, 93, 94
White Material, 212
The White Ribbon, 15, 180, 181, 184–5, 186–90
Whittam Smith, Andreas, 118, 120–1, 121–2, 124, 128n2
Wiberg, Charlotte, 145, 146
The Wild Bunch, 202
wilderness, 61–2, 197
Williams, James, 3
Williams, Linda, 40n2, 44–5, 48, 97, 101n2, 169
Williams, Melanie, 179n1
Williams, Tod, 198
Wimmer, Leila, 13–14, 139
Wimsatt, W. K., 204
Winterbottom, Michael, 170, 179n1, 194
Wiseman, Fred, 172
Witchcraft Through the Ages, 198
Wolf, Alexa, 150, 151
Wolfe, Cary, 101n4
wolf-man archetype, 70, 75–7
Wood, Robin, 41n10, 185
Wrye, Harriet, 185

X certificate, 135–6
xenophobia, 90, 158, 160

Zabriskie Point, 24, 56
Zarchi, Meir, 131
Zilkha, Nathalie, 159, 160
Žižek, Slavoj, 182–3, 186
Zulawski, Andrzej, 18–19

EU representative:
Easy Access System Europe
Mustamäe tee 50, 10621 Tallinn, Estonia
Gpsr.requests@easproject.com

www.ingramcontent.com/pod-product-compliance
Lightning Source LLC
Chambersburg PA
CBHW051636230426
43669CB00013B/2326